Beginning Java MVC 1.0

Model View Controller Development to Build Web, Cloud, and Microservices Applications

Peter Späth

Apress®

Beginning Java MVC 1.0: Model View Controller Development to Build Web, Cloud, and Microservices Applications

Peter Späth
Leipzig, Sachsen, Germany

ISBN-13 (pbk): 978-1-4842-6279-5   ISBN-13 (electronic): 978-1-4842-6280-1
https://doi.org/10.1007/978-1-4842-6280-1

Managing Director, Apress Media LLC: Welmoed Spahr
Acquisitions Editor: Steve Anglin
Development Editor: Matthew Moodie
Coordinating Editor: Mark Powers

Cover designed by eStudioCalamar

Cover image by Janko Ferlic on Unsplash (www.unsplash.com)

Distributed to the book trade worldwide by Apress Media, LLC, 1 New York Plaza, New York, NY 10004, U.S.A. Phone 1-800-SPRINGER, fax (201) 348-4505, e-mail orders-ny@springer-sbm.com, or visit www. springeronline.com. Apress Media, LLC is a California LLC and the sole member (owner) is Springer Science + Business Media Finance Inc (SSBM Finance Inc). SSBM Finance Inc is a **Delaware** corporation.

For information on translations, please e-mail booktranslations@springernature.com; for reprint, paperback, or audio rights, please e-mail bookpermissions@springernature.com.

Apress titles may be purchased in bulk for academic, corporate, or promotional use. eBook versions and licenses are also available for most titles. For more information, reference our Print and eBook Bulk Sales web page at http://www.apress.com/bulk-sales.

Any source code or other supplementary material referenced by the author in this book is available to readers on GitHub via the book's product page, located at www.apress.com/9781484262795. For more detailed information, please visit http://www.apress.com/source-code.

Printed on acid-free paper

To Nicole

Table of Contents

About the Author

Peter Späth graduated in 2002 as a physicist and soon afterward became an IT consultant, mainly for Java-related projects. In 2016, he decided to concentrate on writing books on various aspects, but with a main focus on software development. With two books about graphics and sound processing, three books on Android app development, and a beginner's book on Jakarta EE development, the author continues his effort in writing software development-related literature.

About the Technical Reviewer

 **Luciano Manelli** was born in Taranto, Italy, where he currently resides with his family. He graduated in Electronic Engineering at the Polytechnic of Bari at 24 years of age and then served as an officer in the Navy. In 2012, he earned a PhD in computer science from the IT department, University of Bari - Aldo Moro. His PhD focused on grid computing and formal methods, and he published the results in international publications. He is a professionally certified engineer and an innovation manager, and in 2014, he began working for the Port Network Authority of the Ionian Sea – Port of Taranto, after working for 13 years for InfoCamere SCpA as a software developer. He has worked mainly in the design, analysis, and development of large software systems; research and development; testing; and production with roles of increasing responsibility in several areas over the years. Luciano has developed a great capability to make decisions in technical and business contexts and is mainly interested in project management and business process management. In his current position, he deals with port community systems and digital innovation.

Additionally, he has written several IT books and is a contract professor at the Polytechnic of Bari and at the University of Bari - Aldo Moro. You can find out more at his LinkedIn page: `it.linkedin.com/in/lucianomanelli`.

Introduction

Starting at the very infancy of software creation, developers tried to modularize their applications in order to streamline their projects and increase the maintainability of the software they created. Soon, a very basic segregation scheme was identified: One part of the software must deal with data and persistence, another part must deal with presenting the data to the user, and one last part must handle data input and frontend view propagation.

This segregation scheme showed up in so many projects that it was promoted to a common software design pattern, called Model-View-Controller, or MVC for short. Its power also manifested in its versatility, even with big paradigm changes, like the onset of the Internet age. With database products for the model layer, browsers for the view layer, and some kind of user input processing for the controller layer, the pattern's accuracy and applicability to the majority of software projects became even more apparent with web applications.

Interestingly, even though most web application frameworks under the hood apply some kind of MVC layer demarcation, Java Server products up to JEE 7 did not include a dedicated MVC framework. With JSR-371 (Java Specification Request number 371) only recently and starting with JEE 8/Jakarta EE 8, an MVC specification entered the Java Enterprise application realm, which is one of the reasons this book was born. It does not describe all MVC Frameworks that you can add to Java EE/Jakarta EE as an external library. There are just too many of them and you can learn about them by looking at each library's documentation. Instead, we talk about the genuine Java MVC library as described by JSR-371.

The target version of Java MVC is 1.0, and we use a Jakarta EE version 8.0 compliant server to run Java MVC on it.

The Book's Targeted Audience

The book is for beginning or advanced enterprise software developers with knowledge of Java Standard Edition version 8 or later and some experience in Jakarta EE (or JEE) development. It is also assumed that the reader is able to use the online API references, as this book is not a reference in the sense that all API classes and methods are listed. Instead, it presents techniques and technologies that help professional Java Enterprise level developers leverage web application programming by including Java MVC in their software.

The book uses the Linux operating system as the development platform, although the code can be run on other platforms (Windows and macOS) without complex adaptions. This book also does not talk about hardware issues (in case you don't use a laptop, a PC, or a server).

The readers will in the end be able to develop and run Java MVC programs of mid- to high-level complexity.

Sources

All sources shown or referred to in this book can be accessed via the Download Source Code button located at www.apress.com/9781484262795.

How to Read This Book

You can read this book sequentially from the beginning to the end, or you can read chapters on an ad hoc basis if your work demands special attention on a certain topic.

## CHAPTER 1

About MVC: Model, View, Controller

MVC is a software design pattern. It describes the separation of software into three elements:

- **Model**: Manages the data of an application. This is to be understood in a narrow sense. Of course, any part of a less than trivial application deals with the application's data in one way or another, but the model from MVC corresponds to data items viewable to the user and possibly subject to change by user interactions. The model is agnostic to the way the data is represented to the user or any application workflow, so it can be said that the model is the central part of a MVC application. It is not surprising that developing a model is among the first steps of any MVC software project.

- **View**: Describes the presentation of the data and control elements (inputs, buttons, check boxes, menus, and so on) to the user. A view may provide different modes, like paged or non-paged tables, a formatted list or a link list, and so on. A view also may use different technologies, like a GUI component installed on the user's PC, an app on a mobile phone, or a web page to be viewed in a browser.

- **Controller**: Handles user input and prepares the data set necessary for the view part to do its work. While a view shows model items, the view never has to know how data is stored and retrieved from some persistent storage (database). This is the controller's responsibility. Because the user input determines what an application has to do next, the controller also contains the application logic. Any calculation and data transformation happens in the control part of MVC.

© Peter Späth 2021
P. Späth, *Beginning Java MVC 1.0*, https://doi.org/10.1007/978-1-4842-6280-1_1

For example, consider a book club application. In this case, the model consists of elements such as books (including rental status), book storage location (building, room, or shelf), and member. For search application modules, you normally define lists of books, users, and so on, as model values.

The view part of the book club application will contain pages that show books, show members, show book locations, enable members to rent books, add club members, show book and member lists, as well as various search functionalities, and so on. Technically, this will often go hand in hand with a templating engine that defines placeholders for model elements, shortcuts for loops (for tables and lists), and other view elements like menus and buttons.

The controller handles the data the user enters. If, for example, the view currently shows a search page for books and the user enters a book's name and clicks on the Search button, the controller is informed as to which button was clicked. The controller then reads the request parameters (the book's name in this case) and possibly some model values (for example, the username and whether the user is logged in), queries the database, builds a result list, creates a model from this list, and finally decides which view page to show next.

There exists some fluffiness concerning the implementation details. This comes from the technical details of the data flow between view elements and model elements. MVC makes no assumption about *when* updates to view elements and model elements actually happen and which procedure is chosen to keep them synchronized. This is why, for MVC, you find many different diagrams in the literature.

For Java MVC, we can narrow our ideas about MVC to the following—a model (stored in memory) defines the application's state; a view shows model values and sends user interactions to a controller; and the controller prepares model data, handles user input and accordingly changes model values, and then decides which view page to show next. This kind of MVC model is depicted in Figure 1-1.

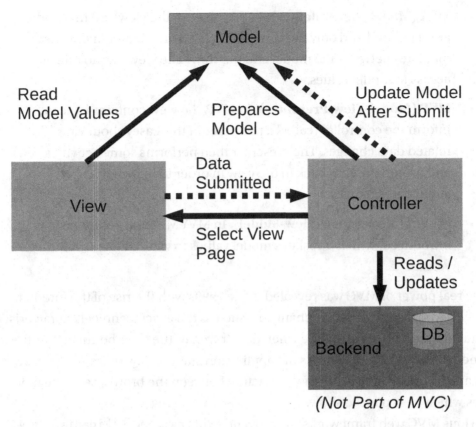

Figure 1-1. *The Java MVC design pattern*

The History of MVC

The advent of MVC dates back to the 1970s. It was introduced into the computer language Smalltalk as a programming concept. At that time, it did not have a name. Only later, in the late 1980s, was the moniker MVC explicitly used. It appeared in an article in the periodical *Journal of Object Technology*.

MVC steadily became more and more widespread, and its ideas were so widely adopted that variants evolved from MVC. We don't talk about these variants in this book, but a short list includes:

- **PAC (Presentation-Abstraction-Control) and HMVC (Hierarchical MVC).** This is a variation of MVC, where submodules have their own MVC-like structure and only later is a view page constructed from them.

- **MVA (Model-View-Adapter).** In this pattern, the view and the model are separated and only the controller (called an adapter in this case) mediates between the model and the view. The view has no direct access to model values.

- **MVP (Model-View-Presenter).** In MVP, the view contains logic to inform the controller (called a presenter in this case) about view-related data changes. The presenter then performs some activities and eventually calls back to the view in order to inform the user about data changes.

- **MVVM (Model-View-View-Model).** In MVVM, some automatism is introduced, which translates model values to view elements and vice versa.

The real power of MVC was revealed in the 1990s with the rise of the Internet. Although some technical details changed—such as the exact technical characteristics of the data flow and the point in time when data traverses the layer boundaries—the idea remained the same: a model holds the application state, a view presents the browser pages, and a controller handles the interaction between the browser and the model, and decides which view page to show.

Various MVC web frameworks were invented; `https://en.wikipedia.org/wiki/Comparison\_of\_web\_frameworks` shows you a comprehensive list (further down on the page, MVC capabilities are also listed).

MVC in Web Applications

Web applications impose some restrictions if we try to let them work the MVC way. The most important distinction comes from the stateless nature of the HTTP protocol, which is used for communication between the view (browser window) and the controller (HTTP server). In fact, the way web application frameworks handle the HTTP protocol leads to decisive differences between the different MVC implementations.

In more detail, important questions concerning MVC for web applications are as follows:

- **Sessions:** We already pointed out the stateless nature of HTTP. So, if the browser sends a request, maybe because the user entered some string into a text field and then pressed the Submit button, how would the server know which user is performing the request? This usually gets handled by a session, which is identified by a session ID transmitted as a cookie, request, or POST parameter. Sessions are transparently handled by the framework, so you don't have to create and maintain sessions from inside the application's code.

- **Accessing model values from the view:** With web applications, some kind of templating engine usually handles the view generation. There, we could have expressions like ${user.firstName} to read the contents of a model entry.

- **Transmitted data extent:** If data is submitted from the web page to the server, we basically have two options. First, the complete form could be transmitted. Second, only the data that changed could be sent to the server. The latter reduces network traffic, but requires some script logic (JavaScript) to perform the data collection on the web page.

- **Updating the view:** With web applications, the way a view is updated is crucial. Either the complete page is loaded after the controller works a request, or only those parts of a web page that actually need an update are transmitted from the server to the browser. Again, the latter method reduces network traffic.

From these points, you can see that programming a MVC framework for web applications is not an utterly trivial task. This is also why there are quite a large number of different MVC frameworks you can use for web applications. In the rest of the book, I will show you why choosing Java MVC is not the worst thing you can do if you need MVC software for your Java platform.

MVC for Java

In the Java ecosystem, a framework named Struts entered the software world around 2000. It is a MVC framework aimed at web applications and integrating with Java EE/Jakarta EE and Tomcat (a server product boiled down to web functionalities). It has been used in many software projects and is still being used, albeit it is not part of the Java EE/Jakarta EE specification. Instead, Java EE/Jakarta EE names JSF (Java Server Faces) as the dedicated web framework. JSF, in contrast to MVC, uses a component-oriented approach for creating web applications.

JSF works out-of-the-box for any Java EE/Jakarta EE 8 or later product. Up to version 7, if you wanted to use MVC, Struts was one of the prominent frameworks you could use. However, in order for Struts to work, an external library had to be added to the application, and Struts always felt like an extension and not so much like something that seamlessly integrated with Java EE/Jakarta EE.

With Java EE 8/Jakarta EE 8, the MVC world reentered the game in form of a Java MVC specification. It is still kind of a second-class citizen in the Java EE/Jakarta EE world, but there are reasons to favor MVC over JSF. We talk about the merits and disadvantages of MVC over other frameworks like JSF at the end of this chapter.

Finally, Java MVC (JSR-371)

The latest Java EE/Jakarta EE MVC implementation operates under the name *Java MVC* and is governed by JSR-371. It is the first MVC framework available for Java EE/Jakarta EE servers version 8 or higher. In fact, the JSR describes an interface. For Java MVC to actually work, you need to add an implementation library.

Note   We use Eclipse Krazo as the Java MVC implementation library. See
`https://projects.eclipse.org/proposals/eclipse-krazo`
or

`https://projects.eclipse.org/projects/ee4j.krazo`

We will later see how to install Eclipse Krazo for your web application.

Java MVC is a lean and clever extension of the REST technology JAX-RS included within Java EE/Jakarta EE. This relationship gives Java MVC a modern touch and allows for a concise and highly comprehensive programming style.

We already learned that MVC allows for some fluffiness concerning the implementation details. Figure 1-1 describes how Java MVC works quite well: A request for a first page in the browser window routes to the controller, which prepares model values (with or without querying some backend for additional data). The controller then decides which view page (browser page) to show next (maybe a login page). The view can access model values. With a data set entered by the user and submitted to the controller, the controller takes request parameters (for example, the login name and password), possibly queries the backend (the user database), updates the model, and finally selects a new view page (for example, a welcome page after successful authentication).

But there is an additional feature that seamlessly integrates with Java MVC. Instead of always loading a complete new page after each HTTP request, you can decide to let parts of your web application use AJAX for more fine-grained frontend-backend communication. Because we use Java MVC in a Java EE/Jakarta EE 8 (or later) environment, we can use JAX-RS for that aim out-of-the-box.

Why MVC

With so many web frontend technologies out there, it is not easy to decide which to use for your project. The new Java MVC certainly is an option and it might very well suit your needs. In order to help you make a decision, here is a list of pros and cons of Java MVC.

Cons:

- MVC seems to be a old-fashioned design pattern. Although this is true, it also has been proven to work well for many projects, and Java MVC allows developers to mix in more modern web development techniques.

- MVC forces the developer to be aware of HTTP internals. MVC is also said to be an action-based design pattern. Actions in a web environment mean HTTP requests and responses. MVC doesn't really hide the internals of the HTTP communication like other frameworks do.

- MVC does not introduce two-way data bindings like other frameworks do. With two-way data bindings, a change in a frontend input field immediately reflects in the model value changes. Instead, in a MVC controller, you have to explicitly implement the update of model values.

Pros:

- Since it's closer to the HTTP communication internals compared to other frameworks, despite introducing some complexity, this introduces less invasive memory management. If you look at JSF, a complete component tree (and component data tree) is built with each browser request. In contrast, a MVC application can be tailored with an extremely small memory footprint.

- Java MVC is part of the Java EE/Jakarta EE 8 specification. This helps to more reliably handle maintenance.

- If you are used to Struts or similar frontend frameworks, switching to Java MVC feels more natural compared to switching to other products with other frontend design patterns.

Where Is Hello World?

In many software-related development instruction books, you find a really simple "Hello World" example in one of the first chapters. For Jakarta EE, this means we must provide a shortcut way to do the following:

- Write a short program that does something simple, like output the string `"Hello World"`.

- Build a deployable artifact from the string (for example, a `.war` file).

- Run a Jakarta EE server.

- Deploy the application (the `.war` file) on the server.

- Connect a client (for example, a browser) to the server.

- Observe the output.

This is a lot of stuff, so instead of building a quick-and-dirty setup to run such an example, I prefer to first talk about Java/Jakarta Enterprise Edition (Java/Jakarta EE) in general, then discuss the development workflow, and only after that, introduce a simple first project. This way, we can make sure your first Java MVC application is developed and runs correctly.

If you think a quick-and-dirty Hello World example will help you, the following paragraphs show you how to create one. Note that we won't use the development processes shown here in the rest of the book—this is simply a simplistic and fast, and maybe not-so-clean, approach. You can also skip this section safely, because we create a proper Hello World project in Chapter 4.

1. First make sure OpenJDK 8 is installed on your PC. Go to `https://jdk.java.net/java-se-ri/8-MR3` to download it. In the rest of this section, we call the OpenJDK 8 folder `OPENJDK8_DIR`.

2. Download and install GlassFish 5.1 from `https://projects.eclipse.org/projects/ee4j.glassfish/downloads` (choose the "Full Profile" variant). In the rest of this section, we call the GlassFish installation folder `GLASSFISH_INST_DIR`.

3. Inside the `GLASSFISH_INST_DIR/glassfish/config/asenv.conf` (Linux) or `GLASSFISH_INST_DIR/glassfish/config/asenv.bat` (Windows) file, add the following lines:

    ```
    REM Windows:
    REM Note, if the OPENJDK8_DIR contains spaces, wrap it
    REM inside "..."
    set AS_JAVA=OPENJDK8_DIR

    # Linux:
    AS_JAVA="OPENJDK8_DIR"
    ```

You must replace `OPENJDK8_DIR` with the installation folder of the OpenJDK 8 installation.

4. Start the GlassFish server:

    ```
    REM Windows:
    chdir GLASSFISH_INST_DIR
    bin\asadmin start-domain
    ```

```
# Linux:
cd GLASSFISH_INST_DIR
bin/asadmin start-domain
```

You must replace GLASSFISH_INST_DIR with the installation folder
of GlassFish.

5. Create a folder called hello_world anywhere on your file system.
   Its contents have to be (instructions follow):

```
build
  |- <empty>
src
  |- java
  |     |- book
  |            |- javamvc
  |                   |- helloworld
  |                           |- App.java
  |                           |- RootRedirector.java
  |                           |- HelloWorldController.java
  |- webapp
  |     |- META-INF
  |     |     |- MANIFEST.MF
  |     |- WEB-INF
  |            |- lib
  |            |     |- activation-1.1.jar
  |            |     |- javaee-api-8.0.jar
  |            |     |- javax.mail-1.6.0.jar
  |            |     |- javax.mvc-api-1.0.0.jar
  |            |     |- jstl-1.2.jar
  |            |     |- krazo-core-1.1.0-M1.jar
  |            |     |- krazo-jersey-1.1.0-M1.jar
  |            |- views
  |            |     |- greeting.jsp
  |            |     |- index.jsp
  |            |- beans.xml
```

```
|            |- glassfish-web.xml
make.bat
make.sh
```

6. Get the JARs for the `lib` folder from `https://mvnrepository.com`.
   Enter each name without the version and the `.jar` extension in
   the search field, select the version, and then get the JAR file.

7. The Java code reads as follows:

```java
// App.java:
package book.javamvc.helloworld;

import javax.ws.rs.ApplicationPath;
import javax.ws.rs.core.Application;

@ApplicationPath("/mvc")
public class App extends Application {
}

// RootRedirector.java
package book.javamvc.helloworld;

import javax.servlet.FilterChain;
import javax.servlet.annotation.WebFilter;
import javax.servlet.http.HttpFilter;
import javax.servlet.http.HttpServletRequest;
import javax.servlet.http.HttpServletResponse;
import java.io.IOException;

/**
 * Redirecting http://localhost:8080/HelloWorld/
 * This way we don't need a <welcome-file-list> in web.xml
 */
@WebFilter(urlPatterns = "/")
public class RootRedirector extends HttpFilter {
    @Override
    protected void doFilter(HttpServletRequest req,
            HttpServletResponse res,
```

11

```java
                FilterChain chain) throws IOException {
            res.sendRedirect("mvc/hello");
        }
    }

// HelloWorldController.java
package book.javamvc.helloworld;

import javax.inject.Inject;
import javax.mvc.Controller;
import javax.mvc.Models;
import javax.mvc.binding.MvcBinding;
import javax.ws.rs.FormParam;
import javax.ws.rs.GET;
import javax.ws.rs.POST;
import javax.ws.rs.Path;
import javax.ws.rs.core.Response;

@Path("/hello")
@Controller
public class HelloWorldController {
    @Inject
    private Models models;

    @GET
    public String showIndex() {
        return "index.jsp";
    }

    @POST
    @Path("/greet")
    public Response greeting(@MvcBinding @FormParam("name")
            String name) {
        models.put("name", name);

        return Response.ok("greeting.jsp").build();
    }
}
```

8. As `MANIFEST.MF`, write the following:

```
Manifest-Version: 1.0
```

9. The view files read as follows:

```jsp
<%-- index.jsp --%>
<%@ page contentType="text/html;charset=UTF-8"
    language="java" %>
<%@ taglib prefix="c"
    uri="http://java.sun.com/jsp/jstl/core" %>
<html>
  <head>
    <meta charset="UTF-8">
    <title>Hello World</title>
</head>
<body>
  <form method="post"
     action="${mvc.uriBuilder('HelloWorldController#
            greeting').build()}">
    Enter your name: <input type="text" name="name"/>
    <input type="submit" value="Submit" />
  </form>
</body>
</html>

<%-- greeting.jsp --%>
<%@ page contentType="text/html;charset=UTF-8"
    language="java" %>
<%@ taglib prefix="c"
    uri="http://java.sun.com/jsp/jstl/core" %>
<html>
<head>
    <meta charset="UTF-8">
    <title>Hello World</title>
</head>
```

```
<body>
  Hello ${name}
</body>
</html>
```

(Remove the line break and the spaces after `HelloWorldController#`.)

10. As `beans.xml`, create an empty file (the file must exist, though!).

11. The contents of `glassfish-web.xml` reads as follows:

```
<?xml version="1.0" encoding="UTF-8"?>
<glassfish-web-app error-url="">
    <class-loader delegate="true"/>
</glassfish-web-app>
```

12. The Linux build file called `make.sh` reads as follows:

```
#!/bin/bash
JAVA_HOME=/path/to/your/openjdk-8

rm -rf build/*
cp -a src/webapp/* build
mkdir build/WEB-INF/classes

$JAVA_HOME/bin/javac \
    -cp src/webapp/WEB-INF/lib/javaee-api-8.0.jar:
        src/webapp/WEB-INF/lib/javax.mvc-api-1.0.0.jar \
    -d build/WEB-INF/classes \
    src/java/book/javamvc/helloworld/*

cd build
$JAVA_HOME/bin/jar cf ../HelloWorld.war *
cd ..
```

(Remove the line break and spaces after the `:`.)

13.   The Windows build file `make.bat` reads as follows:

```
set JAVA_HOME=C:\dev\java-se-8u41-ri

mkdir build
CD build && RMDIR /S /Q .
CD ..
rmdir build

xcopy src\webapp build /s /e /i
mkdir build\WEB-INF\classes

%JAVA_HOME%\bin\javac ^
    -cp src\webapp\WEB-INF\lib\javaee-api-8.0.jar;
        src\webapp\WEB-INF\lib\javax.mvc-api-1.0.0.jar ^
    -d build\WEB-INF\classes ^

    src\java\book\javamvc\helloworld/*

cd build
%JAVA_HOME%\bin\jar cf ..\HelloWorld.war *
cd ..
```

(Remove the line break and spaces after the ;.)

To build the application from inside the console, move into the `hello_world` folder and start the script:

```
# Linux
cd hello_world
./make.sh

rem Windows
chdir hello_world
make
```

Apart from some error messages for the Windows build script that you can safely ignore, you will end up with the `HelloWorld.war` web application in the main folder. From there, you can deploy the application via the following:

```
# Linux
GLASSFISH_INST_DIR/bin/asadmin deploy --force=true \
    HelloWorld.war
```

```
rem Windows
GLASSFISH_INST_DIR\bin\asadmin deploy --force=true ^
    HelloWorld.war
```

For `GLASSFISH_INST_DIR`, you must substitute the GlassFish installation folder.
To see it running, enter the following URL in the address line of your browser:

`http://localhost:8080/HelloWorld`

See Figures 1-2 and 1-3.

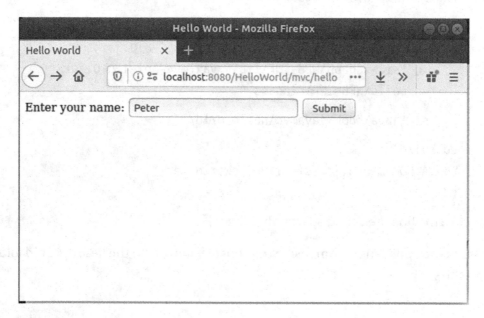

Figure 1-2. *Hello World start page*

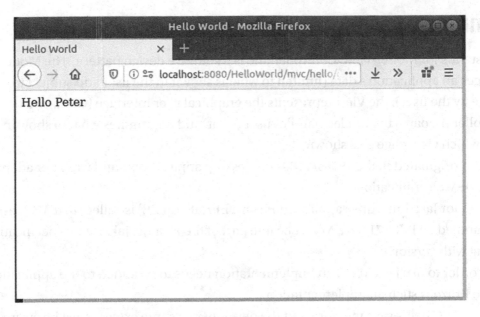

Figure 1-3. Hello World response page

Exercises

Exercise 1: Identify the three constituent elements of MVC.

Exercise 2: True or false: The model's responsibility is to talk with enterprise information systems (e.g., databases).

Exercise 3: True or false: For MVC, passing user-generated data to the model elements is done automatically.

Exercise 4: True or false: Views can read and access model values.

Exercise 5: Which is true: (A) A session is a model object, (B) A session is a property from inside the HTTP protocol, (C) You must create and handle sessions from inside the application code.

Exercise 6: Java MVC became part of the Java EE/Jakarta EE specification with version 7.

Summary

MVC stands for Model-View-Controller and is a software design pattern. The Model manages an application's data (limited to what is shown to the user and subject to change by the user); the View represents the graphical user interface (GUI); and the Controller prepares the model, handles user input, and determines what to show in the view (which view page gets shown).

MVC originated in the 1970s/1980s for desktop applications, and was later adapted to handle web applications.

MVC for Java Enterprise applications (Java EE/Jakarta EE) is called *Java MVC* and it gets handled by JSR-371. Java MVC became part of the Java EE/Jakarta EE specification starting with version 8.

In order to use Java MVC, an implementation needs to be added to the application. Eclipse Krazo is such an implementation.

Java MVC helps save memory, but the developer, to some extent, must be aware of HTTP protocol characteristics. User sessions are handled by a cookie, request, or POST parameter. Sessions are transparently handled by the framework.

In the next chapter, we talk about Java MVC's relationship to Java EE/Jakarta EE in more detail.

CHAPTER 2

Prerequisite: Jakarta EE/Java EE

You can't run Java MVC in a standalone mode. Instead, it must be accompanied by the infrastructure a Java Enterprise Edition Server (Java EE or Jakarta EE) provides. We talk about what this means in this chapter.

The Nature of Java for Enterprise Applications

In a corporate environment, a programming language and software platform like Java has to cover a couple of needs that are important to run a business. It has to be able to connect to one or more databases, reliably establish communication with other IT-based systems in the same company or with connected businesses, and it has to be powerful enough to reliably handle input and perform calculations based on input and database data, and present the appropriate output to clients. As a cross-concern, security also plays an important role. An authentication process needs to be established that forces the users to identify themselves, and an authorization needs to be achieved to limit the amount of resources a particular user is allowed to access. In addition, activities need to be logged for technical maintenance and auditing purposes, and the platform should be able to present monitoring data for technical sanity checks and performance-related investigations.

For all these to work in a desired way, a language and platform must be stable with respect to future changes and enhancements. This has to happen in a way that new language and platform versions can be appropriately handled by the IT staff. Java EE/Jakarta EE follow this trail and thus are very useful in corporate environments.

The Jakarta EE 8 server entirely runs on and depends on Java. Java was invented in 1991 but was first publicly released under version 1.0 by Sun Microsystems in 1996. Java

19

© Peter Späth 2021
P. Späth, *Beginning Java MVC 1.0*, https://doi.org/10.1007/978-1-4842-6280-1_2

has since played an important role as both a language and a runtime environment or platform. There are several reasons that Java became so successful:

- The same Java program can run on different operating systems.

- Java runs in a sandboxed environment. This improves execution security.

- Java can be easily extended with custom libraries.

- The Java language was extended only slowly. While a slow evolution means new and helpful language constructs may be missing in the most current version, it helps developers easily keep track of new features and thoroughly perform transitions to new Java versions in longer running projects. Furthermore, with only a small number of exceptions, Java versions were backward-compatible.

- Java includes a garbage collector that automatically cleans up unused memory.

Since 1998 and the major rebranding as Java 2, the platform was made available in different configurations:

- The standard edition J2SE for running on a desktop. It was further separated into JRE (Java Runtime Environment) for running Java, and JDK (Java Development Kit) for compiling and running Java.

- The micro edition J2ME for mobile and embedded devices.

- The enterprise edition J2EE with enterprise features added to J2SE. Each J2EE configuration includes a complete J2SE installation.

For marketing purposes, the "2" was removed in 2006 and the configurations were named JSE (or JDK, which is JSE plus development tools), JME, and JEE, respectively. In 2018, JEE was moved to the Eclipse foundation and renamed Jakarta EE. The Java language substantially changed from Java 7 to Java 8. We will be using all the modern features of Java 8 in our explanations and code examples.

Java of course continues to be developed. While the latest version of Jakarta EE was 8 while writing this book, and the underlying Java standard edition was version 8 as well, the latest JavaSE (JSE) version you could download was 13. We won't be talking about JavaSE versions 9 or higher in this book.

While knowledge of the Java standard edition JSE version 8 is considered a prerequisite in this book, for readers who are only partly familiar with Java 8, the following new features are worth an investigation before you move to subsequent chapters:

- Functional interfaces

- Lambda calculus (unnamed functions)

- The streams API for working with collections and maps

- The new date and time API

We will be using these where appropriate in the book's examples.

The specifications that describe the parts of Java EE/Jakarta EE tell what each part can do and how it does it, and they keep track of new versions. Java EE/Jakarta EE 8 includes sub-technologies also closely described by exact version numbers. We list them here and include a short description of what each technology does. Note that the list is not exhaustive—it does not include some more advanced APIs, which you can learn about if you look at the official documentation.

- **Java MVC 1.0 - JSR-371:** This is our main concern in this book.

- **Enterprise Java Beans EJB - Version 3.2:** EJBs represent entry points for business logic. Each EJB plays the role of a component in the overall Jakarta EE architecture and is responsible for a dedicate business task. EJBs allow developers to add security, transactional features, JPA features to communicate with databases, and web services functionality, and they can also be entry points for messaging.

- **Java Server Faces JSF - Version 2.3:** JSF is the component-based dedicated primary web frontend technology to be used for browser access. Using Java MVC is somewhat an alternative approach, and nobody hinders you from mixing them freely. JSFs usually communicate over EJBs with the business logic.

- **RESTful Web-Services JAX-RS - Version 2.1:** REST (REpresentational State Transfer) is the original HTTP protocol that defines reading and writing resources. It recently gained increased attention for single page web applications, where the frontend page flow is completely handled by JavaScript running in the browser.

- **JSON Processing JSON-P - Version 1.1:** JSON (JavaScript Object Notation) is a lean data-format particularly useful if a considerable amount of the presentation logic gets handled by JavaScript running in the browser.

- **JSON Binding JSON-B - Version 1.0:** This technology simplifies mapping between JSON data and Java classes.

- **Web Sockets - Version 1.1:** Provides a full-duplex communication between web clients (browsers) and the Jakarta EE server. Other than "normal" access via HTTP, web sockets allow for the server to send messages to a browser client as well!

- **JPA - Version 2.2:** The Java Persistence API provides high-level access to databases.

- **Java EE Security API - Version 1.0:** A new security API that didn't exist prior to Jakarta EE 8. It includes an HTTP authentication mechanism, an identity store abstraction for validating user credentials and group memberships, and a security context API that programmatically handles security.

- **Java Messaging Service JMS - Version 2.0:** This is about messaging, which means messages can be produced and consumed asynchronously. A message sender produces and issues a message and can instantaneously continue its work, even when the message gets consumed later.

- **Java Transaction API (JTA) - Version 1.2:** JTA makes sure that processes that combine several steps acting as a unit can be committed or rolled back as a whole. This can become tricky if distributed partners are involved. JTA helps a lot here to ensure transactionality even for more complex systems.

- **Servlets - Version 4.0:** Servlets are the underlying technology for server-browser communication. You usually configure them only once at the beginning of a project. We describe servlets where necessary to get other technologies to run.

- **Context And Dependency Injection CDI - Version 2.0:** CDI allows developers to bind contexts to elements that are governed by a dedicated lifecycle. In addition, it injects dependencies into objects, which simplifies class associations. We will use CDI to connect JSF elements to the application logic.

- **JavaMail - Version 1.6:** Provides facilities for reading and sending email. This is just an API. For an implementation, you can for example use Oracle's reference implementation: `https://javaee.github.io/javamail/`

- **Bean Validation - Version 2.0:** This allows developers to restrict method call parameters to comply with certain value predicates.

- **Interceptors - Version 1.2:** Interceptors allow you to wrap method calls into invocations of interceptor classes. While this can be done by programmatic method calls as well, interceptors allow developers to do it in a declarative way. You typically use interceptors for crosscutting concerns like logging, security issues, monitoring, and the like.

- **Java Server Pages JSP - Version 2.3:** JSPs can be used to establish a page flow in server-browser communication. JSP is an older technology, but you still can use it if you like. You should however favor JSFs over JSPs, and in this book we don't handle JSPs.

- **JSP Standard Tag Library JSTL - Version 1.2:** Tags used in conjunction with JSPs for page elements.

Java EE/Jakarta EE runs on top of the Java Standard Edition (SE), so you can always use any classes and interfaces of the Java SE if you program for Java EE/Jakarta EE. A couple of technologies included within the Java Standard Edition SE play a prominent role in a Java Enterprise Edition environment:

- **JDBC - Version 4.0:** An access API for databases. All major database vendors provide JDBC drivers for their product. You *could* use it, but you shouldn't. Use the higher-level JPA technology instead. You'll get in contact once in a while, because JPA under-the-hood uses JDBC.

- **Java Naming and Directory Interface JNDI:** In a Jakarta EE 8 environment, objects will be accessed by other objects in a rather loose way. In modern enterprise edition applications, this usually happens via CDI, more precisely, via dependency injection. Under the hood, however, a lookup service plays a role, governed by JNDI. In the past, you'd have to directly use JNDI interfaces to programmatically fetch dependent objects. You could use JNDI for Jakarta EE 8, but you normally don't have to.

- **Java API for XML Processing JAXP - Version 1.6:** A general-purpose XML processing API. You can access XML data via DOM (complete XML tree in memory), SAX (event-based XML parsing), or StAX. This is just an API. Normally you'd have to also add an implementation, but the Jakarta EE server does this automatically for you.

- **Streaming API for XML StAX - Version 1.0:** Used for streaming access to XML data. Streaming here means you serially access XML elements on explicit demand (pull parsing).

- **Java XML Binding JAXB - Version 2.2:** JAXB connects XML elements to Java classes.

- **XML Web Services JAX-WS - Version 2.2:** Web services remotely connect components using XML as a messaging format.

- **JMX - Version 2.0:** JMX is a communication technology you can use to monitor components of a running Jakarta EE application. It is up to the server implementation what information is available for JMX monitoring, but you can add monitoring capabilities to your own components.

The specifications are handled by a community process, and vendors have to pass tests if they want to be able to say their server products conform to a certain version of Jakarta EE (or one of its predecessors, JEE or J2EE). If you are interested, the corresponding online resources provide information about it. As a start, enter "java community process jcp" or "java eclipse ee.next working group" into your favorite search engine.

The Java Enterprise Edition was initially developed by Sun Microsystems and was called J2EE. In 2006, the naming and versioning schema was changed to JEE, and after J2EE version 1.4 came JEE version 5. Since then, major updates happened and versions JEE 6, JEE 7, and JEE 8 were released. In 2010, Sun Microsystems was acquired by Oracle corp. Under Oracle, versions JEE 7 and JEE 8 were released. In 2017, Oracle Corporation submitted Java EE to the Eclipse Foundation, and the name was changed to Jakarta EE 8.

As of the beginning of 2020, the transition from JEE 8 to Jakarta EE 8 was an ongoing process. So depending on when you read this book, it still could be that for online research about Jakarta EE 8, you have to consult pages about both JEE 8 and Jakarta EE 8. This is something you should keep in mind. To keep things simple in this book, we will only talk about Jakarta EE.

When this book was written, there were not many Jakarta EE 8 servers released. There are basically the following:

- GlassFish Server, Open Source Edition, from Oracle Inc.

- WildFly Server, from Red Hat

- JBoss Enterprise Application Platform, from Red Hat

- WebSphere Application Server Liberty, from IBM

- Open Liberty, from IBM

These servers have different licensing models. GlassFish, WildFly, and Open Liberty are free. This means you can use them without charge, both for development purposes and for production. To run the JBoss Enterprise Application Platform, you need a subscription, although the sources are open. WebSphere Application Server Liberty is proprietary.

In this book, we will talk about running Java MVC inside the GlassFish server, open source edition, version 5.1. Due to the nature of Jakarta EE 8, a transition to other servers is always possible, although you'll have to spend a considerable amount of time changing the administration workflow.

GlassFish, a Free Java Server

There are several free Java EE/Jakarta EE servers you can use for evaluation and development. The GlassFish server is a particularly good choice, especially for learning purposes, because it is open source.

Getting GlassFish

The latest version as of the writing of this book is 5.1, and you can download it from the following:

```
https://projects.eclipse.org/
      projects/ee4j.glassfish/downloads
```

Choose the "Full Profile" variant.

Note   At the time this book is published, there are likely later versions for GlassFish available. You could try versions greater than 5.1 and you might not have any problems installing and using them with this book. But to avoid any chance of problems, it will always be possible to use an archived GlassFish 5.1 installer.

After you download the ZIP file, extract it anywhere on your file system. We will henceforth call the installation folder GLASSFISH_INST_DIR. Before GlassFish can be started, you must make sure you have Java 8 JDK installed on your system.

Note   JDK 8 is a requirement for GlassFish 5.1. You cannot use a later version and you should not use an earlier version.

Get the JDK from one of the following links (for the www.oracle.com variant, you must get a paid subscription for commercial projects):

```
https://www.oracle.com/java/technologies/javase/
      javase-jdk8-downloads.html
https://jdk.java.net/java-se-ri/8-MR3
```

The jdk.java.net variant points to the OpenJDK distribution. For Linux, chances are good your distribution's package provider has a pre-built Java installation package for you.

If JDK 8 is not your system default, you can check by entering `java -version` in a console window. You must add the following line

```
REM Windows:
REM Note, if the JDK_INST contains spaces, wrap it
REM inside "..."
set AS_JAVA=JDK_INST
```

```
# Linux:
AS_JAVA="JDK_INST"
```

inside the GLASSFISH_INST_DIR/glassfish/config/asenv.conf (Linux) or GLASSFISH_INST_DIR/glassfish/config/asenv.bat (Windows) file, where you must replace JDK_INST with the installation folder of the JDK 8 installation.

You can now check the installation in a console window. Change the user directory (current directory) to the GlassFish installation folder and then use asadmin to start the server:

```
REM Windows:
chdir GLASSFISH_INST_DIR
bin\asadmin start-domain
```

```
# Linux:
cd GLASSFISH_INST_DIR
bin/asadmin start-domain
```

The output should be something like this:

```
Waiting for domain1 to start .
Successfully started the domain : domain1
domain Location: [...]/glassfish/domains/domain1
Log File: [...]/glassfish/domains/domain1/logs/server.log
Admin Port: 4848
Command start-domain executed successfully.
```

You can also check the indicated log file to see whether the startup worked correctly. You can open your browser at http://localhost:4848 to see whether the web administrator is available (it should be).

Once you verify that the server started up correctly, you can stop it if you like. To do so, enter the following:

```
REM Windows:
bin\asadmin stop-domain

# Linux:
bin/asadmin stop-domain
```

Note   In the rest of this chapter, we assume that you entered `cd GLASSFISH_INST_DIR` to change to the GlassFish installation directory. I will also stop distinguishing between Windows and Linux and write `bin/asadmin`, which on Windows should be `bin\asadmin.bat`.

The GlassFish server has three administrative frontends:

- A shell (or windows command prompt) frontend
- A GUI frontend for browser access
- A REST HTTP frontend

GlassFish Shell Administration

The shell frontend works via the `bin/asadmin` script, which you can call from a shell (or a windows command prompt). This command is extremely powerful; it contains hundreds of options and subcommands. We do not list them all here, so for a complete online list, enter "oracle glassfish server administration guide" in your favorite search engine.

As a starting point, the `asadmin` command also provides a "help" functionality. To see it, enter one of the following:

```
bin/asadmin help
bin/asadmin -?
```

Where the first variant (help) opens a MORE pager. To list all the subcommands, enter the following:

```
# Note: server must be running!
bin/asadmin list-commands
```

To see the help for a particular subcommand, you can write one of the following:

```
bin/asadmin help <SUB-COMMAND>
bin/asadmin -? <SUB-COMMAND>
```

Where you substitute the name of the subcommand for <SUB-COMMAND>.

Note   In order for many subcommands to run properly, the server must be running as well. In the following discussion, we assume that the server has started before you issue any subcommands.

There is also a *multimode* session, where a special subshell is opened. In this subshell you can enter subcommands directly without prepending the bin/asadmin. To start a multimode session, enter the following without arguments:

```
bin/asadmin
```

You can also use the multimode subcommand to start a multimode session:

```
bin/asadmin multimode
```

The subcommand allows for an optional --file <FILE_NAME> argument, which causes the specified file to be read in as a list of subcommands to be executed sequentially:

```
bin/asadmin multimode --file commands_file.txt
```

The file path is relative to the current working directory. In the following paragraphs, we show a list of the most useful options and subcommands. The most useful general options are shown in Table 2-1. You add them as in bin/asadmin --host 192.168.1.37 list-applications.

Table 2-1. *General Options*

Option	Description
--host <HOST>	Specifies the host where the server is running. If you don't specify it, localhost will be used.
--port <PORT>	The administration port. The default is 4848
--user <USER_NAME>	Uses the specified user to authenticate to the server. Use this if you restricted access to the asadmin utility. The default is the admin user.
--passwordfile <FILE_NAME>	If you restricted access to the asadmin utility, and you want to prevent a user password from being prompted, you can specify a file with password information instead. For details, see the output of bin/asadmin -?.

For a complete list of the options you can add to the asadmin command, see the output of bin/asadmin -?.

Subcommands used to inquire various types of information from the server are shown in Table 2-2. You enter them as in bin/asadmin list-applications (obviously, the list will be empty if you haven't installed any applications yet).

Table 2-2. *Inquiring Information*

Subcommand	Description
version	Outputs the GlassFish server version.
list-applications	Lists all applications deployed and running on the server.
list-containers	Containers embrace components (modules, if you like) of a certain type. Use this subcommand to list all the containers running in the server.
list-modules	Lists all OSGi modules running in the server. We won't be talking about OSGi in this book, but in case you are interested, GlassFish incorporates an *Apache Felix* OSGi module management system. You can administer GlassFish components also via an OSGi shell named "Gogo," which needs more configuration work to run.

(*continued*)

Table 2-2. (*continued*)

Subcommand	Description
list-commands	Lists all the subcommands. If you add --localonly the server doesn't have to be running and only subcommands that can be issued with the server not running will be listed.
list-timers	Shows all timers. We don't talk about timers in this book.
list-domains	Lists all domains. In this book, we will be using the preinstalled default domain, called domain1, so this will be the only entry showing up here.

After you perform the installation of the GlassFish server, there will be one administration user named admin without a password. Not having a password makes administrative tasks easy, but it will also leave your server insecure. To remedy that and give the admin user a password, enter the following:

```
bin/asadmin change-admin-password
```

You will then be asked for the actual password, which is empty so just press Enter. Then enter the new password twice.

Once the admin user has a password, you will have to enter the password for most asadmin subcommands.

To start a domain means to start the GlassFish server. We could have several domains in one GlassFish server, but a multi-domain setup is left for advanced users, so we'll go with the single domain1 domain, which is installed by default.

To start, stop, or restart the GlassFish server, enter one of the following commands:

```
bin/asadmin start-domain
bin/asadmin stop-domain
bin/asadmin restart-domain
```

All three subcommands take an optional domain name as a parameter (for example, domain1 or domain2), but since we have only one default domain, it can be left off here.

To see the uptime of the server, which is the time that has elapsed since the default domain started, enter the following:

```
bin/asadmin uptime
```

The Jakarta EE GlassFish server comes with a built-in database. This comes in handy for development purposes, although you probably won't use this database for production setups. This database is an Apache Derby database. It does not run by default when the GlassFish server is started. Instead, to start and stop the database, enter the following:

```
bin/asadmin start-database
bin/asadmin stop-database
```

where the database port by default reads 1527.

GlassFish GUI Administration

After you start the GlassFish server, a GUI console is provided and you should use it to open the following URL in a browser:

```
http://localhost:4848
```

The GUI will then show up, as seen in Figure 2-1.

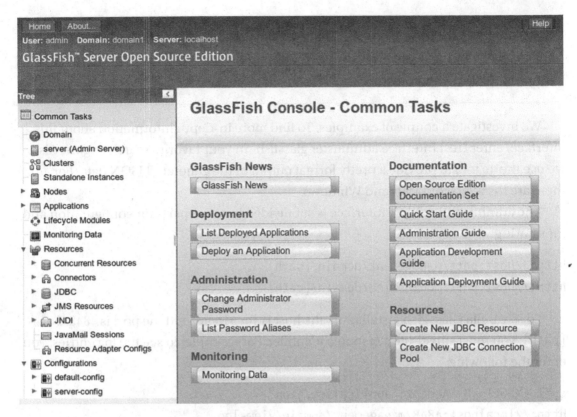

Figure 2-1. *Browser GUI administration*

We don't talk about details of the GUI administration here. We will, however, use and describe it once in a while in this book, and the help button on the top-right corner is a good starting point for your own experiments and investigations.

Note   Many `asadmin` operations that you can enter in a terminal have their counterparts in the admin GUI.

GlassFish REST Interface Administration

The GlassFish Jakarta EE 8 server provides a REST interface that you can use to investigate and control the server. You can issue the following to see the domain logs via REST for example:

```
curl -X GET -H "Accept: application/json" \
http://localhost:4848/monitoring/domain/view-log/details
```

Note   For this to work, the `curl` utility must be installed on your system. Alternatively, you can use any other REST client (Firefox REST-client add-on, REST Client for Eclipse, and others).

We investigate a couple of examples. To find more in-depth information about this interface, enter "rest interface administer glassfish" in your favorite search engine. Also, we use the `jq` tool to provide a pretty format output of the generated JSON data. For `jq`, there are installers for Linux and Windows.

The administrative REST interface is subdivided into two parts for configuration and monitoring:

```
http://host:port/management/domain/[path]
http://host:port/monitoring/domain/[path]
```

For a vanilla GlassFish installation, the host is `localhost` and the port is `4848`. For `[path]`, you must substitute a resource identifier. For example, to see the log entries, you enter the following:

```
curl -X GET -H "Accept: application/json" \
http://localhost:4848/management/domain/view-log
```

(Remove the backslash if you enter this on one line.)

The REST interface is very extensive. You can query a lot of properties using REST's GET verb, and you can alter resources using POST or PUT. As a starting point, you can investigate the verbose output of REST capabilities you will get once you enter the following:

```
curl -X GET -H "Accept: application/json" \
http://localhost:4848/management/domain
```

The output will for example include the following:

```
"commands": [
  ...
  {
    "path": "list-commands",
    "method": "GET",
    "command": "list-commands"
```

```
  },
  {
    "path": "restart-domain",
    "method": "POST",
    "command": "restart-domain"
  },
  {
    "path": "uptime",
    "method": "GET",
    "command": "uptime"
  },
  {
    "path": "version",
    "method": "GET",
    "command": "version"
  }
  ...
]
```

There are lots of others. To see version and uptime, you enter the following:

```
curl -X GET -H "Accept: application/json" \
    http://localhost:4848/management/domain/version | jq .
curl -X GET -H "Accept: application/json" \
    http://localhost:4848/management/domain/uptime | jq .
```

If you use a browser and enter REST URLs there, you get more information about REST resources. If you open a browser and enter http://localhost:4848/management/domain/version, you will get an HTML variant of this CURL output. Both also tell us about child resources.

So this code, for example, shows us about commands referring to installed application:

```
curl -X GET -H "Accept: application/json" \
  http://localhost:4848/management/domain/applications |
jq .
```

It tells us that, for the actual list, we have to enter the following:

```
curl -X GET -H "Accept: application/json" \
  http://localhost:4848/management/domain/applications/ list-applications |
 jq .
```

(No line break after `applications/`.) It tells us about attributes. To get more verbose output, we can add a `?long=true`, as in:

```
curl -X GET -H "Accept: application/json" \
  http://localhost:4848/management/domain/applications/
  list-applications?long=true | jq .
```

Using a Preinstalled Java Server

Java MVC applications usually reside in WAR files (ZIP files ending with `.war`), so they may be installed on any Jakarta EE compliant server.

For this reason, you don't have to use GlassFish. In this book, we will use GlassFish, but if you prefer a different Jakarta EE 8 server, you may use it. Of course, you have to learn how to administer that server by consulting its manual.

Note   If you target a proprietary server, it is generally not recommended to start development with a different product from a different vendor. You should at least try to develop with a free variant of the same server, or try to get a developer license. To learn Jakarta EE 8 first using GlassFish and later switching to a different product or vendor is a reasonable approach, though.

Learning Java for Enterprise Applications

In order to learn the Java language (or the standard edition APIs) or improve your skills, you can choose among a wealth of books and online resources. A good place to start looking is the official Java tutorial from Oracle, found at

```
https://docs.oracle.com/javase/tutorial/
```

Real-world corporate projects may require you to look at other technologies from the Java EE/Jakarta EE technology stack. There is also a tutorial for the enterprise edition Java EE/Jakarta EE, which you can find at:

```
https://javaee.github.io/tutorial/toc.html
```

You may also want to consult the book *Beginning Jakarta EE: Enterprise Edition for Java: From Novice to Professional* (ISBN: 978-1484250785) from the same author. Here, we mainly talk about Java MVC and handle other Java EE/Jakarta EE technologies only where appropriate and needed.

RESTful Services

There is a good reason to also briefly talk about JAX-RS, even though it's an exception to the limitation of this book's scope to Java MVC. JAX-RS is the subtechnology of Java EE/Jakarta EE handling RESTful services. As a matter of fact, Java MVC sits on top of JAX-RS, which was a clever decision of the framework programmers. Not only does it allow developers to let Java MVC very cleanly integrate with the rest of the Java EE/Jakarta EE framework, it also gives a straightforward clue as to how to mix Java MVC development techniques and more fine-grained client-server communication using AJAX and JSON data snippets.

REST is an acronym for *representational state transfer*. It is an architectural style for web related operations. Clients use a predefined set of operations or HTTP methods on data—GET, POST, PUT, and DELETE (and a few more) for communicating with servers. As no state is involved, the client communicates using one of the verbs GET, DELETE, POST, PUT, and so on, and immediately after the server has performed the operation and/or returned data, the server forgets about the communication step. The name "representational state transfer" stems from the fact that, from the client's point of view, the representation of data inquired from the server changes between communication steps (or might change).

The communication verbs have been part of the HTTP specification since the infancy of the web. In more detail, we have the following verbs:

- GET: Used to retrieve a resource. Resources are identified by URIs, so the communication might be described by something like GET http://some.server.com/myclub/member/37. A GET operation is not allowed to change any data (except for access statistics and the like), and it must be idempotent. That means a second GET using the same URI with no intermediate operations between those two GETs must return exactly the same data. Note that GET operations were widely abused for any kind of operations, including changing data. With REST we return to the roots and data must not be changed.

- DELETE: Used to delete information. Again the resource in question gets addressed by an URI, so you write DELETE http://some.server. com/myclub/member/37. A DELETE must be idempotent, which means deleting again using the same URI must not change the data. In this case, the second DELETE is of course superfluous; deleting what was already deleted is not supposed to do anything. As a characteristic of REST concerning a second DELETE, the server must not return an error message, but just ignore the request instead.

- POST: Used to post new information. POSTs commonly happen when the user submits a form. POSTs are not idempotent, so a second post using the same data will lead to a second data set on the server side. A post might be described by POST http://some.server.com/mycl ub/member/37 [data], where [data] stands for the transmitted data, usually in the form of XML or JSON, passed over in the transmitted message body.

- PUT: Used to store data. If the resource described by the data already exists, the resource will be altered according to the data. If it does not exist, the server might decide to act as if a POST were specified. A PUT is idempotent, PUTting again using the same input data will not change the data on the server.

The other verbs are less frequently used in real-world applications. HEAD is for retrieving metadata about a resource (information about it, but not the resource itself). Using a TRACE, you can see what happens to the data on the way to the server. This is more a technical operation and does not pay particular attention to the data payload. A PATCH is like a PUT with partial data. PUTs, with the complete information, are more frequently used over PATCHs. The OPTIONS verb requests the server's capability for a dedicated resource (like telling what can be done with the resource). A CONNECT is used to establish transparent tunnels on the server side. Again this is more a technical facility and does not reveal anything about the transmitted data.

To define a REST endpoint, you write a Java class with annotation `javax.ws.rs.Path` added at class and/or method level. For example, consider a REST controller that returns the current date and time as JSON:

```java
package book.javavmc.restdate;

import java.time.ZonedDateTime;
import javax.ws.rs.*;

/**
 * REST Web Service
 */
@Path("/d")
public class RestDate {
    @GET
    @Path("date")
    @Produces("application/json")
    public String stdDate() {
        return "{\"date\":\"" + ZonedDateTime.now().toString() +
        "\"}";
    }
}
```

The @Path annotations merge, so in the end, we get an endpoint URL such as `http://localhost:8080/theAppName/d/date`.

You will start developing your first Java MVC application soon. This is why I show you this first code snippet without explaining how to build and deploy it. A Java MVC controller looks very similar:

```
package book.javavmc.somecontroller;

import java.util.List;
import javax.inject.Inject;
import javax.mvc.Controller;
import javax.mvc.Models;
import javax.ws.rs.*;

@Path("/pets")
@Controller
public class PetshopController {
    @Inject
    private Models models;

    @GET
    public String showIndex() {
        final List<Pet> pets = ...;
        models.put("pets", pets);
        return "index.jsp";
    }
}
```

You can see that we again use `javax.ws.rs.Path` to define an endpoint. We will later see that the main differences between Java MVC and JAX-RS are the `@Controller` annotation and that the action method returns the name of the next view page instead of data.

Note   You will find more online information about JAX-RS, including the official specification, if you enter "jax-rs" in your favorite search engine.

Exercises

Exercise 1: Describe the relationship between JSE and Java EE/Jakarta EE.

Exercise 2: True or false? Java MVC can run directly inside a PC's or server's operating system.

Exercise 3: True or false? Java MVC is a Jakarta EE server.

Exercise 4: True or false? Jakarta EE is a competitor of Java EE.

Exercise 5: True or false? There is no difference between OpenJDK 8 and Oracle's JSE 8.

Exercise 6: True or false? GlassFish can be used for commercial products without paying for a license.

Exercise 7: Why do we use GlassFish in this book?

Exercise 8: True or false? PURGE is an HTTP verb.

Exercise 9: Describe the relationship between Java MVC and JAX-RS.

Summary

Java MVC is accompanied by the infrastructure that a Java Enterprise Edition server (Java EE or Jakarta EE) provides. In a corporate environment, a programming language and software platform like Java has to cover a couple of needs that are important to run a business. It has to be able to connect to one or more databases, reliably establish communication with other IT-based systems in the same company or with connected businesses, and it has to be powerful enough to reliably handle input and perform calculations based on input and database data, and present the appropriate output to clients.

The Jakarta EE 8 server runs on and depends on Java. There are several reasons that Java became so successful:

- The same Java program can run on different operating systems.

- Java runs in a sandboxed environment. This improves execution security.

41

- Java can be easily extended with custom libraries.

- The Java language was extended only slowly. While a slow evolution means new and helpful language constructs may be missing in the most current version, it helps developers easily keep track of new features and thoroughly perform transitions to new Java versions in longer running projects. Furthermore, with only a small number of exceptions, Java versions were backward-compatible.

- Java includes a garbage collector that automatically cleans up unused memory.

Java continues to be developed. While the latest version of Jakarta EE was 8 while writing this book, and the underlying Java standard edition was version 8 as well, the latest JavaSE (JSE) version you could download was 13. We won't be talking about JavaSE versions 9 or higher in this book.

The specifications that describe the parts of Java EE/Jakarta EE tell what each part can do and how it does it, and they keep track of new versions. Java EE/Jakarta EE 8 includes sub-technologies, which are also closely described by exact version numbers. The specifications are handled by a community process, and vendors have to pass tests if they want to be able to say their server products conform to a certain version of Jakarta EE (or one of its predecessors, JEE or J2EE).

The Java Enterprise Edition was initially developed by Sun Microsystems and was called J2EE. In 2006, the naming and versioning schema was changed to JEE, and after J2EE version 1.4 came JEE version 5. Since then, major updates happened and versions JEE 6, JEE 7, and JEE 8 were all released. In 2010, Sun Microsystems was acquired by Oracle corp. Under Oracle, versions JEE 7 and JEE 8 were released. In 2017, Oracle Corporation submitted Java EE to the Eclipse Foundation, and the name was changed to Jakarta EE 8.

In this book, we will talk about running Java MVC inside the GlassFish server, open source edition, version 5.1. Due to the nature of Jakarta EE 8, a transition to other servers is always possible, although you have to spend a considerable amount of time changing the administration workflow. GlassFish provides three administrative interfaces—command-line tools for a shell or console, a web administrator GUI, and an administrative REST interface.

Java MVC sits on top of JAX-RS, which was a clever decision of the framework programmers. Not only does it allow Java MVC to very cleanly integrate with the rest of the Java EE/Jakarta EE framework, it also gives a straightforward clue as to how to mix Java MVC development techniques and more fine-grained client-server communication using AJAX and JSON data snippets. REST controllers and Java MVC controllers look very similar.

In the next chapter, we handle the development workflow suitable for this book and other Java MVC projects.

CHAPTER 3

Development Workflow

In this chapter, we talk about development techniques, procedures, and tools you can use for the examples in this book and any subsequent projects using Java MVC.

Using Gradle as a Build Framework

Gradle is a modern build framework/build automation tool. It provides for a pure declarative configuration style, but you can also add imperative build code in the form of Groovy (or Kotlin) script snippets, if needed.

Note Best practices indicate that for build scripts, declarative programming (which tells what a build script has to do, not *how* it should do it) is favorable over imperative programming (precise step-by-step instructions).

In the rest of this book, we use Gradle for build automation, because it has a very concise build configuration and can be used from the console (the Linux bash and Windows consoles) and from inside IDEs like Eclipse. Gradle build scripts can be as small as just three lines, but they can also contain arbitrarily long code. We will use Gradle as a tool and a little later in this chapter describe more of its characteristics.

Caution If you want to use OpenJDK 8 to build and run applications, you must add a valid `cacerts` file. Simply install OpenJDK version 10, and then copy the `OpenJDK10-INST-DIR/lib/security/cacerts` to `OpenJDK8-INST-DIR/lib/security/cacerts` file.

© Peter Späth 2021
P. Späth, *Beginning Java MVC 1.0*, https://doi.org/10.1007/978-1-4842-6280-1_3

Using Eclipse as an IDE

Eclipse is an IDE (Integrated Development Environment) with a plethora of functionalities that help to develop Java Enterprise projects. It is freely available and you can use it for both commercial and non-commercial projects without charge.

Eclipse can be extended by plugins, from which many are developed by the community and are free to use. Plugins, however, might also come from vendors and you might have to buy licenses to use them. In this book, we will only use free plugins. If you feel tempted to try proprietary plugins, which under the circumstances might boost your development, visit the Eclipse marketplace at `https://marketplace.eclipse.org` and consult each plugin.eclipse.orgtevelopment, which under censes to use

Installing Eclipse

Eclipse comes in several variants. To download any of them, go to `https://www.eclipse.org/downloads/` or `https://www.eclipse.org/downloads/packages/`. We will use the Eclipse IDE for Enterprise Java Developers variant in this book.

Note   If you choose to download the installer, you will be asked for the variant. To select the Enterprise variant from the start, click the Download Packages link and choose the Enterprise version on the next page.

In this book, we will use Eclipse version 2020-03, but you might be able to use higher versions. Just keep in mind that if you run into trouble without an obvious solution, downgrading to Eclipse 2020-03 is an option.

Use any installation folder suitable for your needs. Plugin installations and version upgrades go in the folder you choose, so ensure appropriate file access rights. On my Linux box, I usually put Eclipse in a folder called:

```
/opt/eclipse-2019-09
```

(Or whatever version you have.) Then I make it writable to my Linux user:

```
cd /opt
USER=...   # enter user name here
GROUP=... # enter group name here
chown -R $USER.$GROUP eclipse-2019-09
```

This changes the ownership of all files of the Eclipse installation, which makes sense for a one-user workstation. If instead you have different users for Eclipse, you can create a new group called eclipse and give that group write access:

```
cd /opt
groupadd eclipse
chgrp -R eclipse eclipse-2019-09
chmod -R g+w eclipse-2019-09
USER=...   # enter your username here
usermod -a -G eclipse $USER
```

The chgrp ... command changes the group ownership and the chmod ... command allows write access for all group members. The usermod ... command adds a particular user to the new group.

Note   You need to be root for these commands. Also note that the usermod command does not affect the currently active window manager session on the PC. You must, for example, restart your system or, depending on your distribution, log out and log in again for that command to take effect.

As a last step, you can provide a symbolic link to the Eclipse installation folder:

```
cd /opt
ln -s eclipse-2019-09 eclipse
```

This makes it easier to switch between different Eclipse versions on your system.

On a Windows system, the installer sets the access rights for you and it is normally possible for any normal user to install plugins. This depends on the Windows version and on your system's configuration. Corporate environments often have more fine-grained access rights, with normal users who are unable to install plugins and to upgrade, and superusers for administrative purposes. These rights can be configured using Windows access rights management.

Configuring Eclipse

Upon startup, Eclipse uses the default Java version installed on your system. In case it cannot find it or you have several Java versions installed, you can explicitly tell Eclipse which Java to choose. For this aim, open this file

```
ECLIPSE-INST/eclipse.ini
```

And add two lines:

```
-vm
/path/to/your/jdk/bin/java
```

Directly above the -vmargs line:

```
...
openFile
--launcher.appendVmargs
-vm
/path/to/your/jdk/bin/java
-vmargs
...
```

Note   The format of the eclipse.ini file depends on the Eclipse version. Check https://wiki.eclipse.org/Eclipse.ini for the correct syntax. On that site you will also find precise instructions for specifying the Java executable path. The syntax shown here is for Eclipse 2020-03.

On Windows PCs, you specify the path as follows:

```
...
-vm C:\path\to\your\jdk\bin\javaw
...
```

Don't use escaped backslashes, like in C:\\path\\to\\..., as you would expect for Java-related files!

In order to see which version Java Eclipse uses for running (not for building projects!), start Eclipse, then navigate to Help➤About Eclipse IDE➤Installation Details➤Configuration tab. In the pane, find the line that starts with `java.runtime.version=....`

Adding Java Runtimes

Eclipse itself is a Java application, and in the preceding section, we learned how to tell Eclipse which Java version to choose for its own interests. For the development itself, you have to tell Eclipse which Java version to use for compiling and running the applications it hosts.

To do so, note the paths of all JDK installations you want to use for Eclipse development. Then, start Eclipse.

Note   When you start Eclipse, it asks you for a *workspace*. This folder can hold several distinct or interrelated projects. It is up to you if you want to choose an existing workspace or prefer to use a fresh new folder for an empty workspace.

Inside Eclipse, go to Window➤Preferences➤Java➤Installed JREs. Usually Eclipse is clever enough to automatically provide the JRE it used for its own startup. If this is enough for you, you don't have to do anything here. Otherwise, click the Add... button to register more JREs. In the subsequent dialog, select Standard VM as the JRE type.

Note   For Java 8, and other than when the name suggests, you must provide the paths to JDK installations, not JRE installations in the strict sense.

Select the check box to mark your primary JRE. Don't forget to click the Apply or Apply and Close button to register your changes.

Adding Plugins

Eclipse can be extended by many useful plugins. Some of them are necessary for your development, and some just improve your development workflow. In this book, we won't use too many extra plugins, and I will provide plugin installation instructions when they are needed.

As an exception, we will now install a Gradle plugin. We will later see that we can use Gradle from the console, but the Gradle plugin in Eclipse allows us to use Gradle directly from inside the IDE. Open Help➤Install New Software... and enter Eclipse Buildship (Gradle) and `http://download.eclipse.org/buildship/updates/latest` in the dialog. Select all the features and finish the wizard.

Eclipse Everyday Usage

Eclipse provides a lot of functions and you can learn about them by opening the built-in help. To give you a starting point, the following are tips that help you get the most out of Eclipse:

- You can get to an identifier's definition by placing the cursor over it and pressing F3. This works for variables (to navigate to their declarations) and classes/interfaces (to navigate to their definitions). You can even inspect referenced and Java standard library classes that way. Eclipse will download sources and show the code. This is a great way to learn about libraries in-depth by looking at the code.

- To rapidly find a resource, such as a file, class, or interface, press Ctrl+Shift+R.

- Start typing code and press Ctrl+Space and Eclipse will show you suggestions on how to finish your typing. For example, type new `SimpleDa` and then press Ctrl+Space. The list provided will contain all the constructors for the `SimpleDateFormat` class. Even better, you can make that shorter by typing new `SiDF` and pressing Ctrl+Space, because Eclipse will guess the missing lowercase letters. An additional goody is that you don't have to write the `import` statements for classes and interfaces you introduce that way. Eclipse will add the `imports` for you.

- Let Eclipse add the `imports` for all classes not yet resolved by pressing Shift+Ctrl+O (think of O as "organize imports").

- Format your code by pressing Ctrl+Alt+F. This also works with XML and other file types.

- Let Eclipse show you super- and subtypes by pressing F4 over a type designator.

- Use F5 to update the Project Explorer view, in case files were added or removed from outside of Eclipse.

- With a new Eclipse installation, open the Problems view by choosing Window➤Show View➤Other...➤General➤Problems. This will readily point you to any problems that Eclipse detects (compiler problems, configuration problems, and others).

- Open the tasks view from Window➤Show View➤Other...➤General➤Tasks to get a list of all occurrences of "TODO" that you entered in code comments.

- In case "TODO" is not fine-grained enough for you, you can add bookmarks by right-clicking the vertical bar anywhere on the left side of the code editor. Bookmarks are then listed in the Bookmarks view.

More About Gradle

With Eclipse and the Gradle plugin at hand, we can improve our knowledge of the Gradle framework. To keep things simple for now, we start with a very simple non-Java MVC project.

Note   You can find the Gradle user manual at `https://docs.gradle.org/current/userguide/userguide.html`.

A Basic Gradle Project

In order to learn more about Gradle, we build a simple `EchoLibrary` library with just one class and one method, printing a string to the console. Start Eclipse, and you'll be asked for a workspace. Choose any folder of your choice.

Note   You may add all example projects from this book to a single workspace called `JavaMVCBook` to keep things together, but this is up to you.

Go to File➤New➤Other...➤Gradle➤Gradle Project. Choose EchoLibrary as the project name. You can use the default settings for the Gradle project options. Upon completion, the New Project wizard prepares the project and adds a few files to the project that holds the Gradle configuration.

The next thing we do is make sure the project can use an existing JSE installation. The Gradle project wizard might try to use a nonexistent JRE and an error marker will appear. See Figure 3-1.

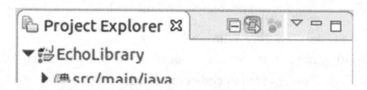

Figure 3-1. *Project error marker (red exclamation mark)*

To fix such a mismatch or to check whether the correct JRE is used, right-click the project, then choose Properties➤Java Build Path➤Libraries. See Figure 3-2.

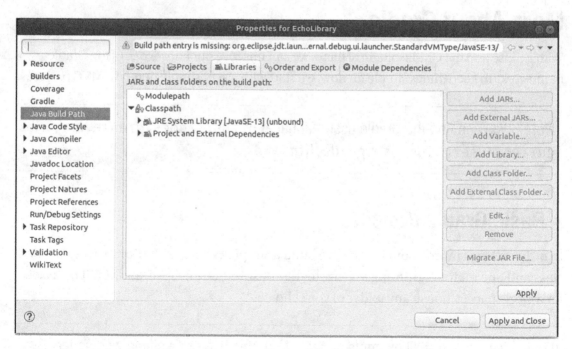

Figure 3-2. *JRE mismatch*

If there is a mismatch, remove the invalid entry by clicking Classpath and then choosing Add Library...➤JRE System Library. Add the version 8 JRE you registered with Eclipse. Then click the Apply and Close button.

Next, add a package called book.javamvc.echo by right clicking src/main/-java➤New➤Package. Inside the package, add an Echo class with these contents:

```
package book.javamvc.echo;

public class Echo {
    public void echo(String msg) {
        System.out.println(msg);
    }
}
```

Gradle Main Concepts

By default, Gradle uses one central build file named build.gradle inside the root folder of the project. Before we start talking about this file, we first need to cover Gradle's main concepts:

- Gradle has a core, which provides the infrastructure for build-related activities. The activities themselves live in Gradle plugins, which need to be specified in the build file and which run on top of the core. For each project, you can specify which plugins are to be used for Gradle builds. There are plugins for compiling Java classes; for packaging artifacts into ZIP, WAR, or EAR files; for running applications; and for publishing applications into a Maven repository. There are also various analysis plugins, IDE integration plugins, utility plugins, and more. And you can of course develop your own plugins.

- Plugins perform tasks. For example, the Java plugin has, among others, a compileJava task for compiling Java classes and a jar task for compressing and gathering several compiled classes.

- Each Gradle build consists of an *initialization*, a *configuration*, and an *execution* phase. In the initialization phase, Gradle determines whether the subprojects need to be included win the build. (We talk about subprojects later.) In the configuration phase, Gradle evaluates dependencies and builds a task graph, which contains all the tasks that need to be executed for a build. Configurations on all objects always run with every Gradle build. This is an important point and a common pitfall for beginning Gradle users. It means that for a task execution, the configuration for seemingly totally unrelated tasks is called as well. So, for performance reasons, the configuration for any task should be really fast. A task's configurations should not do anything that depends on whether the task is actually subject to execution. In the execution phase, the tasks actually do their jobs (compiling, moving, zipping, and so on).

Note   Many Gradle manuals and tutorials at the beginning center around user-defined tasks, which is actually a little bit misleading to the beginning Gradle user. In many, even bigger projects, the corresponding `build.gradle` file specifies and configures plugins, but hardly ever addresses tasks directly. Tasks are important from a technical point of view, but starting Gradle introductions by talking about the different phases and the plugin architecture leads to a more thorough understanding of Gradle's functioning.

Standard Gradle Project Layout

The project layout that all Gradle plugins by default expect is as follows:

```
src
  |- main
  |     |- java
  |     |     |- <java source files>
  |     |- resources
  |           |- <resource files>
  |
  |- test
        |- java
        |     |- <java source files>
        |- resources
              |- <resource files>
build
```

```
|- <any files built by Gradle>

build.gradle        <Gradle build file>
settings.gradle     <(Sub-)Project settings>
gradle.properties   <optional project properties>
```

Note   If you know the Maven build framework, the layout of the `src` folder will look familiar to you.

We will learn how to change the project structure in a later section.

The Central Gradle Build File

The Gradle project wizard from Eclipse creates a sample `build.gradle` file inside the project's root folder. For any Gradle project, including projects that don't use Eclipse, this is the central build file. The Eclipse plugin provides a basic build file with some example entries, but you can of course build this file from scratch.

Caution   The Eclipse Gradle plugin sometimes has a funny idea about when and where to show the build file. If you can't find the file in the Project Explorer, open the Gradle Task view and right-click the project, then choose the Open Gradle Build Script option.

A build file usually starts by defining which plugins are to be used, and then configures the plugins. User-defined tasks with operating instructions can also go to the build file, if needed. It is also possible to add Groovy or Kotlin code to existing tasks, which gives you the power to fine-tune plugins according to your needs.

Note   In this book, we show only Groovy code for Gradle build purposes. Groovy is dynamically typed and because of that maybe just a little bit more concise compared to the statically typed Kotlin. Besides, Groovy dedicatedly is a scripting language, so it's equipped with many utilities for scripting purposes, while Kotlin is a large-scale computer language and a competitor to Java.

Plugins usually have a very precise and reasonable idea about their defaults, so there is not much to configure for your project. For this reason, the build file could be rather small. This convention-over-configuration style is not an invention of Gradle, but Gradle—with its design aiming at elegance-gratefully adopts this idea.

Back to the EchoLibrary sample project. We dismiss the sample build.gradle file created by the wizard and overwrite its contents with the following:

```
// The EchoLibrary build file
plugins {
    id 'java-library'
}

java {
    sourceCompatibility = JavaVersion.VERSION_1_8
    targetCompatibility = JavaVersion.VERSION_1_8
}
repositories {
    jcenter()
}

dependencies {
    testImplementation 'junit:junit:4.12'
}
```

The first three lines plugins { id 'java-library' } specify that we want to use the java-library plugin. The name tells all, we in fact want to build a Java library, but you can learn about the details in the plugins section of the user manual.

The java { sourceCompatibility = JavaVersion.VERSION_1_8; targetCompatibility = JavaVersion.VERSION_1_8 } settings specify the JRE version of our library. Possible values can be looked up in the org.gradle.api.JavaVersion class, but you won't find anything surprising there (JDK 13 = JavaVersion. VERSION_1_13 and so on).

Note   Gradle uses your operating system's default JDK to compile classes. You should *not* use your Gradle project configuration to set the JDK path, because then you'd introduce some unneeded dependency. After all, a JRE 13 can very well handle JRE 8 files and maybe other developers want to use the same build scripts on their own systems. Instead you can change your operating system's JAVA_ HOME environment variable to specify a JDK path prior to Gradle invocations.

The `repositories { jcenter() }` lines indicate where Gradle will try to load libraries that your project depends on. The `jcenter()` points to Bintray's JCenter, but you can also use `google()` for Android projects and `mavenCentral()` for Maven Central. Or, you could specify a custom URL, as in `repositories { maven { url "http:// my.company.com/myRepo" } }`, which comes in handy with private or company-owned repositories. See the Gradle manual section called "Declaring Repositories."

The `dependencies` section indicates which libraries our project needs. For the `EchoLibrary` example, we have no dependency to an external library, but for unit tests, which we did not write in this case but could very well be an exercise for the inclined reader, we add a dependency to the JUnit test library.

All other settings—like the position of the source files, how the generated JAR file is named and where it is written to, where to store and cache downloaded dependencies, and so on—are handled by the plugin defaults.

This build file with a handful of settings can now be used to perform various build tasks.

Running Gradle Tasks

Build-related and user-triggered activities in Gradle are called *tasks*. The main objective of Gradle from a handling perspective is about invoking tasks.

The Eclipse Gradle plugin has a Gradle Tasks and a Gradle Executions view. In addition, diagnostic output goes to the standard Console view. The two Gradle-related views open by default after you install the Gradle plugin. See Figure 3-3.

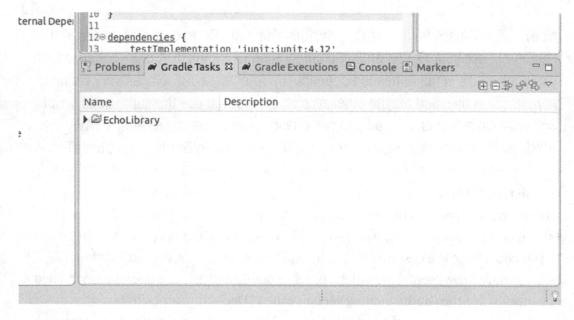

Figure 3-3. *Gradle views*

If this is not the case for you, go to Window➤Show View➤Other...➤Gradle to open a Gradle view. The Console view is available from Window➤Show View➤Console.

The Gradle Tasks view lists all available tasks in a tree view; see Figure 3-4. The scope of the tasks shown can be filtered using the view menu (small down triangle in the menu). If you introduce any custom tasks, this is a good time to enable the Show All Tasks item; otherwise, the custom tasks don't show up in the list. See Figure 3-5.

Name	Description
▼ 📂 EchoLibrary	
▶ 📂 build setup	
▼ 📂 build	
⚙ assemble	Assembles the outputs of this project.
⚙ build	Assembles and tests this project.
⚙ buildDependents	Assembles and tests this project and all projects that depend on it.
⚙ buildNeeded	Assembles and tests this project and all projects it depends on.
⚙ classes	Assembles main classes.
⚙ clean	Deletes the build directory.
⚙ jar	Assembles a jar archive containing the main classes.
⚙ testClasses	Assembles test classes

Figure 3-4. *Gradle tasks view tree*

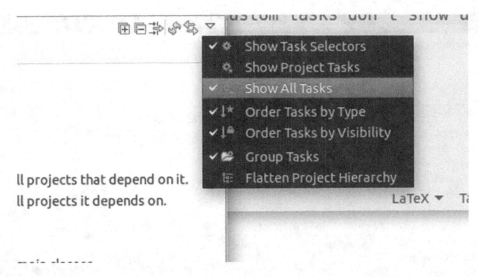

Figure 3-5. *Gradle tasks view menu*

Caution   If you change the project structure, for example by adding, removing, or renaming custom tasks, you must click the Refresh Tasks for All Projects button in the menu (the bent double arrow); otherwise, the view won't reflect the changes.

In order to run a Gradle task from inside the Gradle Tasks view, you first have to locate it inside the tree. Depending on how precise your idea is where to look inside the tree, you can also use the menu filter to find a task. Once you find it, double-click it to run the task. Diagnostic output, including any error messages, is shown in both the Gradle Executions and the Console views.

Tasks might have option parameters that control their functioning. For example, there is a `tasks` task that lists only a certain subset of all tasks. More precisely, tasks have a `group` property, and one of the groups is called `other`. If you run the `tasks` task without a parameter, tasks belonging to the `other` group are not included in the output. To show all tasks using that command, you must add an `--all` parameter. To do so from Eclipse, go to Run➤Run Configurations, navigate to Gradle Task, and add a new entry, as shown in Figure 3-6 (click the Add button twice to enter `tasks` and `--all`). Click Run and switch to the Console view to see the output.

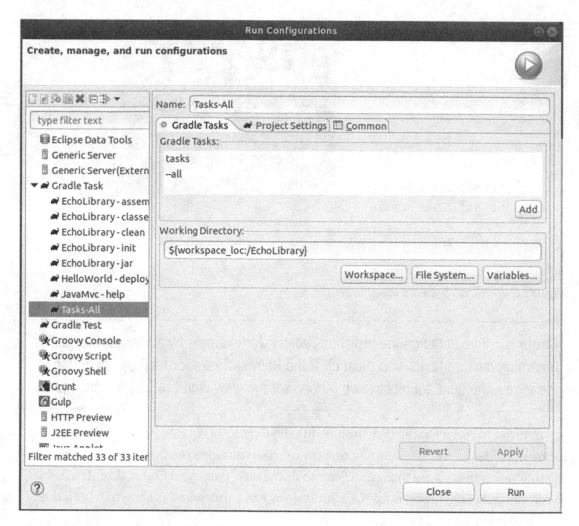

Figure 3-6. *Custom Gradle task run configuration*

For the `EchoLibrary` example, building a library JAR most probably is the main task. You can find it in the `build` section. Once you run it, the final JAR is presented in the `build/libs` folder.

Caution   The `build` folder might be filtered from the Eclipse project view. In this case, if you want to see it, open the project view menu at the small triangle, go to Filters and Customization, and remove the check mark from the Gradle Build Folder entry.

Gradle Tasks Explained

Tasks get defined by plugins, and plugins also might amend or overwrite tasks defined by other plugins, so there is no one-to-one relationship between tasks and plugins. In addition there are plugin-independent tasks defined by Gradle itself. Table 3-1 defines most of the tasks you'll normally use in your Java projects.

Table 3-1. *Gradle Tasks*

Name	Group	Description
help	help	Displays a help message.
projects	help	Shows the name of the project and lists the names of all subprojects, if applicable. We talk about subprojects later in this chapter.
tasks	help	Displays the tasks runnable from the project. You have to add the --all options to include tasks from the other group. To see tasks belonging to a certain group, add the --group <groupName> option (for the groupname, use build, build setup, documentation, help, verification, or other).
dependencies	help	Plugin-independent. Calculates and displays all the dependencies of the project. You can use this to determine which libraries the project depends on, including transitive dependencies (dependencies introduced indirectly, as dependencies of dependencies).
init	build setup	Adds files necessary for the current directory to serve as a root for Gradle builds. You do this normally only once and at the beginning of a new project. With the Eclipse Gradle plugin and the New Gradle Project wizard, this task is called automatically. This task does not depend on Gradle plugins being activated.

(continued)

Table 3-1. (*continued*)

Name	Group	Description
wrapper	build setup	Adds a Gradle wrapper to the project. Gradle builds can then be performed without Gradle being installed at an operating system level (Java must be installed). With the Eclipse Gradle plugin and the New Gradle Project wizard, this task is called automatically. This task does not depend on Gradle plugins being activated.
check	verification	A lifecycle task. Abstractly defined in the base plugin and materialized by activated plugins. Depends on test, but may run additional checks.
test	verification	Runs all unit tests.
assemble	build	A lifecycle task. Abstractly defined in the base plugin and materialized by activated plugins. Any plugin that produces a distribution or other consumable artifacts is supposed to make the assemble task depend on it. In a custom task, you would write something like assemble.dependsOn(someTask). Invoking this task bypasses any tests.
build	build	A lifecycle task. Abstractly defined in the base plugin and materialized by activated plugins. Depends on the check and assemble tasks, and thus performs all tests and then produces a distribution or other consumable artifacts, depending on the activated plugins.
clean	build	A lifecycle task. Deletes the build directory. You invoke this task if you want to make sure a subsequent build performs all build steps, even those that seemingly could have been reused from previous build operations. You do not normally invoke this task in everyday work, because if properly set up, Gradle should be able to determine which preparatory tasks need to be executed and which do not (because of previous builds).

(*continued*)

Table 3-1. (*continued*)

Name	Group	Description
classes	build	Any plugin which, somewhere in its build procedures, needs to build Java classes provided in this task. Its responsibility is to create Java classes from the main section (not test classes) of the sources.
testClasses	build	Similar to the classes task, but handles the test section from the sources.
jar	build	Assembles a JAR archive containing the classes from the main section.
ear	build	Only for the EAR plugin. Assembles an EAR archive from the subprojects (web applications and EJBs).
javadoc	documentation	Generates JavaDoc API documentation for the source code from the main section.
compileJava	other	Compiles Java source from the main section.
compileTestJava	other	Compiles Java source from the test section.

Each plugin's documentation may also describe more tasks of particular interest for that plugin.

Gradle Plugins

If you're developing for Java MVC and other Java and JEE/Jakarta EE related projects, the following list shows you the plugins you will most often encounter:

- **Base**: Provides basic tasks and conventions common for most builds.

- **Java**: Any type of Java project.

- **Java Library**: Extends the Java plugin and provides knowledge about the API exposed to consumers.

- **Java Platform**: Does not contain any sources, but describes a set of interrelated libraries that are usually published together.

- **Application**: Implicitly applies the Java plugin and allows for declaring a main class to be used as an application entry point.

- **WAR**: Extends the Java plugin and adds capabilities to build a web application in the form of a WAR file.

- **EAR**: Allows for creating an EAR file.

- **Maven Publish**: Adds capabilities to publish artifacts to a Maven repository.

- **Ivy Publish**: Adds capabilities to publish artifacts to an Ivy repository.

- **Distribution**: Adds functionalities for simplifying artifact distribution.

- **Java Library Distribution**: Adds functionalities for simplifying artifact distribution, with special attention paid to Java libraries.

- **Checkstyle**: Adds checkstyle checks.

- **PMD**: Adds PMD checks.

- **JaCoCo**: Adds JaCoCo checks.

- **CodeNarc**: Adds CodeNarc checks.

- **Signing**: Adds signing capabilities.

- **Project Report Plugin**: Allows for generating a build report.

You can learn more about each plugin by looking into the Gradle user manual, specifically the chapter entitled "Gradle Plugin Reference."

More About Repositories

Gradle loads libraries from a repository if it determines that the project refers to such libraries. You specify repositories in a repositories { } section inside build.gradle:

```
repositories {
    repoSpec1 (repository specification, see below)
    repoSpec2
    ...
}
```

You can use the following as repository specifications:

- `mavenCentral()`

  Hardcoded to point to the publicly available Maven repository at `https://repo.maven.apache.org/maven2/`

- `jcenter()`

  Hardcoded to point to the publicly available Maven repository at `https://jcenter.bintray.com/`

- `google()`

  Hardcoded to point to the publicly available Android specific Maven repository at `https://maven.google.com/`

- `flatDir { ... }`

  Points to a folder with libraries. The precise syntax is `flatDir { dirs '/path1/to/folder', '/path2/to/folder', ... }`. It does not support meta-information, so if a dependency can be looked up in a `flatDir` repository and in another repository *with* meta-information (Maven, Ivy, and so on), the latter has precedence.

- `maven { ... }`

  Points to a Maven repository given an explicit URL. The precise syntax is

  `maven { url "http://repo.mycompany.com/maven2" }`

- `ivy { ... }`

  Points to an Ivy repository given an explicit URL. The precise syntax is

  `ivy { url "http://repo.mycompany.com/ivy" }`

- `mavenLocal()`

  Uses the local Maven cache (usually in `HOME-DIR/.m2`)

For URLs you specify as repository locations, Gradle also supports the `https:`, `file:`, `sftp:`, and `s3:` (Amazon s3 services) protocols, or `gcs:` (Google cloud storage).

The first three, and of course the standard http:// protocol, use the standard URL syntax. If needed, the Gradle manual explains more about the syntaxes for s3: and gcs.

If you need to provide credentials for connecting to a repository, you can specify them in a credentials { } section:

```
repositories {
    maven {
        url "http://repo.mycompany.com/maven2"
        credentials {
            username "user"
            password "password"
        }
    }
}
```

This is for basic authentication. For more advanced authentication schemes, see the section called "Declaring Repositories" in the Gradle manual.

More About Dependencies

Dependencies in Gradle center on configurations. A (dependency-related) configuration is a dependency scope, which means it describes a usage scenario. Consider for example that you have one set of dependencies important only for testing, another set of dependencies needed for the internal functioning of some library, and yet another set of dependencies needed for internal functioning and forwarded to clients (because they show up in public method calls). All those are different scopes, or *configurations*.

Dependency-related configurations are defined by plugins, but there is a common sense about configuration names, and internally configurations also inherit from each other, which leads to configuration name matches between different plugins. Table 3-2 list the configurations you'll often encounter in Java-related projects.

Table 3-2. *Gradle Configurations*

Name	Description
implementation	Any dependency needed to compile the main section of the sources can use this configuration. The dependency also will be used at runtime.
compile	DEPRECATED. To be replaced by implementation. You find this often in blogs and tutorials, so this is added for your information. Use implementation instead.
compileOnly	Dependency only needed to compile the main section of the sources. During runtime, some kind of container will provide the dependency, so the project is not required to add this kind of dependency to a deliverable artifact.
runtimeOnly	Dependency not needed for compilation of the main section of the sources, but subject to being added to deliverable artifacts.
api	Only for the Java Library plugin, identifies a dependency that must be transferred to library clients as well, because types from the dependency show up in public method calls.
providedCompile	Only for the WAR plugin; same as implementation, but the dependency will *not* be added to the WAR file.
providedRuntime	Only for the WAR plugin; same as runtime, but the dependency will *not* be added to the WAR file.
deploy	Only for the EAR plugin; add the dependency to the root of the EAR file.
earlib	Only for the EAR plugin; add the dependency to the lib folder of the EAR file.
testImplementation	Any dependency needed to compile the test section of the sources can use this configuration. The dependency also will be used at runtime.
testCompile	DEPRECATED. To be replaced by testImplementation. You find this often in blogs and tutorials, so this is added for your information. Use testImplementation instead.
testCompileOnly	Similar to compileOnly, but for the test section of the sources.
testRuntimeOnly	Similar to runtimeOnly, but for the test section of the sources.

Once you identify the configurations you need, you specify a list in the dependencies { } section of your build.gradle file:

```
dependencies {
    implementation 'org.apache.commons:commons-math3:3.6.1'
    // This is the same:
    implementation group:'org.apache.commons',
        name:'commons-math3',
        version:'3.6.1'

    // You can combine:
    implementation 'org.apache.commons:commons-math3:3.6.1',
        'org.apache.commons:commons-lang3:3.10'
    // or like that:
    implementation(
        [ group:'org.apache.commons',
          name:'commons-math3', version:'3.6.1' ],
        [ group:'org.apache.commons',
          name:'commons-lang3', version:'3.10' ]
    )
    // or like that:
    implementation 'org.apache.commons:commons-math3:3.6.1'
    implementation 'org.apache.commons:commons-lang3:3.10'

    testImplementation 'junit:junit:4.12'
}
```

Normally any indirect dependency, which comes from dependencies of dependencies, gets resolved automatically. Such dependencies are called *transitive* dependencies. So if you declare a dependency on some library A, which in turn depends on libraries B and C, Gradle will take care of including B and C in the build, without needing to explicitly declare the dependencies on B and C in build.gradle. If you want to prevent Gradle from including transitive dependencies, you can mark them using transitive = false:

```
dependencies {
    implementation (group: 'org.eclipse.jetty',
                    name: 'jetty-webapp',
```

```
            version: '9.4.28.v20200408') {
        transitive = false
    }
}
```

You can investigate such transitive dependencies if you invoke the `dependencies` task. The output will be a tree-like representation of dependencies and transitive dependencies, as for example, in the following:

```
...
runtimeClasspath - Runtime classpath of source set 'main'.
\--- com.sparkjava:spark-core:2.8.0
    +--- org.slf4j:slf4j-api:1.7.25
    +--- org.eclipse.jetty:jetty-server:9.4.12
    |    +--- javax.servlet:javax.servlet-api:3.1.0
    |    +--- org.eclipse.jetty:jetty-http:9.4.12
    |    |    +--- org.eclipse.jetty:jetty-util:9.4.12
    |    |    \--- org.eclipse.jetty:jetty-io:9.4.12
    |    |         \--- org.eclipse.jetty:jetty-util:9.4.12
...
```

(The noted dependency here is `implementation` `com.sparkjava:spark-core:-` `2.8.0`.)

Changing the Project Structure

We learned that, by adhering to the default project structure, we don't have to spend time in configuring the project, telling it where to find sources and resources.

If for whatever reason you need a custom project layout, add the following lines to your `build.gradle` file:

```
sourceSets {
    main {
        java {
            srcDirs = ['src99/main/java']
        }
        resources {
```

```
                srcDirs = ['src99/main/resources']
            }
        }
        test {
            java {
                srcDirs = ['src99/test/java']
            }
            resources {
                srcDirs = ['src99/test/resources']
            }
        }
    }
}
```

Because all directory settings are specified as lists (seen from [...]), you can also distribute sources and resources over several folders (use commas as separators).

In order to change the build folder where Gradle puts the temporary and final output files, write the following in your build.gradle file:

```
project.buildDir = 'gradle-build'
```

The Gradle Build File Is a Groovy Script

Let's revise the EchoLibrary example build.gradle file:

```
// The EchoLibrary build file
plugins {
    id 'java-library'
}
java {
    sourceCompatibility = JavaVersion.VERSION_1_8
    targetCompatibility = JavaVersion.VERSION_1_8
}
repositories {
    jcenter()
}
```

```
dependencies {
    testImplementation 'junit:junit:4.12'
}
```

Apart from the suspicious () in jcenter() and the strange mixture of A B and A =
B constructs, this file might look like a configuration file with a syntax limited to setting
some properties. The truth is much more gloomy, however. In fact, the build.gradle file
is a Groovy script, and Groovy is a fully fledged scripting language running on top of a
JVM engine.

Although we already stated that, for build definition files, a declarative programming
style is preferable over a declarative programming style, it is, under certain
circumstances, acceptable to add programming language constructs like conditional
statements, switch constructs, loops, and calls to library objects for IO (files and the
console), math, streams, date and time, and whatever else you might think of. Also,
the { } brackets in the build files actually do not denote blocks, but closures. So the
dependencies { } construct is actually a shortcut for dependencies({ }), and any A
B construct in fact is a method call A(B).

For example, if you wanted to add a runtimeOnly dependency only if some system
property is defined, and furthermore wanted to output a corresponding diagnostic
message, you could write the following:

```
...
dependencies {
  if(System.getProperty("add.math") != null) {
    println("MATH added")
    runtimeOnly group: 'org.apache.commons',
                name: 'commons-math3', version: '3.6.1'
  }
  ...
  testImplementation 'junit:junit:4.12'
}
...
```

You could now call any task with the extra option -Dadd.math added to see the
conditional statement and console output working.

Script Variables

For increased readability and maintenance optimization, you can add variables (properties) to your build file. To do so, you can use an ext { } call:

```
...
ext {
    MATH_VERSION = '3.6.1'
    JUNIT_VERSION = '4.12'
}

dependencies {
  implementation group: 'org.apache.commons',
      name: 'commons-math3', version: MATH_VERSION
  testImplementation "junit:junit:${JUNIT_VERSION}"
}
...
```

In order for the ${} substitution to work, the double quotation marks are required—this is a Groovy language feature (GString objects). Otherwise in Groovy you can use both single and double quotation marks to denote strings.

If the variable scope is limited to the current closure (inside a { }), you can also use the standard Groovy local variable declaration:

```
...
dependencies {
  def MATH_VERSION = '3.6.1'
  def JUNIT_VERSION = '4.12'

  implementation group: 'org.apache.commons',
      name: 'commons-math3', version: MATH_VERSION
  testImplementation "junit:junit:${JUNIT_VERSION}"
}
...
```

Custom Tasks

We can define our own tasks inside the build.gradle file. Because we can use the Groovy language inside the build script, the possibilities are endless here. We can add logging, include non-standard files in archives, perform encryption, deploy artifacts on servers, publish files in a non-standard way, perform timing, invoke extra preparation and cleanup steps, and more.

To define your own task, you write the following anywhere in your build.gradle script file:

```
task hello {
  group = 'build'
  description = 'Hello World'

  println 'Hello world! CONFIG'

  doFirst {
    println 'Hello world! FIRST'
  }
  doLast {
    println 'Hello world! LAST'
  }
}
```

The group and description settings are both optional; the default for the group is other, and if you omit the description, an empty string will be taken instead. The possible values for group are build, build setup, documentation, help, verification, and other.

To execute a custom task, you do the same thing as you do for built-in tasks or tasks defined by plugins. However, in order for the Eclipse Gradle plugin to be able to see the new task, you first must right-click the project and then choose Gradle➤Refresh Gradle Project. Then you'll see the new task in the tree view of the Gradle Tasks view and can execute it by double-clicking it.

The instructions inside the main { } are executed during the configuration phase. It is important to know that such instructions are executed unconditionally for all tasks declared! For task-execution matters, you instead put instructions into doFirst { } or doLast { }. Each task has an action list; if you use doFirst, instructions are prepended to the action list, if you use doLast, actions are appended to the action list.

It is possible to add instructions to the task's action list at a later point, by writing:

```
hello.doLast {
  println 'Hello world! MORE LAST'
}

hello.doFirst {
  println 'Hello world! MORE FIRST'
}
```

You can add your custom task to the dependent's list of existing tasks, or add existing tasks to the dependent's list of the new task. To do so, write the following, for example:

```
build.dependsOn hello
hello.dependsOn build
```

The magic behind that is that any task is directly available by its name inside the build.gradle script. So, if you write build.dependsOn hello, any execution of the build task first leads to executing hello. In hello.dependsOn build, an execution of the hello task first yields a build execution. This way, it is possible to add task dependency relations to existing standard and non-standard tasks.

The Gradle Wrapper

If you use the wrapper task or the Eclipse Gradle plugin to start a new project, the wrapper scripts are installed, which allow you to run Gradle without any Gradle installation on the operating system (Java must be working, though). You can see that from the following files:

```
gradlew

gradlew.bat

gradle
  |- wrapper
        |- gradle-wrapper.jar
        |- gradle-wrapper.properties
```

gradlew and gradlew.bat are Gradle startup scripts for Linux and Windows, respectively. The gradle folder contains the standalone Gradle installation.

The Eclipse Gradle plugin does not use these wrapper scripts. Instead, upon starting the first Gradle task, a Gradle *daemon* from inside USER_HOME/gradle is started. This daemon runs in the background and any Gradle task execution triggered from Eclipse contacts this daemon for the actual build work. This allows for faster task executions.

If Gradle gets invoked from the console, the wrapper is used, and such a daemon process will be started as well. We talk about the console-oriented way of development in the "Developing Using the Console" section.

Multi-Project Builds

Gradle projects can have subprojects. Apart from gathering projects that exhibit some kind of inter-relation, such a hierarchy built of one main project and one or more subprojects also is important for EAR projects, where we typically have one web application, maybe some EJBs, and possibly some libraries.

To build such a multi-project from inside Eclipse, first create a normal Gradle project as described previously. Then, open the settings.gradle file and add the following line:

```
include 'proj1', 'proj2'
```

Of course you can choose different names for the subprojects. Next, create two folders inside the project folder, with names proj1 and proj2 (or whatever names you have chosen). Add an empty build.gradle file to each of the new folders. You can later add any subproject-related build instructions there.

Right-click the project and choose Gradle➤Refresh Gradle Project. Eclipse will update the Project Explorer and show the main project and the two subprojects as different entries; see Figure 3-7.

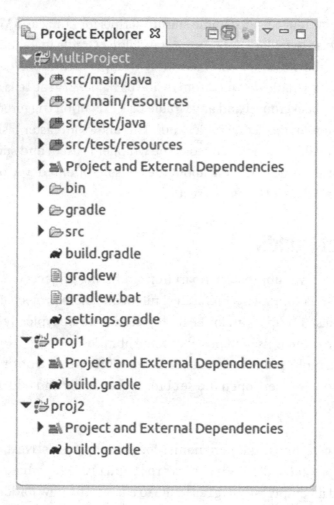

Figure 3-7. *Gradle multi-project in Eclipse*

Due to a bug in the Gradle plugin, you have to fix the JRE library assignment for all three entries. On each of them, right-click and then choose Properties➤Libraries. Remove the wrong entry, then click Add Library (to classpath)➤JRE System Library➤Workspace Default JRE (or whatever suits your needs). The error markers should now be gone, as shown in Figure 3-8.

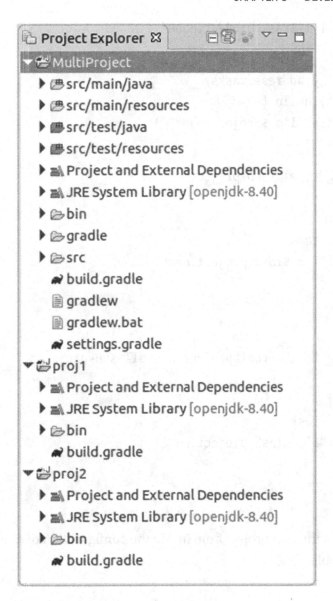

Figure 3-8. *Gradle multi-project in Eclipse, fixed*

Each subproject can be configured independently using its own `build.gradle` file, but it is also possible to refer to subprojects from the root project's `build.gradle` file:

```
// referring to a particular sub-project
project(':proj1') { proj ->
    // adding a new task to proj1
    task('hello').doLast { task ->
```

```
        println "I'm $task.project.name" }
}

// we can directly address tasks
project(':proj1').hello {
  doLast { println "I'm $project.name" }
}

// or, referring to all sub-projects
subprojects {
    task hello {
        doLast { task ->
        println "I'm $task.project.name"
    }
  }
}

// or, referring to the root project and all sub-projects
allprojects {
    task hello {
        doLast { task ->
        println "I'm $task.project.name"
    }
  }
}
```

We can address the root project from inside the configuration of a subproject via the rootProject variable:

```
task action {
    doLast {
        println("Root project: " +
            "${rootProject.name}")
    }
}
```

You can read more about multi-project builds in the sections called "Configuring Multi-Project Builds" and "Authoring Multi-Project Builds" in the Gradle user manual. We will use a multi-project in Chapter 9.

Adding a Deploy Task

A good candidate for a custom task is a deployment process. We can use the standard build task to create a WAR or EAR file, but in order to deploy it on a local development server, a custom Gradle task comes in handy. Throughout the book, we will use the following tasks for deployment and "un-deployment" on a local GlassFish server:

```
task localDeploy(dependsOn: build,
            description:">>> Local deploy task") {
  doLast {
    def FS = File.separator
    def glassfish = project.properties['glassfish.inst.dir']
    def user = project.properties['glassfish.user']
    def passwd = project.properties['glassfish.passwd']

    File temp = File.createTempFile("asadmin-passwd",
        ".tmp")
    temp << "AS_ADMIN_${user}=${passwd}\n"

    def sout = new StringBuilder()
    def serr = new StringBuilder()
    def libsDir = "${project.projectDir}${FS}build" +
        "${FS}libs"
    def procStr = """${glassfish}${FS}bin${FS}asadmin
        --user ${user} --passwordfile ${temp.absolutePath}
        deploy --force=true
        ${libsDir}/${project.name}.war"""
    // For Windows:
    if(FS == "\\") procStr = "cmd /c " + procStr
    def proc = procStr.execute()

    proc.waitForProcessOutput(sout, serr)
    println "out> ${sout}"
```

```
    if(serr.toString()) System.err.println(serr)

    temp.delete()
  }
}

task localUndeploy(
            description:">>> Local undeploy task") {
  doLast {
    def FS = File.separator
    def glassfish = project.properties['glassfish.inst.dir']
    def user = project.properties['glassfish.user']
    def passwd = project.properties['glassfish.passwd']

    File temp = File.createTempFile("asadmin-passwd",
        ".tmp")
    temp << "AS_ADMIN_${user}=${passwd}\n"

    def sout = new StringBuilder()
    def serr = new StringBuilder()
    def procStr = """${glassfish}${FS}bin${FS}asadmin
        --user ${user} --passwordfile ${temp.absolutePath}
        undeploy ${project.name}"""
    // For Windows:
    if(FS == "\\") procStr = "cmd /c " + procStr
    def proc = procStr.execute()

    proc.waitForProcessOutput(sout, serr)
    println "out> ${sout}"
    if(serr.toString()) System.err.println(serr)

    temp.delete()
  }
}
```

These tasks depend on a properties file. Gradle automatically tries to read a properties file named gradle.properties and, if it exists, creates a map from the properties and puts it into the project.properties variable. We create such a file in the project folder, and let it read as follows:

```
glassfish.inst.dir = /path/to/glassfish/inst
glassfish.user = admin
glassfish.passwd =
```

The tasks create a temporary password file; this is just the GlassFish way of avoiding manual password entry. The `"..."`.execute() creates a process running on the operating system; for the Windows variant, we have to prepend a `cmd /c`.

We can now perform a deployment or "un-deployment" by invoking the `localDeploy` or `localUndeploy` task, respectively. Since we added a `dependsOn: build` as a task dependency for deployment, it is not necessary to build a deployable artifact; this is done automatically.

Developing Using the Console

Because the Eclipse Gradle plugin installed wrapper scripts inside the project folder, it is therefore possible to do all build-related work from inside a console (bash terminal in Linux, command interpreter in Windows) instead of from the Eclipse GUI. It is a matter of style; using the console, you can avoid having to switch around Eclipse views and collapsing and scrolling trees. Besides, if you have to add task options or arguments, using the console is much more straightforward and faster compared to the GUI. If you don't have a GUI because you want to do the build on a server, using the console is your only option.

This section covers using the console for Gradle builds. It is possible to freely mix console and GUI triggered builds, so you can use both approaches at the same time.

If you didn't use the Eclipse Gradle plugin to start a Gradle project, you can use the `wrapper` task to create the wrapper. In this case, Gradle must be installed on your OS. The Linux script reads as follows:

```
java -version
# observe output

# if you want to specify a different JDK:
export JAVA_HOME=/path/to/the/jdk

cd /here/goes/the/project

gradle init wrapper
```

For Windows, it reads as follows:

```
java -version
# observe output

# if you want to specify a different JDK: set JAVA_HOME=C:\path\to\the\jdk

chdir \here\goes\the\project

gradle init wrapper
```

This assumes that the gradle is in the PATH (in Windows, gradle.bat is in your PATH). Otherwise, you must specify the complete path to the gradle command. For example: C:\gradle\bin\gradle.bat.

To check the wrapper installation, you can list the available tasks from inside the project directory via the following:

```
./gradlew tasks
# Windows:   gradlew tasks
```

The output should be something like this:

```
> Task :tasks

------------------------------------------------------------
All tasks runnable from root project
------------------------------------------------------------

Build Setup tasks
-----------------
init - Initializes a new Gradle build.wrapper - Generates Gradle wrapper
files.

[...]
```

You can see the complete synopsis of the gradlew (gradlew.bat for Windows) wrapper command if you enter the following:

```
./gradlew -help
# Windows:   gradlew -help
```

A non-exhaustive list of interesting and important option parameters is shown in Table 3-3. Specify any tasks to be executed behind the option list.

Table 3-3. *Gradle Command Options*

Option	Description
-?, -h, -help	Shows this help message.
-Dprop=val	Sets a JVM property. You can use `System.getProperty("prop")` inside the script to read it.
-Pprop=val	Sets a project property. You can use `prop` inside the script to directly read it.
-w, -warn	Adds warning level diagnostic output.
-i, -info	Adds some info level diagnostic output.
-d, -debug	Enables debugging messages when something goes wrong.
-q, -quiet	Shows error level messages only (quiet).
-offline	Normally libraries referred to in a Java build task are downloaded into a cache. If you want to disable network access, use this option.
-status	Shows the status of Gradle daemon(s). Normally upon first startup, a background process (daemon) is started to speed up subsequent Gradle calls. Use this to show the status of the daemon(s).
-stop	Stops the daemon if it is running.
-v, -version	Shows the version info.

Tasks can have options and parameters. In order to use the `tasks` task (show all task), for example, you can add `--all` as an option:

```
./gradlew tasks --all
# Windows:   gradlew tasks --all
```

This shows tasks from the other group (which are normally discarded). If you run `./gradlew help --task <task>`, you can view the info (options) about any particular task.

To troubleshoot build script execution performance problems, there is another option called --profile, which will lead to a performance report being added to build/reports/profile.

For our little EchoLibrary example project, navigate to the project folder and then execute the following:

```
./gradlew build
# Windows:   gradlew build
```

The output JAR called EchoLibrary.jar is generated inside the build/libs folder.

Note   For simplicity in the rest of the book, we will only show console Gradle commands, and only the Linux variant.

Installing MVC

In order to be able to use Java MVC, from a Gradle perspective, we need to check a few things. First, we configure Java MVC as a web application. For this reason, we create a web project and use the WAR plugin. Inside build.gradle, add the following:

```
plugins {
    id 'war'
}
```

Next we add the Jakarta EE 8 API, the Java MVC API, and a Java MVC implementation inside the dependencies section of build.gradle. This comes together with a repository specification, the usual JUnit test library inclusion, and the indication that we want to use Java 1.8:

```
plugins {
    id 'war'
}

java {
    sourceCompatibility = 1.8
    targetCompatibility = 1.8
}
```

84

```
repositories {
    jcenter()
}

dependencies {
  testImplementation 'junit:junit:4.12'

  implementation 'javax:javaee-api:8.0'
  implementation 'javax.mvc:javax.mvc-api:1.0.0'
  implementation 'org.eclipse.krazo:krazo-jersey:1.1.0-M1'

  // more dependencies...
}

// ... more tasks
```

That is it; the build process will make sure that all libraries are downloaded, and that Java MVC is added to the web application during a ./gradlew build.

Exercises

Exercise 1: True or false? Using imperative programming (step-by-step instructions) is the preferred programming style for build scripts.

Exercise 2: True or false? For imperative code snippets, you can use C++ code inside a Gradle build script.

Exercise 3: True or false? Eclipse uses the same JRE for its own functionalities and for building projects.

Exercise 4: Identify the three phases of a Gradle build process.

Exercise 5: True or false? Using the standard Gradle Java project layout, Java classes go into src/java/main.

Exercise 6: True or false? The Gradle plugins to be used are specified in the settings.gradle file.

Exercise 7: Gradle downloads project dependencies as necessary. True or false? Where to download from is specified in a `downloads` { } section inside `build.gradle`.

Exercise 8: Describe what a *configuration* is in Gradle jargon.

Exercise 9: Using the Eclipse Gradle plugin, create a `GraphicsPrimitives` Java library with two classes: `Circle` and `Rectangle`. Configure it to use JRE 1.8. Adapt all Gradle build configuration files as necessary.

Exercise 10: If you have two custom tasks:

```
task a {
    println "Hi, I'm A"
}
task b {
    println "Hi, I'm B"
}
```

Under which condition is `"Hi, I'm A"` printed to the console?

Exercise 11: True or false? The Gradle wrapper works only if Gradle is installed on the operating system.

Exercise 12: Describe what needs to be done to let Gradle use the JDK at `/opt/jdk8` (or for Windows, at `C:\jdk8`).

Summary

In this chapter, we talked about development techniques, procedures, and tools you can use for the examples in this book and any subsequent projects using Java MVC.

Gradle is a modern build framework/build automation tool. You can use a declarative configuration style, but you can also add imperative build code in the form of Groovy (or Kotlin) script snippets. Best practices indicate that, for build scripts, declarative programming (which says *what* a build script has to do, not *how* it should do it) is favorable over imperative programming (precise step-by-step instructions).

Eclipse is an IDE (Integrated Development Environment) with a plethora of functionalities that help to develop Java Enterprise projects. It can be extended by plugins, which add additional functionalities. We use the Eclipse IDE for Enterprise Java Developers variant for this book.

For the book, we need the Eclipse Gradle plugin. Gradle can also be used from the console, but the Gradle plugin in Eclipse allows us to use Gradle directly from inside the IDE. Open Help➤Install New Software and enter Eclipse Buildship (Gradle) and `http://download.eclipse.org/buildship/updates/latest in the dialog`. Select all features and finish the wizard.

To start a Gradle project inside Eclipse, go to File➤New➤Other...➤Gradle➤Gradle Project.

The main Gradle concepts are as follows. Gradle has a core, which provides the infrastructure for build-related activities. Gradle plugins are specified in the main build file. They run on top of the core and add features to it. Each plugin exhibits build-related activities in form of tasks. Each Gradle build consists of an *initialization*, a *configuration*, and an *execution* phase. In the initialization phase, Gradle determines whether or not subprojects need to be included within the build. In the configuration phase, Gradle evaluates dependencies and builds a task graph that contains all the tasks that need to be executed for a build. Configurations on all objects always run with every Gradle build. During the execution phase, the tasks do their jobs (compiling, moving, zipping, and so on).

The default project layout for all Gradle plugins is as follows:

```
src
  |- main
  |    |- java
  |    |    |- <java source files>
  |    |- resources
  |           |- <resource files>
  |
  |- test
       |- java
       |    |- <java source files>
       |- resources
              |- <resource files>
build
```

```
|- <any files built by Gradle>

build.gradle        <Gradle build file>

settings.gradle     <(Sub-)Project settings>

gradle.properties  <optional project properties>
```

The Gradle project wizard from Eclipse creates a sample build configuration `build.gradle` file inside the project's root folder. For any Gradle project, including projects that don't use Eclipse, this is the central build file. The Eclipse plugin provides a basic build file with some example entries.

A build file usually starts by defining which plugins are to be used, and then configures the plugins. User-defined tasks with operating instructions also can go to the build file. Besides, it is possible to add Groovy or Kotlin code to existing tasks, which enables you to fine-tune plugins according to your needs.

Plugins usually have a very precise and reasonable idea about their defaults, so there is probably not much to configure for your project. For this reason, the build file could be rather small. This convention-over-configuration style is not an invention of Gradle, but Gradle gratefully adopts this idea.

The Eclipse Gradle plugin has Gradle Tasks and Gradle Executions views. In addition, diagnostic output goes into the standard Console view. The two Gradle-related views open by default after you install the Gradle plugin.

In order to run a Gradle task from inside the Gradle Tasks view, you first have to locate the task inside the tree. Depending on how precisely you look inside the tree, you can also use the filter from the menu to find a task. Once you find it, double-click it to run the task. Diagnostic output, including any error messages, is shown in the Gradle Executions and Console views.

Gradle loads libraries from repositories if it determines that the project refers to such libraries. You specify repositories in a `repositories { }` section inside `build.gradle`:

```
repositories {
    repoSpec1   (repository specification, see below)
    repoSpec2
    ...
}
```

You can use the following as repository specifications:

- `mavenCentral()`

  Hardcoded to point to the publicly available Maven repository at `https://repo.maven.apache.org/maven2/`

- `jcenter()`

  Hardcoded to point to the publicly available Maven repository at `https://jcenter.bintray.com/`

- `google()`

  Hardcoded to point to the publicly available Android specific Maven repository at `https://maven.google.com/`

- `flatDir { ... }`

  Points to a folder with libraries. The precise syntax is

  `flatDir { dirs '/path1/to/folder', '/path2/to/folder', ... }`

  Does not support meta-information, so if a dependency can be looked up in a `flatDir` repository and in another repository *with* meta-information (Maven, Ivy, and so on), the latter has precedence.

- `maven { ... }`

  Points to a Maven repository given an explicit URL. The precise syntax is

  `maven { url "http://repo.mycompany.com/maven2" }`

- `- ivy { ... }`

  Points to an Ivy repository given an explicit URL. The precise syntax is

  `ivy { url "http://repo.mycompany.com/ivy" }`

- **mavenLocal()**

  Uses the local Maven cache (usually in `HOME-DIR/.m2`).

Dependencies in Gradle center on `configurations`. A dependency-related configuration is a dependency scope, which means it describes a usage scenario like testing, compiling, provisioning, and so on. Dependency-related configurations are defined by plugins, but there is a common sense about configuration names, and internally configurations also inherit from each other, which leads to configuration name matches between different plugins.

Once you identify the configurations you need, you specify a list in the `dependencies` `{ }` section of your `build.gradle` file:

```
dependencies {
    implementation 'org.apache.commons:commons-math3:3.6.1'
    // This is the same:
    implementation group:'org.apache.commons',
        name:'commons-math3',
        version:'3.6.1'

    // You can combine:
    implementation 'org.apache.commons:commons-math3:3.6.1',
        'org.apache.commons:commons-lang3:3.10'
    // or like that:
    implementation(
      [ group:'org.apache.commons',
        name:'commons-math3', version:'3.6.1' ],
      [ group:'org.apache.commons',
        name:'commons-lang3', version:'3.10' ]
)
    // or like that:
    implementation 'org.apache.commons:commons-math3:3.6.1'
    implementation 'org.apache.commons:commons-lang3:3.10'

    testImplementation 'junit:junit:4.12'
}
```

Inside `build.gradle`, it is possible to add programming language constructs like conditional statements, switch constructs, loops, and calls to library objects for IO (files and the console), math, streams, date and time, and whatever else you might think of. Also, the `{ }` brackets in the build files actually do not denote blocks, but closures. So the `dependencies { }` construct is actually a shortcut for `dependencies( { } )`, and any `A B` construct in fact is a method call `A( B )`.

For increased readability and maintenance optimization, you can add variables (properties) to your build file. To do so, use an ext { } call:

```
...
ext {
  MATH_VERSION = '3.6.1'
  JUNIT_VERSION = '4.12'
}

dependencies {
  implementation group: 'org.apache.commons',
      name: 'commons-math3', version: MATH_VERSION
  testImplementation "junit:junit:${JUNIT_VERSION}"
}
...
```

In order for the ${} substitution to work, the double quotation marks are required. This is a Groovy language feature (GString objects). Otherwise, in Groovy, you can use both single and double quotation marks to denote strings.

We can define our own tasks inside the build.gradle file. Because we can use the Groovy language inside the build script, the possibilities are endless. We can add logging, include non-standard files in archives, perform encryption, deploy artifacts on servers, publish files in a non-standard way, perform timing, invoke extra preparation and cleanup steps, and more.

To define your own task, you write the following anywhere in your build.gradle script file:

```
task hello {
  group = 'build'
  description = 'Hello World'

  println 'Hello world! CONFIG'

  doFirst {
    println 'Hello world! FIRST'
  }

  doLast {
```

```
    println 'Hello world! LAST'
  }
}
```

The group and description settings are both optional; the default for group is other, and if you omit the description, an empty string will be taken instead. All possible values for group are build, build setup, documentation, help, verification, and other.

You can add your custom task to the dependent's list of existing tasks, or add existing tasks to the dependent's list of the new task. To do so, write the following, for example:

```
build.dependsOn hello
hello.dependsOn build
```

The magic behind that is that any task is directly available by its name inside the build.gradle script. So, if you write build.dependsOn hello, any execution of the build task first leads to executing hello. With hello.dependsOn build, an execution of the hello task first yields a build execution. This way, it is possible to add task dependency relations to existing standard and non-standard tasks.

Because the Eclipse Gradle plugin installed wrapper scripts inside the project folder, it is therefore possible to do all build-related work from inside a console (bash terminal in Linux, command interpreter in Windows) instead of from the Eclipse GUI. It is a matter of style; using the console, you can avoid having to switch around Eclipse views and collapsing and scrolling trees. Besides, if you have to add task options or arguments, using the console is much more straightforward and faster compared to the GUI. If you don't have a GUI because you want to do the build on a server, using the console is your only option.

If you didn't use the Eclipse Gradle plugin to start a Gradle project, you can use the wrapper task to create the wrapper. In this case, Gradle must be installed on your OS. The Linux script reads as follows:

```
java -version
# observe output

# if you want to specify a different JDK:
export JAVA_HOME=/path/to/the/jdk

cd /here/goes/the/project

gradle init wrapper
```

The Windows script is as follows:

```
java -version
# observe output

# if you want to specify a different JDK:
set JAVA_HOME=C:\path\to\the\jdk

chdir \here\goes\the\project


gradle init wrapper
```

This assumes that the gradle is in the PATH (in Windows, gradle.bat is in your PATH). Otherwise, you must specify the complete path to the gradle command. For example: C:\gradle\bin\gradle.bat.

You can see the complete synopsis of the gradlew (gradlew.bat for Windows) wrapper command if you enter the following:

```
./gradlew -help
# Windows:    gradlew -help
```

Tasks can have options and parameters as well. In order to use the tasks task (show all task), for example, you can add --all as an option:

```
./gradlew tasks --all
# Windows:    gradlew tasks --all
```

This shows tasks from the other group (which are normally discarded). If you run ./gradlew help --task <task>, you can view the info (options) about any particular task.

In order to be able to use Java MVC, from a Gradle perspective, we need to verify a few things. First, we configure Java MVC as a web application. For this reason, we create a web project and use the WAR plugin. Inside build.gradle, add the following:

```
plugins {
    id 'war'
}
```

Next we add the Jakarta EE 8 API, the Java MVC API, and a Java MVC implementation inside the dependencies section of build.gradle. This comes together with a repository specification, the usual JUnit test library inclusion, and the indication that we want to use Java 1.8:

```
plugins {
    id 'war'
}

java {
    sourceCompatibility = 1.8
    targetCompatibility = 1.8
}
repositories {
    jcenter()
}

dependencies {
    testImplementation 'junit:junit:4.12'

    implementation 'javax:javaee-api:8.0'
    implementation 'javax.mvc:javax.mvc-api:1.0.0'
    implementation 'org.eclipse.krazo:krazo-jersey:1.1.0-M1'

    // more dependencies...
}
// ... more tasks
```

In the next chapter, we talk about a clean "Hello World" style project using the development workflow we just described.

CHAPTER 4

Hello World for Java MVC

In Chapter 1, I presented a quick-and-dirty Hello World style Java MVC web application. With the knowledge of how to use Eclipse as an IDE and Gradle as a build framework, we can now investigate a cleaner approach to a Hello World web application. The functionality will be the same: one page serves as a landing page and asks the users for their name. After they submit it, the controller processes the name and shows a submission response page with a personalized greeting.

Starting the Hello World Project

Open Eclipse and choose any suitable workspace. Since in previous chapters we used JavaMVCBook as a workspace, there is no reason not to use it again for this Hello World project. Remember that we added a JDK 1.8 to this workspace, so you don't have to do this again.

Start a new project. Choose File ➤ New ➤ Other ➤ Gradle ➤ Gradle Project. Click Next, which leads to the first page of the Gradle New Project wizard being shown. This is a welcome page and it shows some information about the wizard. See Figure 4-1.

© Peter Späth 2021
P. Späth, *Beginning Java MVC 1.0*, https://doi.org/10.1007/978-1-4842-6280-1_4

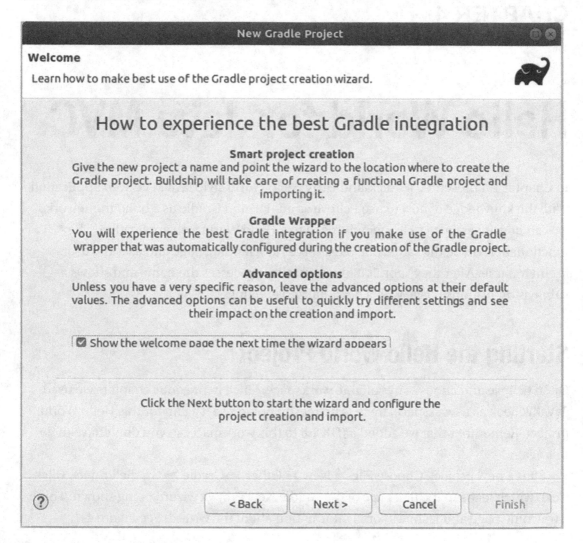

Figure 4-1. *Gradle project wizard welcome page*

If you like, you can uncheck the check box stating whether or not you want to see this wizard welcome page the next time the wizard is started. Click the Next button.

On the second page, shown in Figure 4-2, you are asked for the project name. Enter HelloWorld. On the same page, you can enter a project location. If you select the default location, the project files are created inside the workspace folder. Otherwise, you can enter a folder anywhere on your file system. This makes sense if you, for example, use a version control system and prefer to use a project folder inside a special version control area of your file system.

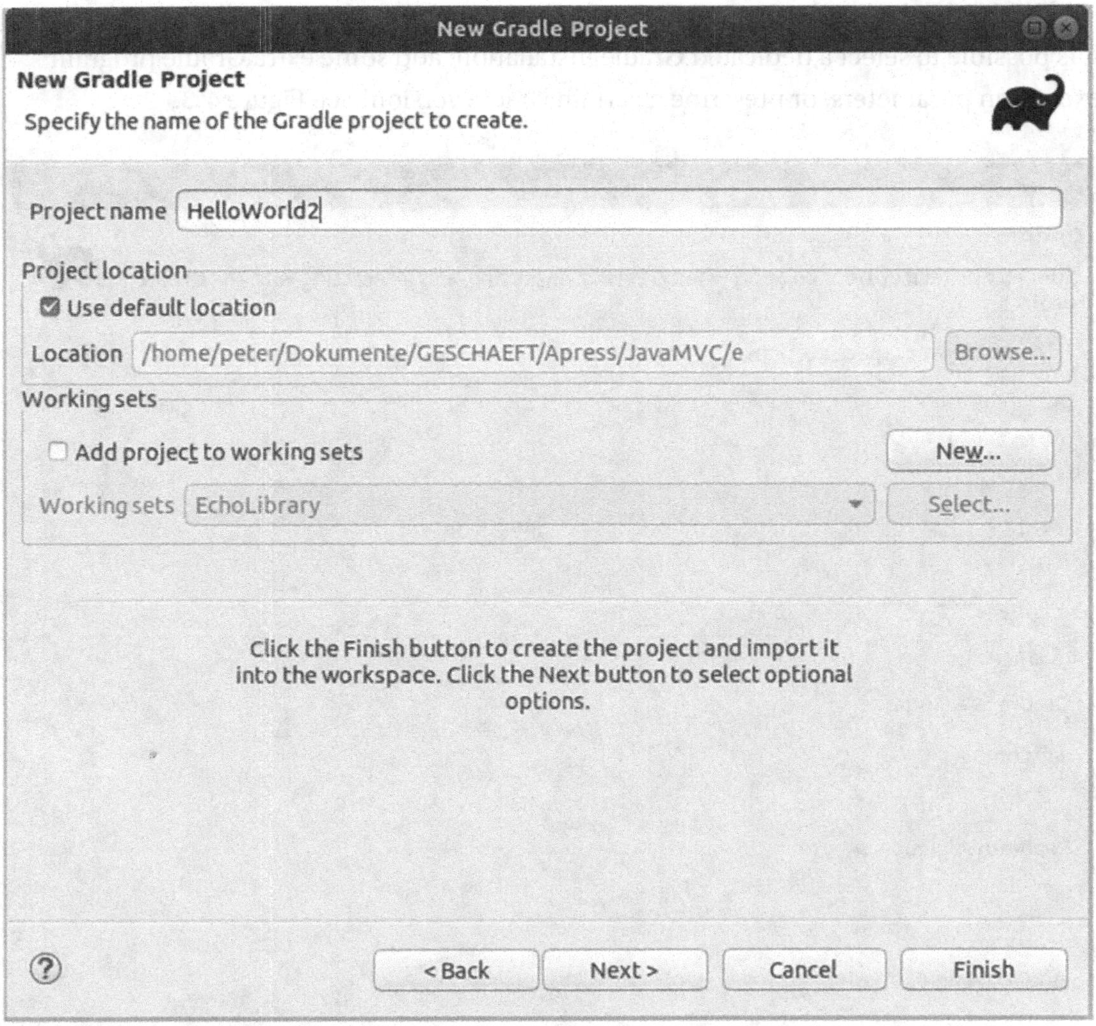

Figure 4-2. *Gradle project wizard page 2*

For learning and working through this book, using the default project location and leaving the appropriate check box checked probably is the most common approach for placing projects. The last setting on this page allows you to define and use a working set for the new project. Working sets are mainly used to filter the projects seen in Eclipse's Project Explorer. It is also possible to apply this setting later, so you safely can leave the Add Project to Working Sets check box unchecked. Click Next to advance to the next page.

On the third wizard page, you can specify some options about Gradle executions. It is possible to select a dedicated Gradle installation, add some extra Gradle program execution parameters, or prescribe a certain Gradle version. See Figure 4-3.

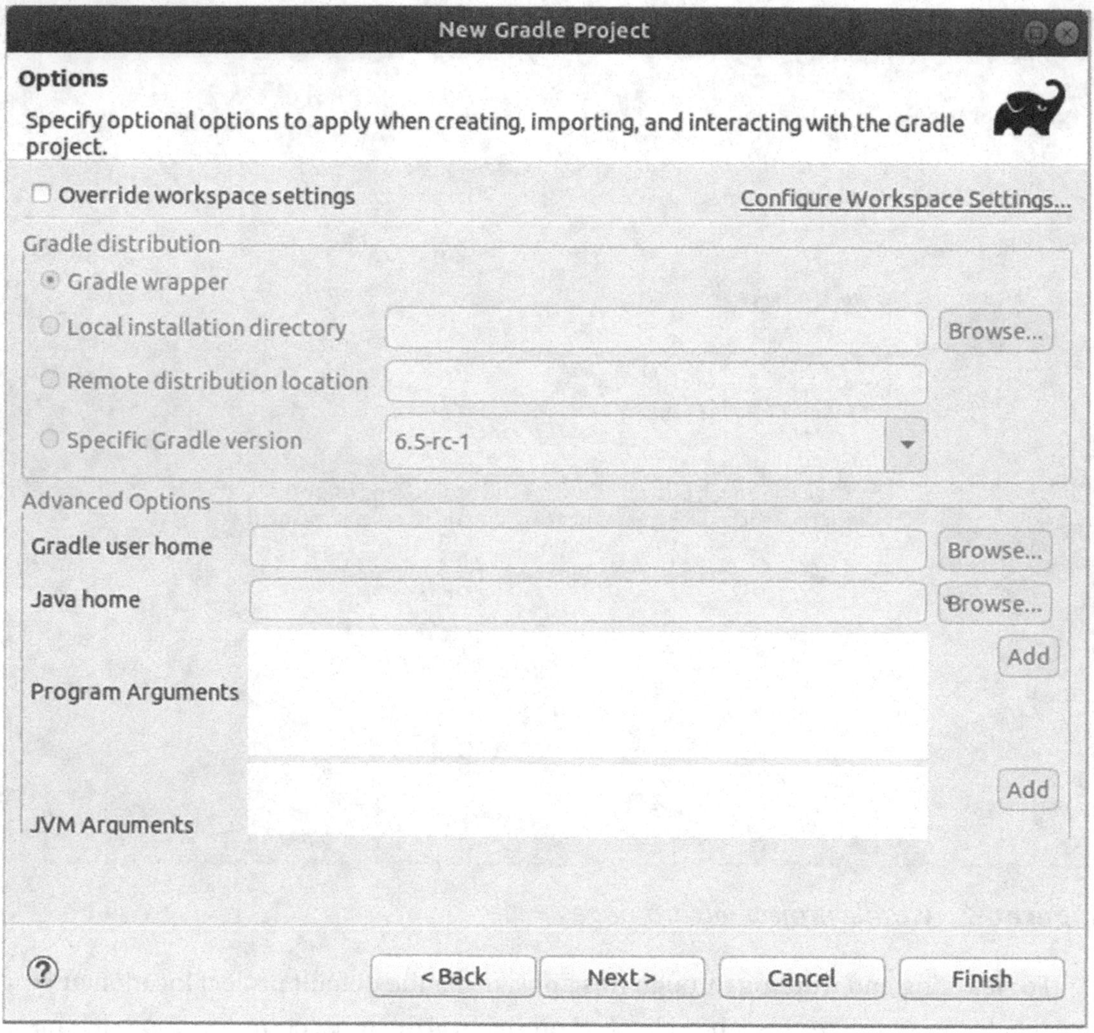

Figure 4-3. Gradle project wizard page 3

For a Hello World style application, you can use the defaults, which leaves the Override Workspace Settings unchecked. In case you are curious: If you click the Configure Workspace Settings, you can investigate or alter these workspace settings. The default is to use the Gradle Wrapper, which means that the Gradle Wrapper that's installed during the project creation and available after the wizard finishes will be used. But you are free to experiment with those options, if you like. Clicking Next will start the actual project generation, and you can see the last page of the wizard, which summarizes the wizard's activities. See Figure 4-4. Clicking Finish completes the wizard.

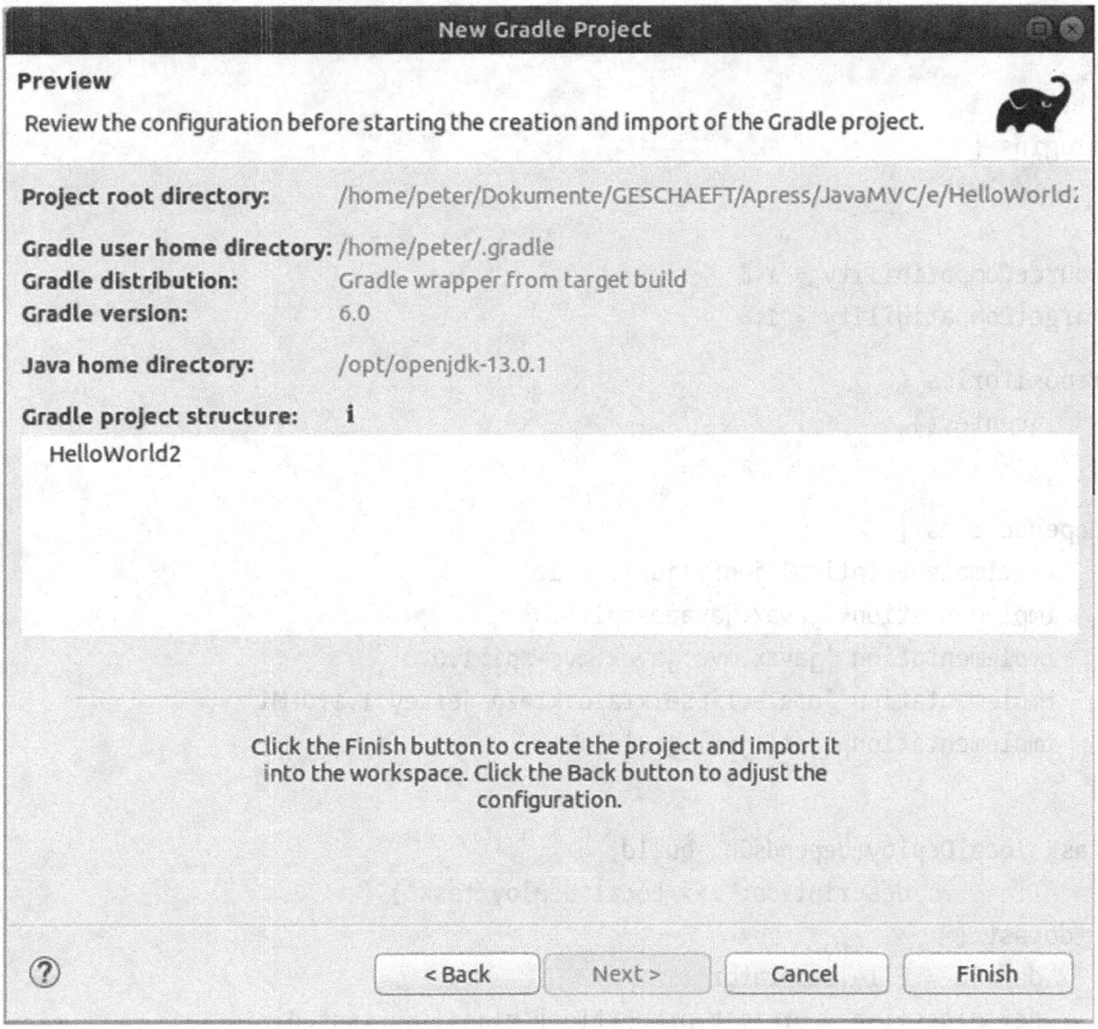

Figure 4-4. *Gradle project wizard page 4*

After the project generation wizard does its work, the new project shows up in the Project Explorer. If an error marker appears, there is probably a JRE version mismatch. Chapter 3 described the procedure to fix this problem in detail. (In short, go to the project settings by right-clicking the project and then clicking Properties, navigate to Java Build Path ➤ Libraries, remove the erroneous JRE assignment, and finally add JRE 1.8 as a library.)

To have the build process correctly add the libraries and construct a WAR web application, we change the `build.gradle` file's content and write the following:

```
/*
 * GRADLE project build file
 */

plugins {
    id 'war'
}
sourceCompatibility = 1.8
targetCompatibility = 1.8

repositories {
    jcenter()
}

dependencies {
    testImplementation 'junit:junit:4.12'
    implementation 'javax:javaee-api:8.0'
    implementation 'javax.mvc:javax.mvc-api:1.0.0'
    implementation 'org.eclipse.krazo:krazo-jersey:1.1.0-M1'
    implementation 'jstl:jstl:1.2'
}

task localDeploy(dependsOn: build,
            description:">>> Local deploy task") {
  doLast {
    def FS = File.separator
    def glassfish = project.properties['glassfish.inst.dir']
    def user = project.properties['glassfish.user']
    def passwd = project.properties['glassfish.passwd']
```

```
    File temp = File.createTempFile("asadmin-passwd",
        ".tmp")
    temp << "AS_ADMIN_${user}=${passwd}\n"

    def sout = new StringBuilder()
    def serr = new StringBuilder()
    def libsDir = "${project.projectDir}${FS}build" +
        "${FS}libs"
    def procStr = """${glassfish}${FS}bin${FS}asadmin
        --user ${user} --passwordfile ${temp.absolutePath}
         deploy --force=true
        ${libsDir}/${project.name}.war"""
    // For Windows:
    if(FS == "\\") procStr = "cmd /c " + procStr
    def proc = procStr.execute()
    proc.waitForProcessOutput(sout, serr)
    println "out> ${sout}"
    if(serr.toString()) System.err.println(serr)

    temp.delete()
  }
}

task localUndeploy(
            description:">>> Local undeploy task") {
  doLast {
    def FS = File.separator
    def glassfish = project.properties['glassfish.inst.dir']
    def user = project.properties['glassfish.user']
    def passwd = project.properties['glassfish.passwd']

    File temp = File.createTempFile("asadmin-passwd",
        ".tmp")
    temp << "AS_ADMIN_${user}=${passwd}\n"

    def sout = new StringBuilder()
    def serr = new StringBuilder()
    def procStr = """${glassfish}${FS}bin${FS}asadmin
```

```
        --user ${user} --passwordfile ${temp.absolutePath}
          undeploy ${project.name}"""
    // For Windows:
    if(FS == "\\") procStr = "cmd /c " + procStr
    def proc = procStr.execute()

    proc.waitForProcessOutput(sout, serr) println "out> ${sout}"
    if(serr.toString()) System.err.println(serr)

    temp.delete()
  }
}
```

This configuration adds the Jakarta EE 8 API (javax:javaee-api:8.0 in the dependencies { } section), the Java MVC libraries (javax.mvc:javax.mvc- api:1.0.0 and org.eclipse.krazo:krazo-jersey:1.1.0-M1), and JSTL as a frontend view templating engine (jstl:jstl:1.2). The build file also contains two custom tasks— localDeploy and localUndeploy—which help you deploy the project on a local development GlassFish server. We talked about these tasks in the previous chapter.

For the build to work correctly, add the gradle.properties file to the project folder:

```
glassfish.inst.dir = /path/to/your/glassfish5.1
glassfish.user = admin
glassfish.passwd =
```

These settings are addressed by the project.properties['..'] expressions in the custom tasks. They tell us where GlassFish is and the user credentials needed to contact it. Adapt the property items according to your needs (admin and an empty password is the default for a GlassFish server). Right-click the project then choose Gradle ➤ Refresh Gradle Project to update the project library assignments.

The project is now set up and you can start adding Java class and resource files.

The Hello World Model

Don't confuse the model layer of the Java MVC application with a database model. All that "model" means in the MVC part of an application is a data holder for values to be transported between different pages, and between the pages and the controller components. For our Hello World application, the model is very small—it consists of a single string that the user enters on the landing page as a username.

For many MVC web applications, it makes sense to introduce Java classes that hold model values. So for this Hello World application, you might want to think about a model class like the following:

```java
public class HelloWorldModel {
    private String userName;
    public String getUserName() {
        return userName; }
    public void setUserName(String userName) {
        this.userName = userName; }
}
```

However, for such easy cases, and generally if for whatever reason you don't want want to introduce model classes, Java MVC provides a model value holder mechanism. In a controller class, you simply use @Inject to let Java MVC (more precisely, the CDI part) inject a javax.mvc.Models instance:

```java
import javax.inject.Inject;
import javax.mvc.Models;
...

public class SomeController {
    @Inject
    private Models models;
    ...
}
```

You can then write the following in the controller:

```java
...
// somehow get String 'name' from the request
String name = ...; models.put("name", name);
...
```

And write this on the web pages:

```
...
Hello ${name}
...
```

For this simple Hello World application, we use the `Models` data container for the username, so we don't introduce any dedicated model classes.

The Hello World View

We need two pages for the view: one landing page where we ask the users for their name, and a greeting page showing the name just entered. We call the landing page `index.jsp` and it has to go into the `src/main/webapp/WEB-INF/views` folder.

The `src/main/webapp` path is a convention dictated by Gradle; the `WEB-INF/views` path underneath marks the page as a Java MVC controlled view. The `index.jsp` page code reads as follows:

```
<%@ page contentType="text/html;charset=UTF-8"
    language="java" %>
<%@ taglib prefix="c"
    uri="http://java.sun.com/jsp/jstl/core" %>
<html>
<head>
  <meta charset="UTF-8">
  <title>Hello World</title>
</head>
<body>
  <form method="post" action="${mvc.uriBuilder(
      'HelloWorldController#greeting').build()}">
    Enter your name: <input type="text" name="name"/>
    <input type="submit" value="Submit" />
  </form>
</body>
</html>
```

Java MVC allows for two templating engines: JSPs and Facelets. We use JSPs (you can see from the <%@ ...>, which doesn't exist in Facelets).

The action attribute from the form tag follows a special syntax dictated by the Java MVC framework—the ${ mvc. ... } by convention connects to a special object provided without further configuration work. This object, for example, has a uriBuilder() method that allows us to generically construct form actions aimed at a certain method from a Java MVC controller. In this case, it is the HelloWorldController controller (the class name of the controller without the package) and its greeting() method.

Placing the view pages somewhere is not enough for the web application to work correctly. As an additional step, we need to announce that index.jsp is the landing page. This means a http://localhost:8080/HelloWo rld/mvc must be redirected to run through the controller and end up in the index.jsp page being loaded. We use two Java classes for that aim. The first one adds /mvc to the target URL:

```
package book.javamvc.helloworld;

import javax.ws.rs.ApplicationPath;
import javax.ws.rs.core.Application;

@ApplicationPath("/mvc")
public class App extends Application {
}
```

You can put it as shown into the book.javamvc.helloworld package. The class is empty by intention—the @ApplicationPath annotation and the javax.ws.rs.core.Application superclass lead to the desired behavior.

The second class, RootRedirector, makes sure the "/" or "" path (behind mvc) is forwarded to mvc/hello, which will later be fetched by the controller as a GET verb (targeting index.jsp):

```
package book.javamvc.helloworld;

import javax.servlet.FilterChain;
import javax.servlet.annotation.WebFilter;
import javax.servlet.http.HttpFilter;
import javax.servlet.http.HttpServletRequest;
import javax.servlet.http.HttpServletResponse;
```

```java
import java.io.IOException;
/**
 * Redirecting http://localhost:8080/HelloWorld/
 * This way we don't need a <welcome-file-list> in web.xml
 */
@WebFilter(urlPatterns = "/")
public class RootRedirector extends HttpFilter {
    private static final long serialVersionUID =
            7332909156163673868L;

    @Override
    protected void doFilter(final HttpServletRequest req,
            final HttpServletResponse res,
            final FilterChain chain) throws IOException {
        res.sendRedirect("mvc/hello");
    }
}
```

The response page is called greeting.jsp, and we put it next to index.jsp in the src/main/webapp/WEB-INF/views folder:

```jsp
<%@ page contentType="text/html;charset=UTF-8"
    language="java" %>
<%@ taglib prefix="c"
    uri="http://java.sun.com/jsp/jstl/core" %>
<html>
<head>
    <meta charset="UTF-8">
    <title>Hello World</title>
</head>
<body>
  Hello ${name}
</body>
</html>
```

You can see that it is extremely limited concerning functionalities. It just outputs the "Hello NAME" string with NAME replaced by whatever was entered in the landing page. It refers to the name via ${name}, which addresses the model value name (see the next section).

The Hello World Controller

The controller class reacts to user input from browser pages and governs navigation between the pages. It is called HelloWorldController and we put it in the book.javamvc.helloworld package:

```
package book.javamvc.helloworld;

import javax.inject.Inject;
import javax.mvc.Controller;
import javax.mvc.Models;
import javax.mvc.binding.MvcBinding;
import javax.ws.rs.FormParam;
import javax.ws.rs.GET;
import javax.ws.rs.POST;
import javax.ws.rs.Path;
import javax.ws.rs.core.Response;

@Path("/hello")
@Controller
public class HelloWorldController {
    @Inject
    private Models models;

    @GET
    public String showIndex() {
        return "index.jsp";
    }

    @POST
    @Path("/greet")
    public Response greeting(
```

```
        @MvcBinding @FormParam("name") String name) {
    models.put("name", name);
    return Response.ok("greeting.jsp").build();
  }
}
```

The controller class looks very similar to a JAX-RS controller for RESTful services. The main difference is that we don't let requests return data values in the form of JSON structures or whatever. Instead, the methods are supposed to return page specifiers. The controller for HelloWorld listens to HTTP GET verbs for URL /hello by virtue of the class' @Path annotation and no extra @Path annotation for the showIndex() method. Thus, for /hello, the landing page index.jsp will be loaded.

The greeting() method connects to POSTs from the hello/greet URL, because the @Path from the class and the @Path from the method are concatenated. We need the HTTP POST verb here, because we want to connect this method to a form submit. Accordingly, for /hello/greet, the response page greeting.jsp will be loaded.

CDI injects the Models instance. It is a general-purpose data container in case you don't want to introduce Java beans to hold model values. It is fed by a POST and can be used inside the response view simply by writing ${someName}, where someName is the name of the POST parameter.

Caution   The Models instance is *request scoped*, which means the model values exist only in direct response to a POST action.

Using Gradle to Build Hello World

In order to build the Hello World web application, you have two options. First, you can use the Eclipse Gradle plugin to build a project that's deployable from inside Eclipse. For this aim, go to the Gradle Tasks view, open the HelloWorld drawer, and find the WAR task in the build section. See Figure 4-5. To start the task, double-click the task name. The view then automatically switches to the Gradle Executions window, as shown in Figure 4-6. There, you get an overview of what exactly Gradle does while performing the task.

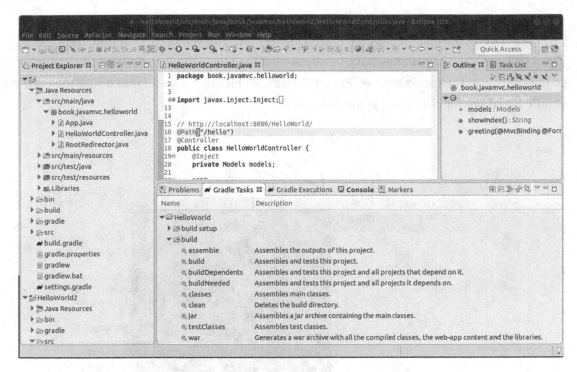

Figure 4-5. *The Hello World Gradle tasks*

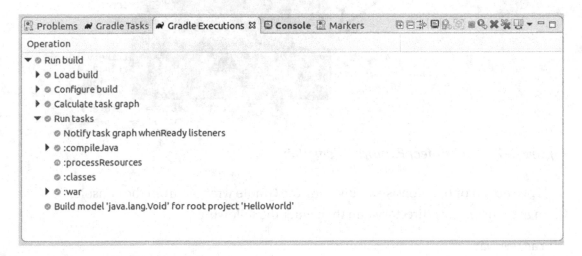

Figure 4-6. *Gradle Executions view*

After the build, you can then find the WAR file inside the build/libs folder. If you can't see it in the Project Explorer, left-click the project and press F5 to update the view. If you still can't see it, you may have to remove a filter. Open the Project Explorer's menu, go to Filters and Customization ➤ Preset Filters (see Figure 4-7), and make sure the Gradle Build Folder check box is unchecked.

Figure 4-7. *The Project Explorer view filter*

The second option consists of invoking the Gradle wrapper from the console. Change to the project directory and then enter the following:

```
./gradlew war
```

Or enter this if your system does not use a decent Java by default (enter your JDK path):

```
JAVA_HOME=/path/to/jdk ./gradlew war
```

After this, you should find the WAR file inside the build/libs folder.

Starting a Jakarta EE Server

Chapter 2 described installing and operating a GlassFish Jakarta EE server. For the Hello World example, make sure you followed that trail and ensured that GlassFish is running on your local system.

Deploying and Testing Hello World

To build and deploy the project, you again have two options. From Eclipse, you first have to make sure that the two custom Gradle tasks—`localDeploy` and `localUndeploy`—are visible to the Eclipse Gradle plugin. For this purpose, open the Gradle Tasks view's menu and make sure the Show All Tasks item is checked; see Figure 4-8.

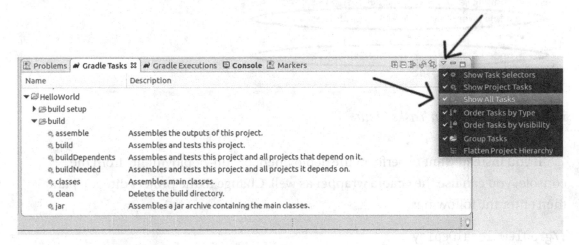

Figure 4-8. *Show All Tasks*

The custom tasks then show up in the Other section of the view, as shown in Figure 4-9. To invoke any of the custom tasks, simply double-click the task name.

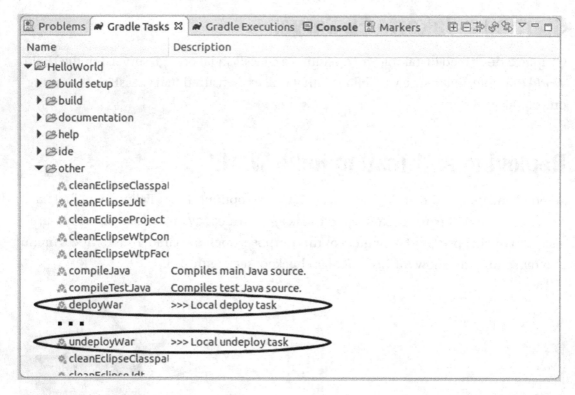

Figure 4-9. *Custom Tasks view*

If you instead want to perform the deployment or "un-deployment" from the console, you can use the Gradle wrapper as well. Change to the project directory and then enter the following:

```
./gradlew localDeploy
# or
./gradlew localUndeploy
```

Or use this if your system does not use a decent Java by default:

```
JAVA_HOME=/path/to/jdk ./gradlew localDeploy
# or
JAVA_HOME=/path/to/jdk ./gradlew localUndeploy
```

In order to test the Hello World web application, open a browser and enter the following URL:

```
http://localhost:8080/HelloWorld
```

The URL is automatically redirected to `http://localhost:8080/HelloWorld/mvc/hello`, which leads to rendering the landing page.

Note   8080 is the default HTTP port for web applications in a GlassFish server. The `/HelloWorld` comes from the WAR file's name (a server-specific feature), the `/mvc` comes from the App class, and the `hello` comes from the `RootRedirector` class.

The landing page and the response page are shown in Figure 4-10.

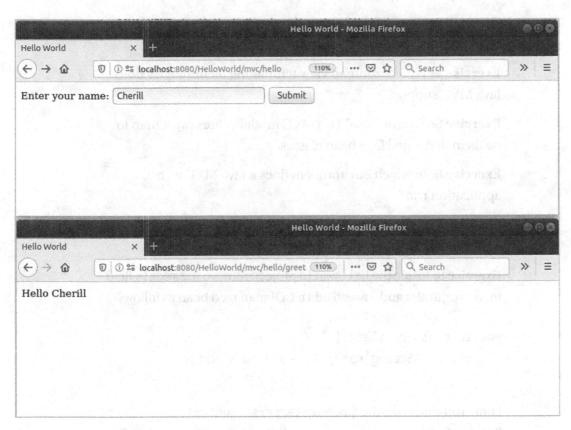

Figure 4-10. Hello World web application

Exercises

Exercise 1: True or false? The Eclipse Gradle plugin's New Gradle project wizard adds a Gradle wrapper to the project by default.

Exercise 2: Which of the following are true? (A) A Gradle wrapper wraps operating system configurations around Gradle invocations. (B) A Gradle wrapper provides a standalone Gradle installation inside the project folder. (C) You can tell the Gradle wrapper which JDK to use. (D) A Gradle wrapper adds the project to the operating system's Gradle project list.

Exercise 3: True or false? Gradle has built-in tasks for deploying WAR files on a Jakarta EE server.

Exercise 4: Which frontend view templating technologies does Java MVC support?

Exercise 5: True or false? Java MVC model values must map to fields in dedicated Java bean classes.

Exercise 6: In which environment does a Java MVC web application run?

Exercise 7: True or false? Gradle is required to build Java MVC web applications.

Exercise 8: Inside the `HelloWorld` project, remove the `models` field in the controller and instead add a CDI managed bean as follows:

```
public class UserData {
    private String name; // + getter / setter
}
```

Hint: You must add the `javax.enterprise.context.RequestScoped` and `javax.inject.Named` annotations to `UserData`. In the controller, you must add a `@Inject userData` field. In the view, you must use `${userData.name}` to access the bean.

Exercise 9: Add a Back link to the response page of the `HelloWorld` example.

Summary

In this chapter, we talked about a Hello World style web application using Eclipse and/or the console, and Gradle as the build framework. In the next chapter, we continue looking at some aspects from a use-case perspective, in order to improve our skills of using Java MVC in projects.

## CHAPTER 5

Start Working with Java MVC

Before we thoroughly handle the Java MVC parts—model, view, and controller—we first need to talk about a number of topics that look upon Java MVC from a use-case perspective. This sits somewhat intermediary between the basic Hello World chapter and the subsequent survey of Java MVC implementation concepts. This chapter's purpose is to gently improve your proficiency in Java MVC development. In detail, we are going to talk about handling data from form posts, parsing query parameters, converting input data types, and handling exceptions.

Handling User Input from Forms

In the Java MVC world, the transmission of data between the frontend (browser) and the controller can happen via `<form>` elements on web pages, a `POST` request initiated by a frontend user's submit, and method parameters in the controller class. The corresponding view code for two example parameters reads as follows:

```
<%@ page contentType="text/html;charset=UTF-8"
    language="java" %>
<%@ taglib prefix="c"
    uri="http://java.sun.com/jsp/jstl/core" %>
<html>
...
<body>
  ...
  <form method="post"
        action="${mvc.uriBuilder(
```

© Peter Späth 2021
P. Späth, *Beginning Java MVC 1.0*, https://doi.org/10.1007/978-1-4842-6280-1_5

```
                    'SomeController#someMethod').build()}">
    P1 Parameter: <input type="text" name="p1" />
    P2 Parameter: <input type="text" name="p2" />
    ...
  </form>
  ...
</body>
</html>
```

The mvc object used here refers to mvc, an automatically provided MvcContext instance (in the javax.mvc package), and its method uriBuilder() enables generic construction of MVC project related URIs/URLs.

As the controller addressed by the <form>'s action attribute, we take a class similar to the following:

```
...
import javax.mvc.binding.MvcBinding;
import javax.ws.rs.FormParam;
...

@Path("/abc")
@Controller
public class SomeController {
    ...

    @POST
    @Path("/xyz")
    public Response someMethod(
          @MvcBinding @FormParam("p1") String p1,
          @MvcBinding @FormParam("p2") String p2,
          ...more parameters...
    ) {
        // handle user input ...
        ...
        return Response.ok("responsePage.jsp").build();
    }
}
```

We talk about the controller later in this chapter, in its own section. For now, the `@Controller` annotation identifies the class as a Java MVC controller, and the `@Path` annotations are used to build the URL (sub) path used by the controller and its methods. The p1 from `@FormParam("p1")` corresponds to a `<input name = "p1" >` inside a submitted `<form>`, and accordingly a `@FormParam("p2")` to a `<input name = "p2">`.

It is also possible to avoid using method parameters and let the user data instead be passed over to controller instance fields. This kind of *data binding* uses the following construct:

```
...
import javax.mvc.binding.MvcBinding;
import javax.ws.rs.FormParam;
...

@Path("/abc")
@Controller
public class SomeController {
    @MvcBinding @FormParam("p1")
    private String p1;

    @MvcBinding @FormParam("p2")
    private String p2;

    ...

    @POST
    @Path("/xyz")
    public Response someMethod() {
    // handle user input via "p1" and "p2" fields
        ...
        return Response.ok("responsePage.jsp").build();
    }
}
```

Normally it is better to declare the parameters in the methods, because other methods might have other parameters and placing all those parameters at the class level will lead to a mess.

For the form parameters, we know that the `@FormParam` annotation directly connects the method parameter or field to a `<form>` input element. See Figure 5-1. We talk about the second parameter annotation shown in the listings, `@MvcBinding`, in the next section.

```
<form method="post"
      action="${mvc.uriBuilder('SomeController#someMethod').build()}">
  Enter your name: <input type="text" name="name" />
  <input type="submit" value="Submit" />
</form>
```

Those must
match

```
@Path("/abc")
@Controller
public class SomeController {
      @MvcBinding @FormParam("name")
      private String name;

      @POST
      @Path("/xyz")
      public Response someMethod() {
          System.out.println("Name: " + name);
          return Response.ok("responsePage.jsp").build();
      }
}
```

Figure 5-1. *Form to controller connection*

Exception Handling in Java MVC

The `@MvcBinding` annotation used in the Java code listings in the previous section introduces some magic about exception handling. Normally, because Java MVC sits on top of JAX-RS, an exception thrown during input data handling can only be caught by a special exception mapper. This procedure does not fit very well into the Java MVC world. We want to have an explicit relationship between a controller and a form submit, and an exception handling mapper class introduces a kind of additional "controller" type, which strictly spoken, has no relation to any MVC concept. Instead, by using the `@MvcBinding` annotation, the same controller and controller method is called whether or not there is an error, and passing-over errors caused by validation mismatches and conversion errors are fed into an injected instance of `javax.mvc.binding.BindingResult`.

You can then check for any errors programmatically by using the methods of the BindingResult instance:

```
...
import javax.mvc.binding.MvcBinding;
import javax.mvc.binding.BindingResult;
import javax.ws.rs.FormParam;
import javax.validation.constraints.Size;
...

@Path("/abc")
@Controller
public class SomeController {
    @Named
    @RequestScoped
    public static class ErrorMessages {
        private List<String> msgs = new ArrayList<>();

        public List<String> getMsgs() {
            return msgs;
        }

        public void setMsgs(List<String> msgs) {
            this.msgs = msgs;
        }

        public void addMessage(String msg) {
            msgs.add(msg);
        }
    }

    // Errors while fetching parameters
    // automatically go here:
    private @Inject BindingResult br;

    // We use this to pass over error messages
    // to the response page:
    private @Inject ErrorMessages errorMessages;

    ...
```

```java
@POST
@Path("/xyz")
public Response someMethod(
        @MvcBinding @FormParam("p1")
        @Size(min=3,max=10)
            String p1,
        @MvcBinding @FormParam("p2")
            String p2)
{
    // ERROR HANDLING ////////////////////////////
    if(br.isFailed()) {
      br.getAllErrors().stream().
            forEach((ParamError pe) -> {
          errorMessages.addMessage(pe.getParamName() +
              ": " + pe.getMessage());
        });
    }
    // END ERROR HANDLING ///////////////////////

    // handle user input via "p1" and "p2" params
    ...

    // advance to response page
    return Response.ok("responsePage.jsp").build();
  }
}
```

Here, we used an inner class for the error messages. Of course, you can also use your own class in your own file for the messages. Also observe the @Size constraint for the p1 parameter. This belongs to bean validation, which we are going to talk about in detail later. The @Size constraint used here means that if you enter a string shorter than three characters or longer than ten characters, a validation error will be handed over via the BindingResult typed br field.

On the response page, you could render errors like the following:

```jsp
<%@ page contentType="text/html;charset=UTF-8"
    language="java" %>
```

```
<%@ taglib prefix="c"
    uri="http://java.sun.com/jsp/jstl/core" %>
<html>
...
<body>
  <div style="color:red">
  <c:forEach var="e" items="${errorMessages.msgs}">
      ${e}
  </c:forEach>
  </div>
...
</body>
</html>
```

The ${errorMessages. ...}, by virtue of the @Named annotation, connects to the injected instance of ErrorMessages (the first letter lowered).

An alternative to presenting error messages in the normal response page consists of deviating the page flow to a different view page instead. This is easy, because we decide where to go next in the controller method. We thus can write the following:

```
...
@POST
@Path("/xyz")
public Response someMethod(...) {
    // ERROR HANDLING ////////////////////////////
    if(br.isFailed()) {
      br.getAllErrors().stream().
          forEach((ParamError pe) -> {
        errorMessages.addMessage(pe.getParamName() +
          ": " + pe.getMessage());
    });
    // advance to error page
    return Response.ok("errorPage.jsp").build();
  }
  // END ERROR HANDLING /////////////////////////

  // handle user input via "p1" and "p2" params
```

```
...

  // advance to response page
  return Response.ok("responsePage.jsp").build();
}
...
```

Non-String POST Parameters

In the previous section, we only used String-typed POST parameters. In Java MVC, you can also use numeric types int, long, float, double, BigDecimal, BigInteger, and boolean (true or false). So it is possible to write the following:

```
<%@ page contentType="text/html;charset=UTF-8"
    language="java" %>
<%@ taglib prefix="c"
    uri="http://java.sun.com/jsp/jstl/core" %>
<html>
...
<body>
  ...
  <form method="post"
        action="${mvc.uriBuilder(
                'SomeController#someMethod').build()}">
    Int Parameter: <input type="text"
        name="theInt" />
    Double Parameter: <input type="text"
        name="theDouble" />
    Boolean Parameter: <input type="text"
        name="theBoolean" />
    ...
  </form>
  ...
</body>
</html>
```

In the controller class, write the following:

```
...
import javax.mvc.binding.MvcBinding;
import javax.ws.rs.FormParam;
...

@Path("/abc")
@Controller
public class SomeController {
    ...

    @POST
    @Path("/xyz")
    public Response someMethod(
        @MvcBinding @FormParam("theInt")
            int theInt,
        @MvcBinding @FormParam("theDouble")
            double theDouble,
        @MvcBinding @FormParam("theBoolean")
            boolean theBoolean)
    {
        // handle user input via the fields
        ...
        return Response.ok("responsePage.jsp").build();
    }
}
```

Java MVC takes care of properly converting the POST parameters into the designated Java types.

If a conversion cannot be performed properly, maybe because an "x" was entered in the theInt input field, for example, an injected BindingResult (as described in the previous section) can be used to catch the conversion error.

Handling Query Parameters

HTTP verbs comprise POST, GET, PUT, DELETE, and others. So far in browser-to-controller communication, we talked about POST requests for transmitting data via HTML <form> elements, and GET requests for requesting the landing page. Consider the following case: On the landing page, the user is asked for some data, and a Submit button is provided which transmits the data to the controller and advances to a response page. On the response page, we want to add a Back button. That button needs the following additional functionality: all data entered in the fields should show up again. How can we do that? The controller @FormParam fields cannot be used, because they only work with form POSTs.

Up to now, we also didn't use session data storage, which prolongs a single request/response cycle. If we had, storing the user input there and later using it to preset input fields would be a valid approach. It is in fact possible to use sessions, but we talk about that later in this chapter. Also, not using sessions decreases the memory footprint and simplifies state housekeeping.

What we can do instead and what Java MVC supports is the use of query parameters. If you have a GET on, for example, http://xyz.com/the-app/start, query parameters are added in an appended string starting with ? and using & as a delimiter:

    http://xyz.com/the-app/start?name=John&birthday=19971230

To fetch such query parameters in a controller, you can use the @QueryParam annotation:

```
...
import javax.mvc.binding.MvcBinding;
import javax.ws.rs.GET;
import javax.ws.rs.Path;
import javax.ws.rs.QueryParam;

@Path("/")
@Controller
public class SomeController {
    private @Inject BindingResult br;

    @GET
    @Path("/start")
    public String someMethod(
```

```
        @MvcBinding @QueryParam("name") String name,
        @MvcBinding @QueryParam("birthday") String birthday
 ) {
    if(name != null) {
      // handle "name" parameter
    }
    if(birthday != null) {
      // handle "birthday" parameter
    }

    // advance to page
    return "index.jsp";
 }
 ...
}
```

Again, as with POST parameters, it is also possible to use fields for fetching the query parameters:

```
...
import javax.mvc.binding.MvcBinding;
import javax.ws.rs.GET;
import javax.ws.rs.Path;
import javax.ws.rs.QueryParam;

@Path("/")
@Controller
public class SomeController {
    private @Inject BindingResult br;

    @MvcBinding @QueryParam("name")
    private String name;

    @MvcBinding @QueryParam("birthday")
    private String birthday);

    @GET
    @Path("/start")
    public String someMethod() {
```

```
      if(name != null) {
        // handle "name" parameter
      }
      if(birthday != null) {
        // handle "birthday" parameter
      }

      // advance to page
      return "index.jsp";
    }
    ...
}
```

On the JSP page, the dedicated element used to issue such a parameterized GET request is a `<a>` link:

```
<a href="${mvc.uriBuilder('SomeController#someMethod').
        queryParam('name', userData.name).
        queryParam('birthday', userData.birthday).
        build()}">Link</a>
```

This snippet uses a `userData` variable, which could have been injected as an instance of the following:

```
@Named
@RequestScoped
public class UserData {
  private String name;
  private String birthday;
  // Getters, setters...
}
```

Obviously, this object has to be filled with data in the controller action, which ends up calling the page with the `<a>` link.

For request parameters, the same conversion rules apply to non-string typed parameters as to POST requests. You can use fields or method parameters of type `string`, numeric types `int`, `long`, `float`, `double`, `BigDecimal`, `BigInteger`, and `boolean` (`true` or `false`). Query parameters that are passed over are appropriately converted. Likewise, because we marked the parameters with @MvcBinding, the same methodology for handling exceptions described for POST parameters applies here.

The detailed procedure for creating a Back link that fills the original page with previously entered values would thus be as follows:

1. On a data input page (called dataInput.jsp), values are posted from inside <form> elements.

2. In the corresponding controller class and method, we retrieve the data via the @FormParam annotated fields or method parameters, and programmatically transport the values into an injected object (marked with @Named).

3. On the follow-up page (called responsePage.jsp), we create a Back link with query parameters taken from the injected object.

4. In the corresponding controller class and method, we retrieve the data via @QueryParam annotated fields or method parameters, and programmatically transport the values into an injected object (marked with @Named).

5. We amend the <input> elements from dataInput.jsp and add value attributes: <input ... value = "${injectedObject. field}">, where injectedObject corresponds to the field of the injected class InjectedObject.

6. For validation and conversion errors, we inject an instance of BindingResult. We use it in the controller methods to check for errors. For this to work, we must add @MvcBinding to all form and query parameters.

Note   It is possible to use form (POST) parameters and query parameters at the same time. Just add queryParam('name', value) method calls to the <form> action's URI builder. However, we don't want to make things too complicated, so we don't further investigate this kind of mixture in this book.

Exercises

Exercise 1: Which of the following is true? A `<form>` element on a web page connects to: (A) The method `userPosts()` of a controller class. (B) A certain method of a controller class determined by the form's `action = "..."` attribute and `@Path` annotations used by the controller class and its methods. (C) A certain model element injected into the controller.

Exercise 2: Describe what is minimally necessary for a Java class to become a Java MVC controller class.

Exercise 3: What is the most obvious similarity between JAX-RS and Java MVC? What is the most prominent difference between the two?

Exercise 4: What is the purpose of the `@MvcBinding` annotation?

Exercise 5: Add error handling, as described in this chapter, to the `HelloWorld` application from the previous chapter.

Exercise 6: Continuing from the previous exercise, add a validation constraint ensuring that the user only enters English letters as names. Hint: A corresponding regular expression reads `[A-Za-z]*`.

Exercise 7: Add a Back link to the response page of the `HelloWorld` application from the previous chapter. Add the username as a query parameter, and make sure the entered username shows up again in the input field from the starting page.

Summary

In the Java MVC world, transmitting data between the frontend (browser) and the controller can happen via `<form>` elements on web pages (and/or query parameters), a `POST` (or `GET`) request initiated by a frontend user's submit (or a link click), and method parameters in the controller class.

The @Controller annotation identifies the class as a Java MVC controller, and the @Path annotations are used to build the URL (sub) path used by the controller and its methods.

Normally, because Java MVC sits on top of JAX-RS, an exception thrown during input data handling can only be caught by a special exception mapper.

This procedure does not fit very well into the Java MVC world. Instead, by using the @MvcBinding annotation, the same controller and controller method are called whether or not there is an error, and passing-over errors due to validation mismatches and conversion errors are fed into an injected instance of javax.mvc.binding. BindingResult.

In addition to posting string-type parameters (and/or transmitting string-type query parameters) in Java MVC, you can also use numeric types int, long, float, double, BigDecimal, BigInteger, and boolean (true or false). Java MVC takes care of properly converting the POST parameters into the designated Java types.

If a conversion cannot be performed properly, maybe because an "x" was entered in an integer typed input field for example, an injected BindingResult can be used to catch the conversion error.

After this somewhat more use-case-centric view of Java MVC, we continue the discussion in the next chapter with a more concept-centric view, starting with the model and commencing with the view and the controller part of Java MVC.

CHAPTER 6

In-Depth Java MVC

In this chapter, we thoroughly handle the various features provided by Java MVC. Note that this chapter is not a substitute for the official Java MVC specification (the latest version is 1.0 as of the writing of this book), which you can find at:

https://download.oracle.com/otndocs/jcp/mvc-1-final-spec

Instead, this chapter covers the patterns you will most often encounter, and we will also work through some example snippets.

The Model

For the *model* part of Java MVC, not to be confused with a database model, the original idea of a MVC framework is rather unagitated. Model classes were just Java bean classes (classes with fields, getters, and setters), and developers would add them to the view programmatically in some way similar to the following (which is pseudo-code, not really Java):

```
...
// inside some controller
String name = ...; // somehow via form POST
int i1 = ...;    // somehow via form POST

    HttpRequest req = ..; // somehow via framework

    MyBean b = new MyBean(); b.setName(name); b.setSomeInt(i1);

    req.setBean("beanName", b);

    // somehow advance to response page
    ...
```

© Peter Späth 2021
P. Späth, *Beginning Java MVC 1.0*, https://doi.org/10.1007/978-1-4842-6280-1_6

In a response view, you would then probably access the model beans using some expression similar to the following:

```
Hello ${beanName.name}
```

where `beanName` corresponds to the `setBean()` method parameter from the pseudo-code, and `name` corresponds to a field name.

CDI in Java MVC

Java MVC is a modern framework and its model capabilities supersede the idea of simply referring to beans. It does so by incorporating the CDI (Context and Dependency Injection) technology for Jakarta EE 8 in version CDI 2.0. CDI is not a small technology—its specification PDF has more than 200 pages! Needless to say, we cannot introduce every concept of CDI, but we discuss the most important ideas and center our survey on the way Java MVC uses CDI.

Note   You can find the CDI specification at `https://jakarta.ee/specifications/cdi/2.0/`.

The basic idea is the same: we want to instantiate bean classes (data classes that contain mainly fields and their getters and setters) and provision those instances to both the controllers and the views. The main difference between the pre-CDI and the CDI way is that we don't instantiate such model classes ourselves and instead let CDI do it.

To tell Java MVC that we want a model class to be controlled by CDI and available to the view pages, we use the @Named annotation from the `javax.inject` package:

```
import javax.enterprise.context.RequestScoped;
import javax.inject.Named;

@Named
@RequestScoped
public class UserData {
  private String name;
  private String email;
  // Getters and setters...
}
```

We also use the @RequestScoped annotation to bind the lifecycle of the object instance to a single HTTP request/response cycle. We talk more about scopes in the next section.

Once we announce a bean via @Named to the CDI framework, two things happen in Java MVC. First we can use @Inject (package javax.inject) to refer to the bean instance from inside any Java MVC controller and from inside any other CDI controlled class. Second, we can use the instance from the view pages by using the class name with the first letter lowercased: ${userData.name} and ${userData.email}. See Figure 6-1.

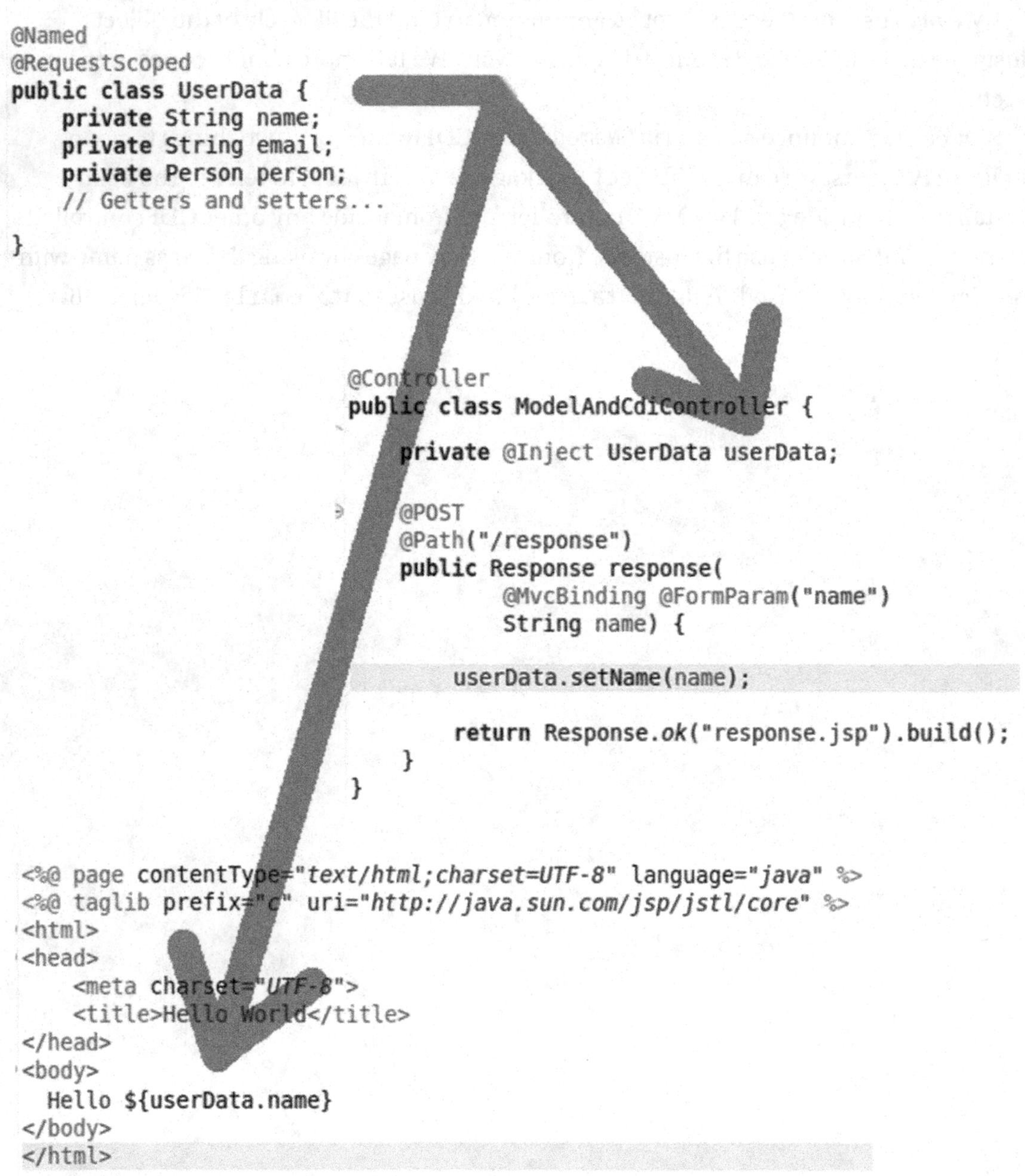

```java
@Named
@RequestScoped
public class UserData {
    private String name;
    private String email;
    private Person person;
    // Getters and setters...

}
```

```java
@Controller
public class ModelAndCdiController {

    private @Inject UserData userData;

    @POST
    @Path("/response")
    public Response response(
            @MvcBinding @FormParam("name")
            String name) {

        userData.setName(name);

        return Response.ok("response.jsp").build();
    }
}
```

```jsp
<%@ page contentType="text/html;charset=UTF-8" language="java" %>
<%@ taglib prefix="c" uri="http://java.sun.com/jsp/jstl/core" %>
<html>
<head>
    <meta charset="UTF-8">
    <title>Hello World</title>
</head>
<body>
  Hello ${userData.name}
</body>
</html>
```

Figure 6-1. *CDI in Java MVC*

If you want to use a different name for the CDI beans, you can use @Named with a parameter:

```
import javax.enterprise.context.RequestScoped;
import javax.inject.Named;
@Named("user")
@RequestScoped
public class UserData {
  private String name;
  private String email;
  // Getters and setters...
}
```

You can then use the altered name in a view page: ${user.name}. Since, in @Inject, the reference happens by class name and not by an annotation parameter, for injection into a Java class, you still use @Inject private UserName userName;, even with the altered name.

Model Object Scopes

If you're using CDI to manage model data, model class instances subordinate to a lifecycle control governed by CDI. This means CDI decides when to construct beans and when to abandon them. In injected beans, the way CDI controls the lifecycle of instances is by a characteristic called *scope*. In Java MVC, the following scopes exist:

- **Request scope:** An instance of an injected bean is created during an HTTP request and prevails only for the lifespan of the HTTP request and the response sent to the client (the browser). A typical usage scenario of request scope variables is when communicating POST form data or GET query parameters to the view layer page defined in the response. So you inject @Named request scope beans into controllers, set their fields there, and use the beans in the view layer. Because the lifespan of request scoped beans is short, they help keep the memory footprint of a web application low and avoid memory leaks.

- **Session scope:** A session is bound to a browser window and spans several HTTP request/response cycles. A session is started whenever the user enters a web application and terminates upon some timeout or an explicit session cancellation. Session scoped data objects prevail until some timeout is fired or the session is explicitly closed. You use session scoped objects when you need to maintain state with a lifecycle exceeding a single HTTP request/response cycle. Session data simplifies state handling, but significantly increases the danger of having a memory consuming web application or of establishing destabilizing memory leaks.

- **Redirect scope:** In order to support the POST-redirect-GET design pattern, Java MVC defines a *redirect scope* for CDI beans. You use this pattern if you want to avoid reposts when a browser user clicks the reload button prior to a POST action being terminated. The lifecycle of beans with a redirect scope span the POST and a subsequent GET (because the browser was made to receive a redirect code 303). In the Java MVC controller, you start POST-redirect-GET by either returning a `Response.seeOther( URI.create("response/path" )).build()` or a string `"redirect:response/path"` from inside the method that handles the POST. The process is as follows:

  1. The user enters data in a form and submits it. The Java MVC controller is invoked.

  2. The controller works through the form parameters, and the method in the end returns `Response.seeOther( URI.create("response/path" )).build()` or `"redirect:response/path"`.

  3. The browser automatically sends a *redirect* to the given path.

  4. The `response/path` path (adapt it accordingly) points to another controller method with the GET verb. It advances to a view page showing the appropriate response to the user's request.

The redirect scope CDI beans span a lifetime from the original POST request to the response generated by the subsequent GET request, which is two HTTP request/response cycles.

- **Application scope:** Any application-wide user-independent data can use this scope. Data prevails until the web application is undeployed or the server is stopped.

- **Dependent scope:** This is a pseudo-scope. It means the CDI bean gets the same scope as the bean it was activated from. The dependent scope is the default if no scope is explicitly set.

In order to define the scope for an injected bean, you use one of the following annotations:

```
@RequestScoped
@SessionScoped
@ApplicationScoped
@RedirectScoped
@Dependent
```

They are all from the `javax.enterprise.context` package, except for RedirectScoped, which is a Java MVC extension and belongs to the `javax.mvc.annotation` package.

The Simplified Model Data Container

Instead of using CDI beans marked with the @Named annotation, you can use an injected instance of Models (in the `javax.mvc` package). In a controller, you can then write the following:

```
import javax.inject.Inject;
import javax.mvc.Controller;
import javax.mvc.Models;
...

@Path("/abc")
@Controller
public class SomeController {
```

```
@Inject private Models models;

...
// inside any method:
models.put("name", name);

...
}
```

The model values are then available from inside view pages without a prefix:

```
Hello ${name}
```

Use the Models interface only when you need to handle a small amount of data. Otherwise, you risk unstructured, incomprehensible code.

Note   Models data has a request scope.

If you need model values from the Models object (still inside the same request/ response cycle!), you can use the get() method:

```
Object o = models.get("someKey");
```

```
// or, if you know the type
String s = models.get("someKey", String.class);
}
```

The View: JSPs

The view part of Java MVC is responsible for presenting the frontend to the client (the browser), for both input and output. Those Java MVC view files, which are connected to controller methods, are in the WEB-INF/views folder, or, because we are using Gradle as a build framework, in the src/main/webapp/WEB-INF/views folder.

Java MVC, out-of-the-box, supports two view engines—JSPs (JavaServer Pages) and Facelets (the view declaration language for JSF, JavaServer Faces). By design, other view engines can be included by an extension mechanism based on CDI. In this section, we talk about the JSP variant of Java MVC views.

> **Note**   For the JSP specification, see `https://download.oracle.com/otndocs/jcp/jsp-2_3-mrel2-spec/`.

JSP Basics

JSPs allow developers to interleave static content, for example HTML, and dynamic content, represented by JSP elements. A JSP page is internally compiled into one big Java class inheriting from `Servlet`. A file containing JSP code has the ending `.jsp`.

> **Note**   For GlassFish, you can see the generated servlets in the `GLASSFISH_INST/glassfish/domains/domain1/generated/jsp/-[PROJECT-NAME]` folder.

Directives

JSP directives provide directions to the container. Table 6-1 gives a description of the directives and Table 6-2 specifically lists the JSP page directives.

Table 6-1. *JSP Directives*

Name	Description
`<% page ... %>`	Page-dependent attributes.
	Possible parameters are shown in Table 6-2 (space-separated list).
`<% include file="relative url" %>`	Include another file in this place. For example: `<% include file = "header1a.jsp" %>`
`<% taglib uri="uri" prefix="prefix" %>`	Include a tag library. The precise syntax is shown in the tag library documentation.

Table 6-2. *JSP Page Directives*

Name	Description
`buffer="..."`	Use this to set the output buffer's size. Possible values: none (no buffer), or Nkb, where N is a number and kb stands for kilobytes (for example: 8kb).
`autoFlush="true"|"false"`	Auto-flushes the output buffer once it's filled. Otherwise, an exception will be thrown. Default is `true`.
`contentType="..."`	Sets the output's content type. Examples: `text/html`, `text/xml`. To also specify the character encoding, add `;charset=...`, as in `contentType = "text/html;charset=UTF-8"`
`errorPage="..."`	Specify an error page to be shown if an exception is thrown. This is a relative URL. Example: `errorPage = "error.jsp"`
`isErrorPage="true"|"false"`	If `true`, qualifies this JSP as an error page.
`extends="some.pckg.SomeClass"`	Makes the generated servlet extend the given class. This way you can provide your own servlet implementation.
`import="..."`	Works exactly like a Java `import` statement.
`info="..."`	Add any text here that describes the JSP.
`isThreadSafe="true"|"false"`	If `false`, only one thread at a time will be working the JSP. Default is `true`.
`language="..."`	Indicates the programming language used. Write `java` here.
`session="true"|"false"`	If `true`, sessions will be enabled. Default is `true`.
`isELIgnored="true"|"false""`	If `true`, expression language constructs ${ ... } are not evaluated. Default is `false`.
`isScriptingEnabled="true"|"false"`	If `true`, dynamic JSP scripting is enabled. Default is `true`, and setting this to `false` normally makes no sense except for truly static pages.

A basic JSP file header with the most common directives reads as follows:

```
<%@ page language="java"
    contentType="text/html;charset=UTF-8" %>
<%@ taglib prefix = "c"
    uri = "http://java.sun.com/jsp/jstl/core" %>
<%@ taglib prefix = "fmt"
    uri = "http://java.sun.com/jsp/jstl/fmt" %>
```

This implies that the text editors use UTF-8 (I presume this is the case). The two taglibs refer to the JSTL (JavaServer Pages Standard tag Library) tag library. The core and fmt parts of this taglib refer to useful tags common to many web applications.

Note JSTL has more parts, which we don't use for Java MVC. If you want to learn more about JSTL, go to https://jcp.org/aboutJava/communityprocess/final/jsr052/index.html.

Static Content

To produce static content, you just write it verbatim in the JSP file:

```
<%@ page language="java"
    contentType="text/html;charset=UTF-8" %>
<%@ taglib prefix = "c"
    uri = "http://java.sun.com/jsp/jstl/core" %>
<%@ taglib prefix = "fmt"
    uri = "http://java.sun.com/jsp/jstl/fmt" %>

<html>
<head>
    <meta charset="UTF-8">
    <title>Model And CDI</title>
</head>
<body>
    <%-- The string inside action is dynamic contents --%>
    <form method="post"
```

```
        action="${mvc.
                uriBuilder('ModelAndCdiController#response').
                build()}">
    Enter your name: <input type="text" name="name" />
    <input type="submit" value="Submit" />
  </form>
</body>
</html>
```

This code will be output as is, with three exceptions. The directives on top, the
`<%-- ... --%>`, which embraces a comment, and the `${ ... }`, which stands for an
expression to be handled by a processing step inside the JSP engine.

Java Scriptlets and Java Expressions

Because JSPs are transcribed into Java classes, JSP allows Java code and expressions to be
included in JSP pages. The syntax is as follows:

```
<%=
    Any Java code
    ...
%>

<%=
    Any Java expression (semicolons not allowed)
    ...
%>
```

The second construct, `<%= ... %>`, adds the expression result to the servlet's output
stream.

Caution   Do not overuse these constructs. After all, Java is an object oriented
language, not a frontend templating language.

Implicit Objects

Inside <%= ... %> or <% ... %>, there are a couple of implicit objects you can use:

- out: The servlet's output stream of type JspWriter (extends java.io.Writer).

- request: The request, type HttpServletRequest.

- response: The response, type HttpServletResponse.

- session: The session, type HttpSession.

- application: The application, type ServletContext.

- config: The servlet configuration, type ServletConfig.

- page: The servlet itself, type Object (runtime type javax.servlet.http.HttpServlet).

- pageContext: The page context, type PageContext.

You can use these objects to achieve fancy results, but bear in mind that you somehow leave official development patterns if you use them. This might make your code hard for others to read, and by putting functionality into the view pages, the natural demarcation between the model, the view, and the controller is broken.

JavaBeans Components

CDI beans with the @Named annotation are directly provisioned to the JSPs:

```
@Named
public class UserName {
  private String name;
  // Getters and setters...
}

JSP:
...
Hello ${userName.name}
```

If you add model data to an injected `javax.mvc.Models` CDI bean, you can directly access it without a prefix:

Controller:

```
import javax.mvc.Models;
...
@Controller
public class SomeController {
  @Inject private Models models;
  ...
  // inside any method:
  models.put("name", name);
  ...
}
```

JSP:

```
...
Hello ${name}
```

In both cases, you use an *expression language* construct ${ ... } inside the JSP. We talk about the expression languages in the next section.

Caution   Because of the implicit objects, you can refer to POST or query parameters directly from inside the JSPs. This is not MVC-like, however, because it introduces a second model layer out of reach to the controllers, and it moves controller responsibilities to the view. So don't do that and always use injected CDI beans instead.

Expression Languages

Constructs in JSP pages like ${ ... } are treated as an expression and are processed by an expression language handler. Expression elements are:

- `name`: Directly refers to a CDI managed bean or an implicit object. While rendering the view, the expression leads to using the `toString()` method for generating output. Example: ${user}.

- `value.property`: Refers to a `property` field of a `value` object (there must be a getter), or a map entry keyed by `property` if `value` is a map. Examples: `${user.firstName}` (there must be a `getFirstName()` in the `user` CDI bean) and `${receipt.amount}` (`receipt` is a map, and `amount` a key therein).

- `value[property]`: Refers to a field value-of-`property` of a `value` object (there must be a getter), or a map entry keyed by value-of-`property` if `value` is a map, or an item of a list or array if `property` evaluates to an `int` (for the index) and if `value` is a list or array. The `property` can also be a literal, like `42` or `1.3` or `'someString'` or `"someString"`. Examples: `${user['firstName']}` (same as `${user.firstName}`) and `${list[2]}` (third element in a list or array).

- `unaryOperator value`: Applies `unaryOperator` to value. Unary operators are − (negate), `not` or `!`, and `empty` (value is `null` or empty).

- `value1 binaryOperator value2`: Applies `binaryOperator` to `value1` and `value2`. Binary operators are:

  - Arithmetical: `+`, `-`, `*`, `/`, and `div`, `%`, and `mod` (modulo)

  - Logical: `and` and `&&`, `or` and `||`

  - Relational: `==` and `eq`, `!=` and `ne`, `<` and `lt`, `>` and `gt` `<=`, and `le`, `>=`, and `ge`

- `value1 ternaryOperatorA value2 ternaryOperatorB value3`: Applies `ternaryOperator` to `value1`, `value2`, and `value3`. There is just one: `a ? b : c` evaluates to `b` if `a` is true; otherwise, it evaluates to `c`.

There are several implicit objects you can use in expressions, as outlined in Table 6-3.

Table 6-3. *EL Implicit Objects*

Name	Description
pageScope	A map with scoped variables from page scope.
requestScope	A map with scoped variables from request scope.
sessionScope	A map with scoped variables from session scope.
applicationScope	A map with scoped variables from application scope.
paramValues	A map with request parameters as collections of strings. In a Java MVC application, you normally don't access such data via expressions, so don't use it.
param	A map with request parameters as strings (the first of each request parameter). In a Java MVC application, you normally don't access such data via expressions, so don't use it.
headerValues	A map with HTTP request headers as collections of strings.
header	A map with HTTP request headers as strings (the first of each header). To access a certain header, you'd for example write ${header["user-agent"]}.
initParam	A map with context initialization parameters.
cookie	Maps cookie names to instances of javax.servlet.http.Cookie.
pageContext	An object of type javax.servlet.jsp.PageContext. Allows you to access various objects, like the request, the response, and the session.

Output

If you prefer to use a tag for dynamic output, you can use the `<c:out>` tag as follows:

```
Hello <c:out value="${userData.name}" />

<%-- Similar to --%>
Hello ${userData.name}
```

They are not exactly the same, though. Without an additional escapeXml = "false", the tag will for example replace > with > and < with <. If ${userData.name} happens to be `<John>`, you won't see anything in the browser window for `Hello ${userData.name}`. The browser sees a `<John>`, which it interprets as an (invalid) tag. The tag variant instead outputs a `<John>` which shows up as a `<John>`.

The attributes of `<c:out>` are as follows:

- `escapeXml`: Whether to escape special XML characters. Not required; the default is `true`.

- `value`: The value to print. Required. Typically you write an expression like `${someBean.someProperty}` here.

- `default`: The default to write if something goes wrong with the value. Not required.

Variables

Using the `<c:set>` tag, we can introduce variables for further use on the page. In the Java MVC world, the most common usage scenario is introducing aliases for improving readability. Tasks like setting session scope variables should not be done from inside JSPs, since this is the controller's responsibility.

```
<c:set var="firstName" value=${user.firstName} />
<%-- We can henceforth use 'firstName' in expressions
     Instead of 'user.firstName' --%>
Hi ${firstName}
```

The complete attribute set for the `<c:set>` tag reads as follows:

- `value`: The value to be used for the new variable (or property). Typically, you write an expression like `${someBean.someProperty}` here.

- `var`: The name of a new variable that stores the value. Not required, but if not given, `target` and `property` must be used.

- `scope`: The scope of the variable given in `var="..."`. The default is `page` (only the currently rendered page).

- `target`: An object or map that stores the value. Not required.

- `property`: The name of a property (field) or key (for maps) if `target` is specified. Not required.

Loops

For loops over lists or arrays, you can use the `<c:forEach>` tag (the c signifies the `jstl/ core` taglib):

```
<c:forEach items="${theList}" var="item">
  ${item} <br/>
</c:forEach>
```

The expression inside `items="..."` can be any array or a list of strings, primitives, or other objects.

You will often use such loops for HTML tables. In the controller, you construct a list of item objects, with each item representing a row in the table:

```java
// probably inside a models package:
@Named
@RequestScoped
public class Members {
  private List<Member> list = new ArrayList<>();
  public void add(Member member) {
    list.add(member);
  }
  // Getters, setters...
}

public class Member {
  private int id;
  private String firstName;
  private String lastName;
  // Constructors, getters, setters...
}

// probably inside a controllers package:
@Controller
public class MyController {
    @Inject private Members members;

    // inside a method:
    members.add(new Member(...));
```

```
members.add(new Member(...));
...
}
```

In the JSP, we can now access the Members object via ${members. ...} and build a
table from the list:

```
<%@ page contentType="text/html;charset=UTF-8"
    language="java" %>
<%@ taglib prefix="c"
    uri="http://java.sun.com/jsp/jstl/core" %>
<html>
<head>
    <meta charset="UTF-8">
    <title>Table</title>
</head>
<body>
  <table>
    <thead>
      <tr>
        <th>ID</th>
        <th>Last Name</th>
        <th>First Name</th>
      </tr>
    </thead>
    <tbody>
      <c:forEach items="${members.list}" var="item">
        <tr>
          <td>${item.id}</td>
          <td>${item.lastName}</td>
          <td>${item.firstName}</td>
        </tr>
      </c:forEach>
    </tbody>
  </table>
</body>
</html>
```

All possible attributes for the `<c:forEach>` tag are as follows:

- `items`: The items to iterate through. Not required, but if missing, the loop will iterate over an integer. This is where you probably write an expression like `${someBean.someListOrArray}`.

- `var`: The name of a page scope variable that will be generated and then will hold each item of the loop. Not required.

- `begin`: Element to start with. Not required; the default is 0 (the first item).

- `end`: Element to end with. Not required; the default is the last element.

- `step`: The step. Not required; the default is 1.

- `varStatus`: The name of a loop status variable (the page scope). Not required. The variable will hold an object of type `javax.servlet.jsp.jstl.core.LoopTagStatus`.

If you want to use the `<c:forEach>` tag for an integer-valued range loop, you don't specify the `items` attribute, but use the `begin` and `end` attributes instead:

```
<c:forEach begin="1" end="10" var="i">
  ${i}<br/>
</c:forEach>
```

Conditional Branching

For conditional branching inside a JSP, you can use one of the `<c:if>` and `<c:choose>` tags. The simple `<c:if>` test allows for a simple condition check without alternatives and without an else branch:

```
<c:if test="${showIncome}">
  <p>Your income is: <c:out value="${income}"/></p>
</c:if>
```

An `if-else` can be painlessly achieved by using the following construct:

```
<c:if test="${showIncome}">
    <p>Your income is: <c:out value="${income}"/></p>
</c:if><c:if test="${!showIncome}">
    <p>Your income is: ***</p>
</c:if>
```

However, for a real `if-elseif-elseif-...-else`, the `<choose>` tag is the better candidate:

```
<c:choose>
    <c:when test="${income <= 1000}">
        Income is not good.
    </c:when>
    <c:when test="${income > 10000}">
        Income is very good.
    </c:when>
    <c:otherwise>
        Income is undetermined...
    </c:otherwise>
</c:choose>
```

Cookies

Cookies can be read directly from inside JSPs by using the implicit `cookie` object:

```
Cookie name: ${cookie.theCookieName.name} <p/>
Cookie value: ${cookie.theCookieName.value} <p/>
```

where `theCookieName` is replaced with the cookie name. The `${cookie.theCookieName}` then refers to an object of type `javax.servlet.http.Cookie`. However, only the name and the value are available.

For testing purposes, you can create a cookie named `theCookieName` in a controller method (set the cookie properties at will):

```
@Controller
@Path("abc")
public class MyController {
```

```
@GET
public Response myResponse() {
    ...
    // This is a subclass of Cookie:
    NewCookie ck = new NewCookie("theCookieName",
        "cookieValue",
        "the/path",
        "my.domain.com",
        42,
        "Some Comment",
        3600*24*365,
        false);

    return Response.
        ok("responsePage.jsp").
         cookie(ck).
        build();
  }
  ...
}
```

In the response page (or some later page), you can then write the JSP code shown to investigate the cookie.

Caution   For a local test server, you must set `localhost` as the cookie domain. Also, you must set the appropriate path value, maybe / for simplicity (it matches all paths).

The View: Facelets

The other view technology that Java MVC supports, apart from JSP, are *Facelets*. Facelets is the templating framework especially created for JSF, and JSF (JavaServer Faces) is the dedicated main frontend technology for Jakarta EE. JSF is component-based, in contrast to Java MVC, which is action-based. This is where a problem shows up: Java MVC is somewhat of a competitor to JSF, so Java MVC and Facelets at first sight don't seem to match. The good news is that, because JSF and Facelets are highly decoupled, we don't have to use JSF components, and Facelets as a mere templating engine can be used for Java MVC as well. This is nice, because Facelets is more apt to a modern programming style compared to JSP, which is sometimes considered old-school, although venerable.

We didn't put Facelets at second place as a templating engine for Java MVC without intention, though. JSPs have proven to be valuable for decades now, and they are a little bit closer to basic programming paradigms often used by frontend developers. Besides, if you have some experience programming in JSF, using Facelets obviates the danger of trying to use JSF features for Java MVC, which easily messes up your application design. Facelets, in contrast, applies a higher degree of abstraction, and, if it's used by a skilled developer, allows for a leaner and cleaner application design.

Having said that, it is totally up to you which frontend technology you use. This section shows you how to use Facelets for Java MVC.

Facelets Files

Facelets files for Java MVC go in the same folder as JSP files: the WEB-INF/views folder, or, because we are using Gradle as a build framework, in the src/main/webapp/WEB-INF/views folder.

Facelets files are XML files, which is maybe the most noticeable difference between JSPs and Facelets. You don't have directives like \ci{<\% ... \%>} in Facelets, and you can't use legacy HTML constructs which are not valid XML, but nevertheless allowed for JSPs.

Facelets Configuration

What we achieved in JSP programming, avoiding the need to provide a web.xml configuration file, can be achieved in Facelets as well. At first, we provide an App class to add mvc to the URL context path:

```
package any.project.package;

import javax.ws.rs.ApplicationPath;
import javax.ws.rs.core.Application;

@ApplicationPath("/mvc")
public class App extends Application {
}
```

This class is empty by intention; the context path element is added by the annotation alone.

Next, we add a redirector, which allows us to use the base URL http://the. server:8080/WarName/ to start the application (this is for GlassFish, WarName needs to be replaced with the WAR filename). The redirector forwards such a request to http:// the.server:8080/WarName/mvc/facelets, which we will use as an entry point for the landing page configured in the controller class. The name doesn't matter; we call it RootRedirector:

```java
package any.project.package;

import javax.servlet.FilterChain;
import javax.servlet.annotation.WebFilter;
import javax.servlet.http.HttpFilter;
import javax.servlet.http.HttpServletRequest;
import javax.servlet.http.HttpServletResponse;
import java.io.IOException;

@WebFilter(urlPatterns = "/")
public class RootRedirector extends HttpFilter {
  private static final long serialVersionUID =
       73329091561636738668L;

@Override
  protected void doFilter(final HttpServletRequest req,
       final HttpServletResponse res,
       final FilterChain chain) throws       IOException {
    res.sendRedirect("mvc/facelets");
  }
}
```

What is left is to take care that in the controller a "facelets" path will lead to a GET on the landing page:

```java
import javax.mvc.Controller;
import javax.ws.rs.GET;
import javax.ws.rs.Path;
import javax.ws.rs.core.Response;
```

```
@Path("/facelets")
@Controller
public class MyFaceletsController {
    @GET
    public Response showIndex() {
        return Response.ok("index.xhtml").build();
    }
    ...
}
```

Templating via Facelets

Facelets allow us to introduce parameterized template HTML pages, HTML snippets (components) to be included in pages, placeholders for such snippets, and decorators and repetitions for things like elaborated list views. In the following pages, we first enlist the Facelets tags, and after that develop a sample application to get you started.

To use Facelets, you have to add the Facelets namespace to the XHTML files:

```
<?xml version='1.0' encoding='UTF-8' ?>
<!DOCTYPE html>
<html lang="en"
      xmlns="http://www.w3.org/1999/xhtml"
      xmlns:ui="http://java.sun.com/jsf/facelets">
    <h:head>
        <title>Facelet Title</title>
    </h:head>
<body>
  ...
</body>
</html>
```

In the following sections, we explain the Facelets tags you can include in a XHTML file to apply or mix templates, include XHTML snippets, or pass parameters.

The <ui:include> Tag

Include another XHTML file, as in

```
<ui:include src="incl.xhtml" />
```

If the included file contains a `<ui:composition>` or a `<ui:component>`, only the inner contents of the `<ui:composition>` or `<ui:component>` tag will be included. This allows designers to style the included files independent of their later plumbing together by the server.

The <ui:composition> Tag, First Variant

If it's used *without* `template="..."`, as in

```
<ui:composition>
    ...
</ui:composition>
```

it defines a subtree (collection) of HTML elements. The idea behind that is, if you use `<ui:include>` and the included file contains a `<ui:composition> ... </ui:composition>`, only the inner contents of the `<ui:composition> ... </ui:composition>` will be included. The tag itself and anything around it will be ignored. So you can let page designers create a completely valid XHTML file, put a `<ui:composition> ... </ui:composition>` around the interesting parts, and write `<ui:include>` in any other JSF page to extract exactly such parts.

The <ui:composition> Tag, Second Variant

If it . used *with* `template="..."`, as in

```
<ui:composition template="templ.xhtml">
    ...
</ui:composition>
```

it defines a collection of XHTML snippets to be passed into placeholders inside the template file (corresponding to the `template = "..."` attribute).

This is a completely different usage scenario compared to `<ui:composition>` without `template="..."`. In the template file, you have one or more elements like `<ui:insert name="name1" />` and in the file with the `<ui:composition template="...">`,

you use <ui:define> tags *inside* the <ui:composition template="..."> ... </
ui:composition>

```
<ui:composition template="templ.xhtml">
    <ui:define name = "someName"> ... </ui:define>
    <ui:define name = "someName2"> ... </ui:define>
    ...
</ui:composition>
```

to define contents to be used for the <ui:insert> tags. Anything around the
<ui:composition> tag will be ignored again, so you can let designers create the
snippets using non-JSF aware HTML editors and only later extract interesting parts with
<ui:define name = "someName"> ... </ui:define> to be used for materializing the
template file.

The <ui:insert> Tag

Use this to define placeholders inside template files. A <ui:insert name="name1"/>
tag inside a template file thus means that any file referring to this template may define
contents for the placeholders. This definition has to happen inside <ui:composition>,
<ui:component>, <ui:decorate>, or <ui:fragment>.

Usually you don't provide contents in this tag. If you add contents, such as

```
<ui:insert name="name1">
    Hello
</ui:insert>
```

it will be taken as a default if the placeholder is not defined otherwise.

The <ui:define> Tag

This tag declares what will be inserted at the insertion points:

```
<ui:define name="theName">
    Contents...
</ui:define>
```

Since insertion points can only exist in template files, the <ui:define> tag can only
show up in files referring to template files via <ui:composition template = "...">

159

The <ui:param> Tag

Specifies a parameter that gets passed to an <ci:include>-ed file, or to the template specified in <ui:composition template = "..."> ... Simply add it as a child element, as in the following:

```
<ui:include src="comp1.xhtml">
    <ui:param name="p1" value="Mark" />
</ui:include>
```

Inside the referred-to file, add #{paramName} to use the parameter:

```
<h:outputText value="Hello #{p1}" />
```

The <ui:component> Tag

This is the same as <ui:composition>, first variant without template specification, but it adds an element to the JSF component tree. This tag supports the following attributes:

- id: The element's ID in the component tree. Not required; JSF generates an automatic ID if you don't specify it. May be an EL (expression language) string value.

- binding: For binding the component to a Java class (must inherit from javax.faces.component.UIComponent). Not required. May be an EL string value (class name).

- rendered: Whether or not the component is to be rendered. Not required. May be an EL boolean value.

It is common practice to use <ui:param> to pass parameters to components. You can, for example, tell the component to use a particular ID. The caller is as follows:

```
<ui:include src="comp1.xhtml">
    <ui:param name="id" value="c1" />
</ui:include>
```

The callee (comp1.xhtml) is as follows:

```
<ui:component id="#{id}">
    ...
</ui:component>
```

The <ui:decorate> Tag

Similar to <ui:composition>, but this tag does *not* disregard the XHTML code around it:

```
...
I'm written to the output!
<ui:decorate template="templ.xhtml">
    <ui:define name="def1">
        I'm passed to "templ.xhtml", you can refer to
        me in "templ.xhtml" via
        <ui:insert name="def1"/&gth;
    </ui:define>
</ui:include>
...
```

In contrast to <ui:composition>, the file with the <ui:decorate> will contain the completely valid XHTML code, including html, head, and body, and the template file will be inserted where the <ui:decorate> appears. Therefore, it must not contain html, head, or body. This is more or less an extended include, where passed-over data is not given by the attributes but listed in the tag body instead.

You usually apply the <ui:decorate> tag to further elaborate code snippets. You can wrap them into more <div>s to apply more styles, add a label or a heading, and more.

The <ui:fragment> Tag

This tag is the same as <ui:decorate>, but it creates an element in the JSF component tree. It has the following attributes:

- id: For the element's ID in the component tree. Not required; JSF generates an automatic ID if you don't specify it. May be an EL (expression language) string value.

- binding: For binding the component to a Java class (must inherit from javax.faces.component.UIComponent). Not required. May be an EL string value (class name).

- rendered: Whether or not the component is rendered. Not required. May be an EL boolean value.

You can use this to extract existing code snippets and to convert them partly to a component. For example, consider the following code:

```
<DOCTYPE html>
<html ...><head>...</head>
<h:body>
  ...
  <table>
      [Some table|
  </table>
  ...
</h:body></html>
```

If we now extract the table to a different file, called table1_frag.xhtml:

```
<!-- Caller: ########################### -->
<!-- original file                     -->
<DOCTYPE html>
<html ...><head>...</head>
<h:body>
  ...
  <ui:include src="table1_frag.xhtml"/>
  ...
</h:body></html>

<!-- Callee: ########################### -->
<!-- table1_frag.xhtml                  -->
<div xmlns="http://www.w3.org/1999/xhtml"
  xmlns:h="http://xmlns.jcp.org/jsf/html"
xmlns:f="http://xmlns.jcp.org/jsf/core"
xmlns:ui="http://java.sun.com/jsf/facelets"
xmlns:pt="http://xmlns.jcp.org/jsf/passthrough">
  <div>I am the table caption</div>
  <ui:fragment>
    <table>
```

```
    [Some table|
  </table>
</ui:fragment>
</div>
```

We have introduced XHTML (the caption) and a new component (the table).

The <ui:repeat> Tag

This is not necessarily a templating related tag, but it gets used to loop over a collection or an array. Its attributes are:

- begin: Not required. If it's specified, the iteration begins in the list or array. May be an int valued value expression.

- end: Not required. If specified, the iteration ends (inclusive) in the list or array. May be an int valued value expression.

- step: Not required. If specified, steps inside the list or array. May be an int valued value expression.

- offset: Not required. If specified, an offset is added to the iterated-over values. May be an int valued value expression.

- size: Not required. If specified, it's the maximum number of elements to read from the collection or array. Must not be greater than the array size.

- value: The list or array to iterate over. An Object valued expression. Required.

- var: The name of an expression language variable to hold the current item of the iteration. May be a String value expression.

- varStatus: Not required. The name of a variable to hold the iteration status. A POJO with read-only values: begin (int), end (int), index (int), step (int), even (boolean), odd (boolean), first (boolean), or last (boolean).

- rendered: Whether the component is to be rendered. Not required. May be an EL boolean value.

> **Note**   The JSTL (Java Standard Tag Library) collection provides a `<c:forEach>` tag for looping. JSF and JSTL do not work together very well because of conceptual differences. In tutorials and blogs, you will find lots of examples for loops with JSTL. It is, however, better to use `<ui:repeat>` instead to avoid problems.

The <ui:debug> Tag

Add this to your page during the development phase of your project. Using a hotkey, the tag will then lead to the JSF component tree and the other information to be shown on the page. Use the `hotkey="x"` attribute to change the hotkey. Shift+Ctrl+x will then display the component (note that the default d does not work with the Firefox browser!). The second optional attribute is `rendered="true|false"` (you can also use an EL boolean expression) to switch on or off this component.

> **Note**   This tag only works in the development project stage. Inside `WEB-INF/web.xml`, you can add this tag:
>
> ```
> <context-param>
>     <param-name>javax.faces.PROJECT_STAGE</param-name>
>     <param-value>Development</param-value>
> </context-param>
> ```
>
> to specify the project stage (any of `Development` (default), `UnitTest`, `SystemTest`, or `Production`).

An Example Facelets Project

We build an example Facelets project with a music box database, which shows similarly designed pages for titles, composers, and performers. We have a header, a footer, and a menu to appear on every page of the web application, no matter which functionality the user is currently using. Facelets does a good job of letting us factor out common page parts, so we have to code them only once. See Figure 6-2.

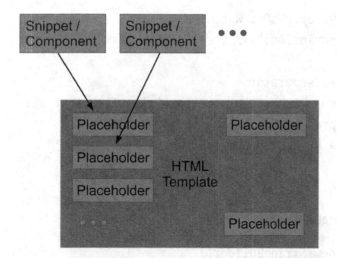

Figure 6-2. *Templating with Facelets*

Start a new Gradle project in Eclipse and name it MusicBox. Use the build.gradle file and replace its contents with:

```
plugins {
    id 'war'
}

java {
    sourceCompatibility = JavaVersion.VERSION_1_8
    targetCompatibility = JavaVersion.VERSION_1_8
}

repositories {
    jcenter()
}

dependencies {
    testImplementation 'junit:junit:4.12'
    implementation 'javax:javaee-api:8.0'
    implementation 'javax.mvc:javax.mvc-api:1.0.0'
    implementation 'org.eclipse.krazo:krazo-jersey:1.1.0-M1'
    implementation 'jstl:jstl:1.2'
    implementation 'com.google.guava:guava:28.0-jre'
}
```

```
task localDeploy(dependsOn: war,
            description:">>> Local deploy task") {
  doLast {
    def FS = File.separator
    def glassfish = project.properties['glassfish.inst.dir']
    def user = project.properties['glassfish.user']
    def passwd = project.properties['glassfish.passwd']

    File temp = File.createTempFile("asadmin-passwd",
        ".tmp")
    temp << "AS_ADMIN_${user}=${passwd}\n"

    def sout = new StringBuilder()
    def serr = new StringBuilder()
    def libsDir =
        "${project.projectDir}${FS}build${FS}libs"
    def proc = """${glassfish}${FS}bin${FS}asadmin
      --user ${user} --passwordfile ${temp.absolutePath}
      deploy --force=true
      ${libsDir}/${project.name}.war""".execute()
    proc.waitForProcessOutput(sout, serr)
    println "out> ${sout}"
    if(serr.toString()) System.err.println(serr)

    temp.delete()
  }
}

task localUndeploy(
            description:">>> Local undeploy task") {
  doLast {
    def FS = File.separator
    def glassfish = project.properties['glassfish.inst.dir']
    def user = project.properties['glassfish.user']
    def passwd = project.properties['glassfish.passwd']

    File temp = File.createTempFile("asadmin-passwd",
        ".tmp")
```

```
    temp << "AS_ADMIN_${user}=${passwd}\n"

    def sout = new StringBuilder()
    def serr = new StringBuilder()
    def proc = """${glassfish}${FS}bin${FS}asadmin
        --user ${user} --passwordfile ${temp.absolutePath}
        undeploy ${project.name}""".execute()
    proc.waitForProcessOutput(sout, serr) println "out> ${sout}"
    if(serr.toString()) System.err.println(serr)

    temp.delete()
  }
}
```

Apart from dependency handling, this build file introduces two custom tasks for deploying and undeploying the `MusicBox` web application on a local server. The *Guava* library is just a collection of useful tools for streamlining basic development needs.

To connect to the `asadmin` tool, we create another file, called `gradle.properties`, in the project root:

```
glassfish.inst.dir = /path/to/glassfish5.1
glassfish.user = admin
glassfish.passwd =
```

You should enter your own GlassFish server installation path. An empty `admin` password is An empty password is Glassfish' default setting. If you changed this, you must enter the password in this file.

For the `musicbox` data, we create three Java classes. For simplicity they return static information. In real life, you would connect to a database to get the data. Create a package called `book.javamvc.musicbox.model` and add the following:

```
// Composers.java:
package book.javamvc.musicbox.model;

import java.io.Serializable;
import java.util.List;

import javax.enterprise.context.SessionScoped;
import javax.inject.Named;
```

```java
import com.google.common.collect.Lists;

@SessionScoped
@Named
public class Composers implements Serializable {
    private static final long serialVersionUID =
        -5244686848723761341L;

    public List<String> getComposers() {
        return Lists.newArrayList("Brahms, Johannes",
            "Debussy, Claude");
    }
}

// Titles.java:
package book.javamvc.musicbox.model;

import java.io.Serializable;
import java.util.List;

import javax.enterprise.context.SessionScoped;
import javax.inject.Named;

import com.google.common.collect.Lists;

@SessionScoped
@Named
public class Titles implements Serializable {
    private static final long serialVersionUID =
        -1034755008236485058L;

    public List<String> getTitles() {
        return Lists.newArrayList("Symphony 1",
            "Symphony 2", "Childrens Corner");
    }
}

// Performers.java:
package book.javamvc.musicbox.model;
```

```
import java.io.Serializable;
import java.util.List;

import javax.enterprise.context.SessionScoped;
import javax.inject.Named;

import com.google.common.collect.Lists;

@SessionScoped
@Named
public class Performers implements Serializable {
    private static final long serialVersionUID =
        6941511768526140932L;

    public List<String> getPerformers() {
        return Lists.newArrayList(
            "Gewandhausorchester Leipzig",
            "Boston Pops");
    }
}
```

For CDI to work correctly, create an empty file called src/main/webapp/WEB-INF/beans.xml. Add one more file, called src/main/webapp/WEB-INF/glassfish-web.xml. It should contain the following:

```
<?xml version="1.0" encoding="UTF-8"?>
<glassfish-web-app error-url="">
    <class-loader delegate="true"/>
</glassfish-web-app>
```

Before we get into the view coding, Figure 6-3 shows an impression of what we want to achieve. To apply the Facelets functionalities, we add a template file called src/main/webapp/WEB-INF/frame.xhtml:

```
<!DOCTYPE html>
<html lang="en"
      xmlns="http://www.w3.org/1999/xhtml"
      xmlns:ui="http://java.sun.com/jsf/facelets">
<head>
```

```
    <title>Musicbox</title>
    <link rel="stylesheet" href="../../css/style.css" />
</head>

<body>
    <div class="header-line">
        <ui:insert name="header">
          <h2>Top Section</h2>
        </ui:insert>
    </div>
    <div class="center-line">
        <div class="menu-column">
          <ui:insert name="menu">
            <ul><li>Menu1</li><li>Menu2</li></ul>
          </ui:insert>
        </div>
        <div class="contents-column">
          <ui:insert name="contents">
              Contents
          </ui:insert>
        </div>
    </div>
    <div class="bottom-line">
        <ui:insert name="footer">Footer</ui:insert>
    </div>
</body>
</html>
```

This template file defines a common page structure and declares a couple of placeholders via <ui:insert> tags. The CSS file we are referring to is called style.css and it goes to src/main/webapp/css/style.css:

```
body { color: blue; }
.header-line { height: 3em; background-color: #CCF000; }
.bottom-line { clear: both; height: 1.5em; }
.menu-column { float: left; width: 8em;
    background-color: #FFC000; height: calc(100vh - 7em); }
```

```
.menu-column ul { margin:0.5em; padding: 0;
    list-style-position: inside; }
.contents-column { float: left; padding: 0.5em;
    background-color: #FFFF99;
    width: calc(100% - 9em); height: calc(100vh - 8em); }
.bottom-line { padding-top: 1em;
    background-color: #CCFFFF; }
```

For common page elements, we define a couple of XHTML files inside the src/main/webapp/common folder:

```
<!-- File commonHeader.xhtml -->
<!DOCTYPE html>
<div xmlns="http://www.w3.org/1999/xhtml"
    xmlns:ui="http://java.sun.com/jsf/facelets">
  <h2>Musicbox</h2>
</div>

<!-- File commonMenu.xhtml -->
<!DOCTYPE html>
<div xmlns="http://www.w3.org/1999/xhtml"
      xmlns:ui="http://java.sun.com/jsf/facelets">
  <ul>
    <li><a href="titles">Titles</a></li>
    <li><a href="composers">Composers</a></li>
    <li><a href="performers">Performers</a></li>
  </ul>
</div>

<!-- File commonFooter.xhtml -->
<!DOCTYPE html>
<div xmlns="http://www.w3.org/1999/xhtml"
      xmlns:ui="http://java.sun.com/jsf/facelets">
  (c) The Musicbox company 2019
</div>
```

Inside commonMenu.xhtml, we provide <a> links to the titles, composers, and performers pages. The href attributes do not directly correspond to XHTML pages;

instead, they point to methods inside the controller. This is a Java class called
MusicBoxController.java inside the book.javamvc.musicbox.controller package:

```java
package book.javamvc.musicbox.controller;

import java.util.ArrayList;
import java.util.List;

import javax.enterprise.context.RequestScoped;
import javax.inject.Inject;
import javax.inject.Named;
import javax.mvc.Controller;
import javax.mvc.binding.BindingResult;
import javax.mvc.binding.MvcBinding;
import javax.mvc.binding.ParamError;
import javax.ws.rs.FormParam;
import javax.ws.rs.GET;

import javax.ws.rs.POST;
import javax.ws.rs.Path;
import javax.ws.rs.core.NewCookie;
import javax.ws.rs.core.Response;

@Path("/musicbox")
@Controller
public class MusicBoxController {
    private @Inject BindingResult br;

    @GET
    public Response showIndex() {
        return Response.ok("titles.xhtml").build();
    }

    @GET
    @Path("/titles")
    public Response showTitles() {
        return Response.ok("titles.xhtml").build();
    }
```

```
@GET
@Path("/composers")
public Response showComposers() {
    return Response.ok("composers.xhtml").build();
}

@GET
@Path("/performers")
public Response showPerformers() {
    return Response.ok("performers.xhtml").build();
}

@POST
@Path("/response")
public Response response(
        @MvcBinding @FormParam("name")
        String name) {
    if(br.isFailed()) {
        // ... handle errors
    }

    // ... handle user POSTs

    // ... advance to response page
    return Response.ok("response.xhtml").build();
}
}
```

The response() method is not implemented in this example. It is shown here to get you started if you want to include forms.

The three page files—titles.xhtml, composers.xhtml, and performers.xhtml—inside the src/main/webapp/WEB-INF/views folder refer to the template file and the common page elements:

```
<!-- File titles.xhtml ********************* -->
<!DOCTYPE html>
<html lang="en"
    xmlns="http://www.w3.org/1999/xhtml"
```

```
        xmlns:ui="http://java.sun.com/jsf/facelets">

<body>
<ui:composition template="frame.xhtml">

  <ui:define name="header">
    <ui:include src="/common/commonHeader.xhtml" />
  </ui:define>

  <ui:define name="menu">
    <ui:include src="/common/commonMenu.xhtml" />
  </ui:define>

  <ui:define name="contents">
    <h2>Titles</h2>
    <ul>
      <ui:repeat var="t" value="${titles.titles}"
           varStatus="status">
        <li>${t}</li>
      </ui:repeat>
    </ul>
  </ui:define>

  <ui:define name="footer">
    <ui:include src="/common/commonFooter.xhtml" />
  </ui:define>

</ui:composition>

</body>
</html>

<!-- File composers.xhtml ******************** -->
<!DOCTYPE html>
<html lang="en"
      xmlns="http://www.w3.org/1999/xhtml"
      xmlns:ui="http://java.sun.com/jsf/facelets">
```

```
<body>
<ui:composition template="frame.xhtml">

  <ui:define name="header">
    <ui:include src="/common/commonHeader.xhtml" />
  </ui:define>

  <ui:define name="menu">
    <ui:include src="/common/commonMenu.xhtml" />
  </ui:define>

  <ui:define name="contents">
    <h2>Composers</h2>
    <ul>
      <ui:repeat var="c" value="${composers.composers}"
          varStatus="status">
        <li>${c}</li>
      </ui:repeat>
    </ul>
  </ui:define>

  <ui:define name="footer">
    <ui:include src="/common/commonFooter.xhtml" />
  </ui:define>

</ui:composition>
</body>
</html>

<!-- File performers.xhtml ******************** -->
<!DOCTYPE html>
<html lang="en"

      xmlns="http://www.w3.org/1999/xhtml"
      xmlns:ui="http://java.sun.com/jsf/facelets"
      xmlns:c="http://java.sun.com/jsp/jstl/core">
<body>
<ui:composition template="frame.xhtml">
```

```
<ui:define name="header">
  <c:if test="true">
  <ui:include src="/common/commonHeader.xhtml" />
  </c:if>
</ui:define>

<ui:define name="menu">
  <ui:include src="/common/commonMenu.xhtml" />
</ui:define>

<ui:define name="contents">
  <h2>Performers</h2>
  <ul>
    <ui:repeat var="p" value="${performers.performers}"
         varStatus="status">
      <li>${p}</li>
    </ui:repeat>
  </ul>
</ui:define>

<ui:define name="footer">
  <ui:include src="/common/commonFooter.xhtml" />
</ui:define>

</ui:composition>
</body>
</html>
```

You can see that we use the `<ui:composition>` tag to apply the page template.

Caution   The pages deliberately do not use any JSF tags. If you look for Facelets tutorials, in most cases they will include JSF tags. I consider it a dangerous practice to use Facelets *and* JSF tags in Java MVC projects. The different design paradigms for Java MVC (action based) and JSF (component based) will very likely lead to problems that are hard to fix. It is however possible to use Facelets and JSTL together; see the following section.

Build and deploy the application by running the Gradle task `localDeploy`. Then point your browser to `http://localhost:8080/MusicBox` to see the application running. See Figure 6-3.

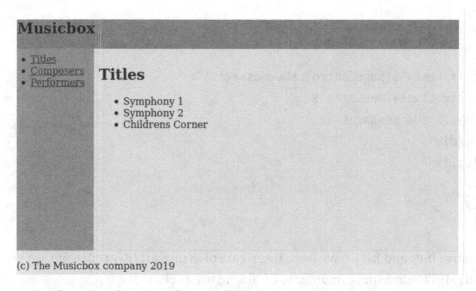

Figure 6-3. *The Musicbox Facelets application*

Mixing Facelets and JSTL

We already pointed out that, with Java MVC, we don't want to mix-in JSF components and Facelets pages for stability reasons. This however leads to a severe lack of functionalities, including a missing `if-else` construct. In the JSF world, you switch on and off components (or component subtrees) via the `rendered` attribute. So what can we do if we want to use Facelets for Java MVC and need conditional branching on a view page? The answer is astonishingly simple. Because we don't use JSF components, we can simply add the JSTL tag libraries without any danger of breaking proper page rendering. Then we can use the `<c:if>` and `<c:choose>` tags.

Consider, for example, that we want to add a messages box based on some condition. It is then possible to write the following:

```
<!DOCTYPE html>
<html lang="en"
      xmlns="http://www.w3.org/1999/xhtml"
```

```
        xmlns:ui="http://java.sun.com/jsf/facelets"
        xmlns:c="http://java.sun.com/jsp/jstl/core">
<head>
  ...
</head>
<body>
    ...
    <c:if test="${pageControl.showMessages}">
      <div class="messages">
        ... the messages ...
      </div>
    </c:if>
    ...
</body>
</html>
```

Because JSPs and JSTL have been taken care of in our `build.gradle` file, we just have to add the JSTL namespace in order to be able to use JSTL.

Unified Expressions

For JSF, the expression language handling has been extended to use *deferred* expressions, denoted by #{ ... } instead of ${ ... }. Such deferred expressions aren't evaluated prior to the JSF component reacting to the requests initiated by forms. This way, it was possible to use expressions as `lvalues`, meaning you can assign user input to them. A #{ `someBean.someProperty` } thus can serve both output and input.

The combination of immediate expressions and deferred expressions, more precisely the enhanced expression language, is also called *unified expressions*.

For Java MVC, form input is exclusively handled by controller methods. There is by design no such thing as autowiring form input to CDI beans. For this reason, we don't need deferred expressions, and to make things clear as a rule of thumb consider:

Caution   Don't use deferred expressions #{ ... } in Java MVC Facelets views.

The Controller

Controller classes describe the action part of a Java MVC application. They are responsible for preparing the model, taking user requests, updating the model, and deciding which view pages to show after a request.

Controller Basics

To mark a class as a Java MVC controller, add the @Controller annotation (in the javax. mvc package) and the @Path annotation (in the javax.ws.rs package) to the class:

```
...
import javax.mvc.Controller;
import javax.ws.rs.Path;
...

@Path("/controllerPath")
@Controller
public class MyController {
    ...
}
```

The @Path will make sure the controller acts on URLs starting with WEB_ APPLICATION_BASE/mvc/controllerPath, where WEB_APPLICATION_BASE depends on the Jakarta EE server product (for GlassFish, for example, it e http://the.server:8080/ TheWarName), and /mvc is configured as the application path in some class:

```
...
import javax.ws.rs.ApplicationPath;
import javax.ws.rs.core.Application;
...

@ApplicationPath("/mvc")
public class App extends Application {
}
```

You don't have to use controllerPath for the @Path parameter; this is just an example.

Getting Pages

For pages that are *not* the result of some form post, you use the GET verb and mark the corresponding methods:

```java
import javax.mvc.Controller; import javax.ws.rs.GET; import javax.ws.rs.Path;
import javax.ws.rs.core.Response;

@Path("/controllerPath")
@Controller
public class MyController {
    @GET
    public Response showIndex() {
        return Response.ok("index.jsp").build();
    }

    @GET
    @Path("/b")
    public String showSomeOtherPage() {
        return "page_b.jsp";
    }
}
```

In this snippet, you can see the two possible return types—you return a string pointing to a JSP (or Facelets page) and then use suffix .xhtml, or you return a Response object. While returning a string is easier, with the Response instance, you have more options. For example, you can precisely specify the HTTP status code, and actually specify status codes (like OK, Server Error, Accepted, Created, No Content, Not Modified, See Other, Temporary Redirect, or Not Acceptable). You can also set the encoding, the cache control, HTTP headers, the language, the media type, expired and last modification times, and add cookies. For details, see the API documentation of the javax.ws.rs.core.Response class.

The triggering path is calculated by concatenating the classat@Path annotation and the methodng @Path annotation, and then prepending the applications' URL path. If you, for example, deployed a WAR named TheWAR.war on a local GlassFish server with an HTTP connector running on port 8080 (the default), and furthermore added this class anywhere in your package hierarchy:

```
...
import javax.ws.rs.ApplicationPath;
import javax.ws.rs.core.Application;
...

@ApplicationPath("/mvc")
public class App extends Application {
}
```

Then this controller:

```
import javax.mvc.Controller;
import javax.ws.rs.GET;
import javax.ws.rs.Path;
import javax.ws.rs.core.Response;

@Path("/controllerPath")
@Controller
public class MyController {
    @GET
    public Response showIndex() {
        return Response.ok("index.jsp").build();
    }

    @GET
    @Path("/b")
    public String showSomeOtherPage() {
        return "page_b.jsp";
    }
}
```

will ensure the following mappings apply:

```
http://localhost:8080/TheWAR/mvc/controllerPath
    -> method showIndex()
http://localhost:8080/TheWAR/mvc/controllerPath/b
    -> method showSomeOtherPage()
```

See Figure 6-4.

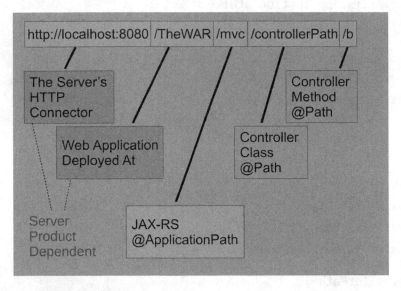

Figure 6-4. *Controller URLs*

Preparing the Model

If you need to prepare model values for the called page to use, you can inject CDI beans in the controller and adjust their values from inside the controller methods.

```
import javax.mvc.Controller;
import javax.ws.rs.GET;
import javax.ws.rs.Path;
import javax.ws.rs.core.Response;
import javax.inject.Inject;

@Path("/controllerPath")
@Controller
public class MyController {
    // The controller is under custody of CDI, so
    // we can inject beans.
    @Inject private SomeDataClass someModelInstance;

    @GET
    public Response showIndex() {
```

```
    // Preparing the model:
    someModelInstance.setVal(42);
    ...

    return Response.ok("index.jsp").build();
  }
  @GET
  @Path("/b")
  public String showSomeOtherPage() {
    // Preparing the model:
    someModelInstance.setVal(43);

    return "page_b.jsp";
  }
}
```

The updated or initialized model can then be used from inside the called view page. We described that in the previous view-related text sections.

Posting Data into Controllers

In order to transport user input from a form to a controller method, you mark the method with a @POST annotation and add the form fields as parameters of the method:

```
@POST
@Path("/response")
public Response response(
    @MvcBinding @FormParam("name") String name,
    @MvcBinding @FormParam("userId") int userId) {

    // Handle form input, set model data, ...

    return Response.ok("response.jsp").build();
}
```

For the parameter type, you can choose String, int, long, float, double, BigDecimal, BigInteger, and boolean (true or false). Java MVC makes sure that user input is appropriately converted if you choose any type other than String.

The @MvcBinding allows Java MVC to pass over validation and conversion errors in an injected BindingResult object. You can then handle the errors programmatically inside the POST method:

```
...
import javax.mvc.binding.MvcBinding;
import javax.mvc.binding.ParamError;
import javax.mvc.binding.BindingResult;
import javax.ws.rs.FormParam;
...

@Path("/controllerPath")
@Controller
public class MyController {

    // Errors while fetching parameters
    // automatically go here:
    private @Inject BindingResult br;

    @POST
    @Path("/response")
    public Response response(
        @MvcBinding @FormParam("name") String name,
        @MvcBinding @FormParam("userId") int userId) {

        // ERROR HANDLING //////////////////////////
        if(br.isFailed()) {
          br.getAllErrors().stream().
              forEach((ParamError pe) -> {
            ...
          });
        }
        // END ERROR HANDLING ///////////////////////

        // Handle form input, set model data, ...

        return Response.ok("response.jsp").build();
    }
}
```

Instead of passing the form input as method parameters, you can also use controller fields to receive the data:

```
import javax.mvc.Controller;
import javax.ws.rs.GET;
import javax.ws.rs.Path;
import javax.ws.rs.core.Response;
import javax.inject.Inject;

@Path("/controllerPath")
@Controller
public class MyController {
    // Errors while fetching parameters
    // automatically go here:
    private @Inject BindingResult br;

    @MvcBinding @FormParam("name")
    private String name;

    @MvcBinding @FormParam("userId")
    private int userId;

    @POST
    @Path("/response")
    public Response response() {
        // Handle form input, set model data, ...

        return Response.ok("response.jsp").build();
    }
}
```

Generally, it is recommended to use method parameters, because class instance fields somehow suggest that parameter passing is the controller classeqresponsibility, without respecting which method is used, while it actually depends on the method as to which parameters make sense.

If you need to make query parameters (a and b in http://xyz.com/app?a=3&b=4) available to controller methods, you basically do the same thing as for posted parameters. What is different though is that you must use the QueryParam annotation for query parameters, as follows:

```
...
import javax.mvc.binding.MvcBinding;
import javax.ws.rs.GET;
import javax.ws.rs.Path;
import javax.ws.rs.QueryParam;

@Path("/")
@Controller
public class SomeController {
    private @Inject BindingResult br;
    @GET
    @Path("/start")
    public String someMethod(
        @MvcBinding @QueryParam("name") String name,
        @MvcBinding @QueryParam("birthday") String birthday
    ) {
        if(name != null) {
        // handle "name" parameter
        }
        if(birthday != null) {
        // handle "birthday" parameter
        }

        // advance to page
        return "index.jsp";
    }
    ...
}
```

This is possible for @GET and @POST annotated methods.

Exercises

Exercise 1: In the `HelloWorld` application from two chapters ago, remove the `Models` field in the controller and instead add a new request scoped model class called `UserData` with one field, `name`. Update the controller and the views accordingly.

Exercise 2: Which one is true? JSPs are handled by one `Servlet`. Or, each JSP is transformed into one new `Servlet`.

Exercise 3: Which view technology is newer—Facelets or JSPs?

Exercise 4: True or false? In order to use Facelets in Java MVC, you must also use JSF.

Summary

For the *model* part of Java MVC, the original idea of a MVC framework is rather unchanged. Model classes were just Java bean classes (classes with fields, getters, and setters), and developers would add them to the view programmatically. In a response view, you then would access the model beans using some expression similar to `Hello ${beanName.name}`. Java MVC however is a modern framework and its model capabilities supersede the idea of simply referring to beans. It does so by incorporating the CDI (Context and Dependency Injection) technology for Jakarta EE 8 in version CDI 2.0. The basic idea is still the same: we want to instantiate bean classes (data classes that contain mainly fields and their getters and setters) and provision those instances to the controllers and the views. The main difference between the pre-CDI and CDI way is that we don't instantiate model classes ourselves and let instead CDI do it.

To tell Java MVC that we want a model class to be controlled by CDI and available to the view pages, we use the `@Named` annotation from the `javax.inject` package. We can also add the `@RequestScoped` annotation to bind the lifecycle of the object instance to a single HTTP request/response cycle.

Once we announce a bean via `@Named` to the CDI framework, two things happen in Java MVC. First, we can use `@Inject` (in the `javax.inject` package) to refer to the bean instance from inside any Java MVC controller and from inside any other CDI controlled class. Second, we can use the instance from view pages by using the class name with the first letter lowercase: `${userData.name}` and `${userData.email}`.

If you're using CDI to manage model data, model class instances subordinate to a lifecycle control governed by CDI. This means CDI decides when to construct beans and when to abandon them. In injected beans, the way CDI controls the lifecycle of instances is by a characteristic called *scope*. In Java MVC, the following scopes exist: request scope, session scope, redirect scope, and application scope.

Instead of using CDI beans marked with the @Named annotation, you can also use an injected instance of Models (in the javax.mvc package). The model values are then available from inside view pages without a prefix: Hello ${name}.

The view part of Java MVC is responsible for presenting the frontend to the client (the browser), for both input and output. Those view files for Java MVC, which are connected to controller methods, go in the WEB-INF/-views folder, or, because we are using Gradle as a build framework, in the src/main/webapp/WEB-INF/views folder.

Java MVC, out-of-the-box, supports two view engines—JSPs (JavaServer Pages) and Facelets (view declaration language for JSF, JavaServer Faces). By design, other view engines can be included with an extension mechanism based on CDI.

JSPs allow you to interleave static content, for example HTML and dynamic content, represented by JSP elements. A JSP page is internally compiled into one big Java class inheriting from Servlet. A file containing JSP code has the ending .jsp. JSP directives <% ... %> provide directions to the container. To produce static content, you just write it verbatim in the JSP file. Because JSPs are transcribed into Java classes, JSP allows for the inclusion of Java code and Java expressions into JSP pages. Inside <%= ... %> or <% ... %>, there are a couple of implicit objects you can use:

- out: The servlet's output stream of type JspWriter (extends java.io.Writer).

- request: The request, type HttpServletRequest.

- response: The response, type HttpServletResponse.

- session: The session, type HttpSession.

- application: The application, type ServletContext.

- config: The servlet configuration, type ServletConfig.

- page: The servlet itself, type Object (runtime type javax.servlet.http.HttpServlet).

- pageContext: The page context, type PageContext.

You can use these objects to achieve fancy things, but bear in mind that you somehow leave official development patterns if you use them. This might make your code hard for others to read, and by putting functionality into the view pages, the natural demarcation between the model, the view, and the controller is broken.

CDI beans with the @Named annotation are directly provisioned to the JSPs: Hello ${userName.name}. If you add model data to an injected javax.mvc.Models CDI bean, you can directly access it without a prefix, as in Hello ${name}.

Constructs in JSP pages like ${ ... } are treated as expressions and are processed by an expression language handler. There are several implicit objects you can use in expressions: pageScope, requestScope, sessionScope, applicationScope, paramValues, param, headerValues, header, initParam, cookie, and pageContext.

If you prefer to use a tag for dynamic output, you can use the <c:out> tag as follows: Hello <c:out value="${userData.name}" />.

By using the <c:set> tag, you can introduce variables for further use in the page.

For loops over lists or arrays, you can use the <c:forEach> tag (the c signifies the jstl/core taglib). If you want to use the <c:forEach> tag for an integer-valued range loop, you use the begin and end attributes, such as <c:forEach begin="1" end="10" var="i">.

For conditional branching inside a JSP, you can use one of the <c:if> and <c:choose> tags.

Cookies can be read directly from inside JSPs by using the implicit cookie object.

The other view technology that Java MVC supports apart from JSP is called *Facelets*. Facelets is the templating framework especially created for JSF. Facelets files for Java MVC go in the same folder as JSP files, the WEB-INF/views folder, or, because we are using Gradle as a build framework, in the src/main/webapp/WEB-INF/views folder. Facelets files are XML files, which is maybe the most noticeable difference between JSPs and Facelets.

Facelets allow you to introduce parameterized template HTML pages, HTML snippets (components) to be included in pages, placeholders for such snippets, and decorators and repetitions for things like elaborated list views.

For Java MVC, we don't want to mix JSF components into Facelets pages for stability reasons. This, however, leads to a severe lack of functionalities, including a missing if-else construct. In the JSF world, you switch on and off components (or component subtrees) via the rendered attribute. So what can we do if we want to use Facelets for Java MVC and need a conditional branching on some view page? The answer is astonishingly simple. Because we don't use JSF components, we can simply add the JSTL tag libraries without danger of breaking proper page rendering. Then we can use the `<c:if>` and `<choose>` tags.

For JSF, expression language handling has been extended to use *deferred* expressions, denoted by #{ ... } instead of ${ ... }. These deferred expressions aren't evaluated prior to the JSF component reacting to the requests initiated by forms. This way, it was possible to use expressions as `lvalues`, meaning you can assign user input to them. A #{ `someBean.someProperty` } thus can serve for both output and input. The combination of immediate expressions and deferred expressions, more precisely the enhanced expression language, is also called *unified expressions*. For Java MVC, form input is exclusively handled by controller methods. There is by design no such thing as autowiring form input to CDI beans. For this reason, we don't need deferred expressions.

Caution   Don't use deferred expressions #{ ... } in Java MVC Facelets views.

Controller classes describe the action part of a Java MVC application. They are responsible for preparing the model, taking user requests, updating the model, and deciding which view pages to show after a request. To mark a class as a Java MVC controller, add the `@Controller` annotation (in the `javax.mvc` package) and the `@Path` annotation (in the `javax.ws.rs` package) to the class.

For pages that are *not* the result of some form post, you use the `GET` verb and mark the corresponding methods with the `@GET` annotation.

In controller methods marked with `@GET` or `@POST`, you either return a string pointing to a JSP (or Facelets page) and then use suffix `.xhtml`, or you can return a `Response` object. While returning a string is easier, with the `Response` instance you have more options. For example, you can precisely specify the HTTP status code and actually specify status codes (like OK, Server Error, Accepted, Created, No Content, Not Modified, See Other, Temporary Redirect, or Not Acceptable). You can also set the encoding, the cache control, HTTP headers, the language, the media type, expired and last modification times, and add cookies.

The triggering path is calculated by concatenating the class' `@Path` annotation and the method's `@Path` annotation, and then prepending the applications' URL path.

If you need to prepare model values for the called page to use, you can inject CDI beans in the controller and just adjust their values from inside the controller methods. The updated or initialized model can then be used from inside the called view page.

In order to transport user input from a form to a controller method, you mark the method with a @POST annotation and add the form fields as parameters of the method. For the parameter type, you can choose `String`, `int`, `long`, `float`, `double`, `BigDecimal`, `BigInteger`, and `boolean` (`true` or `false`). Java MVC makes sure that user input is appropriately converted if you choose any type other than `String`.

The `@MvcBinding` allows Java MVC to pass over validation and conversion errors in an injected `BindingResult` object. You can then handle the errors programmatically inside the `POST` method.

If you need to make query parameters (a and b in `http://xyz.com/app?a=3&b=4`) available to controller methods, you basically do the same thing as with posted parameters. What is different though is that you must use the `QueryParam` annotation for query parameters. This is possible for `@GET` and `@POST` annotated methods.

In the next chapter, we cover more advanced topics of Java MVC.

CHAPTER 7

In-Depth Java MVC: Part II

In this chapter, we continue our in-depth survey of Java MVC. We talk about some topics that you'll encounter less frequently compared to the topics discussed in the last chapter, but that could be important to your project, depending on the circumstances. This includes bean validation, injectable context, partial page updates, and observer classes. We also deepen our knowledge about state handling, and we include some configuration topics.

Adding Bean Validation

Bean validation (version 2.0) is described by the JSR 380 specification. The full specification can be downloaded from `https://jcp.org/en/jsr/detail?id=380`.

This technology is about constraints defined by annotations. You can add checks to determine whether a field or method parameter is null, whether a number exceeds some lower or upper bound, whether a string's size is within a certain range, whether a date is in the past or future, and more. You even can define your own custom annotations to check certain parameters or fields.

We don't talk about the full gamut of possibilities of bean validation—the specification and many tutorials on the Internet readily tell you more. We talk about where bean validation fits into Java MVC, and we cover some built-in constraints that you will often use, as well as a couple of custom constraints.

You can easily use bean validation in Java MVC next to form and query parameters inside controllers. If you have constraints, such as @CONSTRAINT1, @CONSTRAINT2, and so on (we will talk about possible values and constraint parameters soon), you can use any of the following:

```
public class SomeController {

// constraints for fields:
@MvcBinding @FormParam("name")
```

© Peter Späth 2021
P. Späth, *Beginning Java MVC 1.0*, https://doi.org/10.1007/978-1-4842-6280-1_7

```
@CONSTRAINT1
@CONSTRAINT2
...
private String formParam; // or other type

// or, for query parameters:

@MvcBinding @QueryParam("name")
@CONSTRAINT1
@CONSTRAINT2
...
private String queryParam; // or other type

// or, in controller action:

@POST
@Path("/xyz")
public Response someMethod(
 @MvcBinding @FormParam("name")
 @CONSTRAINT1
 @CONSTRAINT2
 ...
 String name )
{
 ...
}

// or, for query parameters:

@GET
@Path("/xyz")
public Response someMethod(
  @MvcBinding @QueryParam("name")
  @CONSTRAINT1
  @CONSTRAINT2
  ...
```

```
    String name )
  {
...
  }
}
```

Any violation will be forwarded as an error inside an injected `BindingResult`:

```
@Controller
@Path("/xyz")
public class SomeController {
  @Inject BindingResult br;
  ...
}
```

For example, if we want to limit a form parameter string to have more than two, but less than ten, characters, we write the following:

```
@Controller
@Path("/xyz")
public class SomeController {
  @Inject BindingResult br;

  @MvcBinding @FormParam("name")
  @Size(min=3,max=10)
  private String formParam;

  ...
}
```

The most interesting built-in bean validation constraints are defined in Table 7-1.

Table 7-1. *Built-in Bean Validation Constraints*

Name	Description
@Null	Checks whether the value is null.
@NotNull	Checks whether the value is not null.
@AssertTrue	Checks whether the boolean value is true.
@AssertFalse	Checks whether the boolean value is false.
@Min(min)	Checks whether the numerical value (short, int, long, BigDecimal, or BigInteger) is greater or equal to the supplied parameter.
@Max(max)	Checks whether the numerical value (short, int, long, BigDecimal, or BigInteger) is less or equal to the supplied parameter.
@Negative	Checks whether the numerical value (short, int, long, BigDecimal, or BigInteger) is less than zero.
@NegativeOrZero	Checks whether the numerical value (short, int, long, BigDecimal, or BigInteger) is less than or equal to zero.
@Positive	Checks whether the numerical value (short, int, long, BigDecimal, BigInteger) is greater than zero.
@PositiveOrZero	Checks whether the numerical value (short, int, long, BigDecimal, BigInteger) is greater than or equal to zero.
@Size(min=minSize, max=maxSize)	Checks whether the string value has a length between the specified bounds. Both bounds are optional; if omitted, 0 or Integer. MAX_VALUE is assumed. Example: @Size(max=10) means size ten or less.
@NotEmpty	Checks whether the value is not empty. For strings, this means the string length must be greater than 0.
@NotBlank	Checks whether the string value contains at least one non-whitespace character.

(continued)

Table 7-1. (*continued*)

Name	Description
@Pattern(regexp=regExp, flags={f1,f2,...})	Checks whether the string value matches the given regular expression. The optional `flags` parameter may be a list of `javax.validation.constraints.Pattern.Flag.*` constants controlling the match, such as case insensitiveness. As is usually the case for annotations, you can omit the { } if you have only one element in the list.
@Email(regexp=regExp, flags={f1,f2,...})	Checks whether the string value represents an email address. The optional `regexp` and `flags` parameters specify an additional pattern, with the same meaning as the `@Pattern` constraint.

You can see that there is no min or max check for float or double values. These were left out intentionally. Because of possible precision errors, these types of checks cannot reliably be performed.

It is also possible to define your own bean validators. For the lack of a double valued bound check, you might for example want to define a double (float) range validator (including some precision grace). For such an annotation, you would write the following:

```
package book.javamvc.validation;

import javax.validation.Constraint;
import javax.validation.Payload;
import static java.lang.annotation.ElementType.*;
import java.lang.annotation.Retention;
import static java.lang.annotation.RetentionPolicy.RUNTIME;
import java.lang.annotation.Target;

@Constraint(validatedBy = FloatRangeValidator.class)
@Target({ PARAMETER, FIELD })
@Retention(RUNTIME)
public @interface FloatRange {
    String message() default
      "Value out of range [{min},{max}]";
    Class<?>[] groups() default {};
```

```
    Class<? extends Payload>[] payload() default {};
    String[] value() default { };
    double min() default -Double.MAX_VALUE;
    double max() default Double.MAX_VALUE;
    double precision() default 0.0;
}
```

The important parts are as follows:

- validatedBy = FloatRangeValidator.class

    The implementation class, see next code section.

- @Target

    We want to allow this annotation for fields and method parameters.

- @Retention(RUNTIME)

    RUNTIME is important here, so the annotation won't get lost during compilation.

- message()

    The message to be shown if the validation fails, with placeholders for the parameters.

- value()

    This is the default parameter if there is no named parameter. We want to introduce three named parameters—min, max, and precision—so we don't use a default parameter.

- min(), max(), precision()

    The three named parameters, as methods.

- groups(), payload()

    Not used here.

The implementation class checks the code and reads as follows:

```
package book.javamvc.validation;

import javax.validation.ConstraintValidator;
import javax.validation.ConstraintValidatorContext;

public class FloatRangeValidator implements
        ConstraintValidator<FloatRange, Number> {
  private double min;
  private double max;
  private double precision;

  @Override
  public void initialize(FloatRange constraint) {
    min = constraint.min();
    max = constraint.max();
    precision = constraint.precision();
}

  @Override
  public boolean isValid(Number value,
      ConstraintValidatorContext context) {
    return value.doubleValue() >=
     (min == -Double.MAX_VALUE ? min :
        min - precision)
      && value.doubleValue() <= (max == Double.MAX_VALUE ?
        max : max + precision);
  }
}
```

The overwritten isValid() method performs the actual validation. In this case, we have to make sure the precision grace is not applied to the default values +/- Double. MAX_VALUE.

To add the new constraint to a Java MVC controller, we use the same method as for the built-in constraints:

```
...
import book.javamvc.validation.FloatRange;
```

...

```
@Path("/abc")
@Controller
public class SomeController {
    @MvcBinding @FormParam("theDouble")
    @FloatRange(min=1.0, max=2.0, precision = 0.000001)
    private double theDouble;

    ...
}
```

As another custom bean validator using the value annotation default parameter, consider a check that allows string values only from a certain set. We call it StringEnum and its code is as follows:

```
package book.javamvc.validation;

import javax.validation.Constraint;
import javax.validation.Payload;
import static java.lang.annotation.ElementType.*;
import java.lang.annotation.Retention;
import static java.lang.annotation.RetentionPolicy.RUNTIME;
import java.lang.annotation.Target;

@Constraint(validatedBy = StringEnumValidator.class)
@Target({ PARAMETER, FIELD })
@Retention(RUNTIME)
public @interface StringEnum {
    String message() default
      "String '${validatedValue}' not inside {value}";
    Class<?>[] groups() default {};
    Class<? extends Payload>[] payload() default {};
    String[] value() default { };
}
```

This time, no named parameters are introduced, only the default `value` attribute is. The implementation then looks as follows:

```
package book.javamvc.validation;

import java.util.Arrays;
import javax.validation.ConstraintValidator;
import javax.validation.ConstraintValidatorContext;

public class StringEnumValidator implements
    ConstraintValidator<StringEnum, String> {
  private String[] val;

  @Override
  public void initialize(StringEnum constraint) {
    this.val = constraint.value();
}

  @Override
  public boolean isValid(String value,
      ConstraintValidatorContext context) {
    return Arrays.asList(val).contains(value);
  }
}
```

Because there is only one default parameter, we don't need the name to use it:

```
...
import book.javamvc.validation.StringEnum;
...

@Path("/abc")
@Controller
public class SomeController {
  @MvcBinding @FormParam("fruit")
  @StringEnum({"grape", "apple", "banana"})
  private String fruit;

  ...
}
```

So far, for validation failure messages, we have seen named parameter placeholders in the form {paramName} or {value} for the annotation's default value, and an expression language construct for the checked value, ${validatedValue}. In an internationalized application, it would be better if we could add a reference to a localized message file. This is possible, and the name of the bundle file is ValidationMessages.properties. The localized properties files then have the following names:

```
ValidationMessages.properties        (default)
ValidationMessages_en.properties     (English)
ValidationMessages_fr.properties     (French)
ValidationMessages_de.properties     (German)
...
```

In a Gradle project layout, you'd place them inside the src/main/resources folder. In the properties files, you then write messages like this:

```
myapp.user.name.error = Invalid User Name: \
    ${validatedValue}
myapp.user.address.error = Invalid Address
...
```

In the message method of the bean validation annotation, you use curly brackets and the property key name:

```
String message() default
    "{myapp.user.name.error}";
```

Note   Resource bundles like these belong to the JRE standard. Using Validation-Messages as a base name is a bean validation technology convention.

Injectable Context

Inside a Java MVC controller class, we can use a couple of context objects. There are basically two methods to access them. First, we can use the @Inject annotation provided by CDI on a class instance level, as follows:

```
...
import javax.servlet.http.HttpSession;
import javax.mvc.MvcContext;
import javax.servlet.http.HttpServletRequest;
import javax.servlet.ServletContext;
import javax.mvc.binding.BindingResult;
import javax.ws.rs.core.Application;
import javax.enterprise.inject.spi.BeanManager;
...

@Controller
public class SomeController {
    // Access to the session. You can use it to retrieve
    // the session ID, the creation time, the last
    // accessed time, and more.
    @Inject private HttpSession httpSession;

    // Access to the MVC context. This is a context
    // object provided by Java MVC. You can use it to
    // construct URIs given the simple controller name
    // and method name, to retrieve the current
    // request's locale, to look up the base URI, and
    // more.
    @Inject private MvcContext mvcContext;

    // Access to the current servlet request. You can use
    // it to get various HTTP request related properties,
    // like headers, user information, and many more.
    @Inject private HttpServletRequest httpServletRequest;

    // Access to the servlet context. There you can for
    // example get the URI of a resource file, or an
```

```
    // info about the server (container), and more.
    @Inject private ServletContext servletContext;

    // Use this to fetch conversion and validation errors.
    // Parameters (@FormParam or @QueryParam) must have
    // been marked with @MvcBinding for this error
    // fetching process to work.
    @Inject private BindingResult bindingResult;

    // Use this to access the application scope
    // Application object. You can for example register
    // and retrieve application-wide custom properties.
    @Inject private Application application;

    // In case you ever need to have programmatic access
    // to CDI, you can inject the BeanManager. This can
    // also be handy for diagnostic purposes.
    @Inject private BeanManager beanManager;

    ...
}
```

Second, and as an additional feature of Java MVC, it is also possible to inject `javax.ws.rs.core.Request` and `javax.ws.rs.core.HttpHeaders` directly into controller methods:

```
...
import javax.ws.rs.core.Context;
import javax.ws.rs.core.HttpHeaders;
import javax.ws.rs.core.Request;
import javax.ws.rs.GET;
import javax.ws.rs.POST;
...

@Controller
public class SomeController {
...

@GET    // or @POST
```

```
public String someMethod(
    ... query and post parameters...,
    @Context HttpHeaders httpHeaders,
    @Context Request request)
{
...
}

...
}
```

It does not matter where in the method's parameter list you add such @Context parameters. The httpHeaders parameter then enables to access HTTP header values, the language, cookie values, and more. The request parameter provides helper methods for preconditions and variants (we don't talk about preconditions and variants in this book).

For more details about such injected types, consult the API documentation (Jakarta EE, JAX-RS, and Java MVC).

Persisting State

If you need to persist state between several requests, the HttpSession class from the javax.servlet.http package is your friend. Whenever a user starts a web application on a browser, an instance of HttpSession is created. Once it exists, the very same session object is transparently assigned to any subsequent HTTP request/response cycles, provided all the following are met:

- The user stays inside the same web application on the same server

- The user uses the same browser instance (the browser wasn't restarted)

- The session was not destroyed by the container because of a timeout

- The session was not destroyed explicitly by the web application

From your web application, you usually don't have to take any precautions in order to use sessions. All you have to do is register sessions-scoped CDI beans:

```
...
import javax.enterprise.context.SessionScoped;
...
@Named
@SessionScoped
public class UserData {
...
}

@Controller
public class SomeController {
    @Inject UserData userData;
    // <- same object inside a session
    ...
}
```

The container automatically ensures that, inside the same browser session, exactly one instance of each session-scoped CDI bean is used.

Note   The server transparently maintains session identification by cookies, automatically adding session IDs in URL query parameters, or adding invisible fields in forms.

We already know that to programmatically access session data, we can inject the session as a class instance field:

```
...
import javax.servlet.http.HttpSession;
...

@Controller
public class SomeController {
  @Inject private HttpSession httpSession;
  ...
}
```

This is also the place where we can programmatically ask for the session ID: httpSession.getId() (a string). Or we can invalidate a session: httpSession. invalidate().

Session data can be important for your web application to work properly, but bear in mind that for many concurrently working web users, you also have many concurrently active sessions. Therefore, if you store many data items in the session storage, the memory footprint of your web application will rise, possibly destabilizing the application.

Dealing with Page Fragments

We learned that verbatim output from JSP view pages is not checked for syntactical correctness. So a file like this, for example:

```
<%@ page language="java"
    contentType="text/html;charset=UTF-8" %>
<%@ taglib prefix = "c"
    uri = "http://java.sun.com/jsp/jstl/core" %>
<%@ taglib prefix = "fmt"
    uri = "http://java.sun.com/jsp/jstl/fmt" %>

This is a JSP generated page. Hello ${userData.name}
```

Is literally a correct JSP page, even though it does not produce valid HTML. The output complies to the text/plain media type though, so a corresponding controller method could read the following:

```
...
import javax.mvc.Controller;
import javax.ws.rs.POST;
import javax.ws.rs.Path;
import javax.ws.rs.core.MediaType;
import javax.ws.rs.core.Response;

@Path("/abc")
@Controller
public class SomeController {
```

```
// Assuming the JSP is stored at
// WEB-INF/views/fragm1.jsp
@POST
@Path("/fragm1")
public Response fragm1(...) {
...
 return Response.ok("fragm1.jsp").
    type(MediaType.TEXT_PLAIN).build();
}
}
```

You can even send this response to a browser client, which typically produces simple text output (most browsers that I'm aware of do so, at least). Such text/plain pages neither contain any formatting instructions nor do they possibly present any input fields, so the question is how an application can take advantage of this fragmentary output.

When MVC was invented, the usual paradigm was to reload the *whole* page after any user submit, or to load a *complete* new page if the navigation demands it. Web developers felt uncomfortable from the very beginning about even very small changes to the resulting page leading to a full page being passed over the network. It just seemed to be an unnecessary waste of network resources. For this reason, in the mid 2000s, AJAX started to become more and more popular. AJAX (Asynchronous JavaScript and XML) allowed browsers to request data from the server using JavaScript and work the result into the page, again using JavaScript. To ensure maximum frontend usability, this happens in the background (asynchronously) and the user can operate the browser while the AJAX process is still active.

Modern and highly dynamic web applications use AJAX quite often, so this begs the question as to whether we can also use AJAX from inside Java MVC.

The answer is yes, because we learned that we can ask the server for page snippets. All that is missing are a couple of JavaScript functions to initiate an AJAX server request and later work in the result from the server into corresponding page parts. You could use plain JavaScript for this purpose, but using a JavaScript library like jQuery comes handy to even out browser differences and to simplify AJAX handling.

As an example, we revive the HelloWorld application from Chapter 4 and add a second form for an AJAX request and an area for showing AJAX call results.

First we add the jQuery library, which you can download from `https://jquery.com/download/`. Any decent version should do (the examples are tested with version 3.5.1). Move the file to `src/main/webapp/js`.

Note   The jQuery library provides many more tool functions apart from AJAX. You also get functions for finding HTML elements, traversing the DOM, manipulating HTML elements, and more.

Next, we update `index.jsp` to include jQuery and add a new form and an area to receive AJAX responses:

```
...
<head>
  ...
  <script type="text/javascript"
    src="${mvc.basePath}/../js/jquery-3.5.1.min.js">
  </script>
</head>
<body>
  ...
  <form>
    <script type="text/javascript">
      function submitAge() {
        var age = jQuery('#age').val();
        var url = "${mvc.uriBuilder(
          'HelloWorldController#ageAjax'). build()}";
        jQuery.ajax({
          url : url,
          method: "POST",
          data : { age: age },
          dataType: 'text',
          success: function(data, textStatus, jqXHR) {
            jQuery('#ajax-response').html(data);
          },
          error: function (jqXHR, textStatus,
```

```
                    errorThrown) {
                console.log(errorThrown);
            }
        });
        return false;
    }
    </script>
    Enter your age: <input type="text" id="age" />
    <button onclick="return submitAge()">Submit</button>
    </form>
    <div>
        <span>AJAX Response: </span>
        <div id="ajax-response">
        </div>
    </div>
    ...
</body>
...
```

A couple of important notes on this JSP code seem appropriate:

- The `<div id = "ajax-response">` is just a placeholder. It is filled by JavaScript once the AJAX call returns data.

- The `${ ... }` inside the JavaScript function is an expression language construct, and it is handled correctly only if the JSP engine sees it. So you *cannot* export this JavaScript code to a `script.js` file without further precautions. What you could do prior to exporting the code to its own file is to add the URL as a parameter to the function: `function submitAge( url ) { ... }`. In the `onclick = ...` event handler declaration, you then must write `onclick = "return submitAge( '${ ... }' )"`.

- The form is never submitted. This is why it does not have an `action` attribute and the `onclick` handler returns `false`. The `<form>` is not actually required if you're using AJAX. We add it here for clarity.

- To use jQuery objects, you usually apply the shortcut notation $ (it has the same meaning as in jQuery). We can't do that in JSP pages, because, there, a $ starts a JSP expression.

- An AJAX error for simplicity just writes to the console. In real-world applications, you should place error messages to a place visible to the users.

- In the <head> script tag, you must of course refer to the jQuery version you downloaded.

- The dataType: 'text' refers to the AJAX call returning text/plain data. If the server returns something different, for example XML or JSON, you must change this.

You add a new AJAX-related method to the controller class:

```
@POST
@Path("/ageAjax")
public Response ageAjax(
  @MvcBinding @FormParam("age")
  int age)
{
  if(br.isFailed()) {
    br.getAllErrors().stream().
      forEach((ParamError pe) -> {
        errorMessages.addMessage(
          pe.getParamName() + ": " +
          pe.getMessage());
      });
  }
  userData.setAge(age);
  return Response.ok("ageAjaxFragm.jsp").
      type(MediaType.TEXT_PLAIN).build();
}
```

This assumes that we use a `private @Inject UserData userData;` field in the controller class and that `UserData` gets a new age field:

```
package book.javamvc.helloworld;

import javax.enterprise.context.RequestScoped;
import javax.inject.Named;

@Named
@RequestScoped
public class UserData {
    private String name;
    private int age;
    // Getters and setters...
}
```

We introduced this class in one of the exercises in Chapter 4.

The fragment page `ageAjaxFragm.jsp` inside `src/main/webapp/-WEB-INF/views` is addressed from the controller class. As a result, the AJAX request reads as follows:

```
<%@ page language="java"
    contentType="text/html;charset=UTF-8" %>
<%@ taglib prefix = "c"
    uri = "http://java.sun.com/jsp/jstl/core" %>
<%@ taglib prefix = "fmt"
    uri = "http://java.sun.com/jsp/jstl/fmt" %>

This is a JSP generated fragment. Your age is: ${userData. age}
```

Observers

Java MVC, by virtue of CDI, provides an elegant observer mechanism, which you can use for cross-cutting concerns like logging, monitoring, and performance measurement, or for just diagnostic purposes.

All you have to do is provide a CDI bean class with one or more methods with a parameter of an event type from the `javax.mvc.event` package. It should be marked with `@Observes` (in the `javax.enterprise.event` package):

```java
package book.javamvc.helloworld.event;

import java.io.Serializable;
import java.lang.reflect.Method;

import javax.enterprise.context.SessionScoped;
import javax.enterprise.event.Observes;
import javax.mvc.event.AfterControllerEvent;
import javax.mvc.event.AfterProcessViewEvent;
import javax.mvc.event.BeforeControllerEvent;
import javax.mvc.event.BeforeProcessViewEvent;
import javax.mvc.event.ControllerRedirectEvent;

@SessionScoped
public class HelloWorldObserver implements Serializable {
private static final long serialVersionUID =
    -2547124317706157382L;

public void update(@Observes BeforeControllerEvent
        beforeController) {
  Class<?> clazz = beforeController.getResourceInfo().
    getResourceClass();
  Method m = beforeController.getResourceInfo().
    getResourceMethod();
  System.err.println(this.toString() + ": " +
    clazz + " - " + m);
}

public void update(@Observes AfterControllerEvent
        afterController) {
  System.err.println(this.toString() + ": " +
    afterController);
}

public void update(@Observes ControllerRedirectEvent
        controllerRedirect) {
  System.err.println(this.toString() + ": " +
    controllerRedirect);
}
```

```
public void update(@Observes BeforeProcessViewEvent
        beforeProcessView) {
    String view = beforeProcessView.getView();
    System.err.println(this.toString() + ": " +
        view);
}

public void update(@Observes AfterProcessViewEvent
        afterProcessView) {
    System.err.println(this.toString() + ": " +
        afterProcessView);
    }
}
```

That is all. Java MVC takes care of calling the appropriate observer methods during its processing requests.

Marking the observer class with @SessionScoped is not a requirement for the observer class to work. If you, however, need to collect elapsed times, as in the following:

```
package book.javamvc.helloworld.event;

import java.io.Serializable;
import java.lang.reflect.Method;
import java.time.Instant;

import javax.enterprise.context.SessionScoped;
import javax.enterprise.event.Observes;
import javax.mvc.event.AfterControllerEvent;
import javax.mvc.event.BeforeControllerEvent;

@SessionScoped
public class HelloWorldObserver implements Serializable {
    private long controllerStarted;

    public void update(@Observes BeforeControllerEvent
        beforeController) {
     controllerStarted = Instant.now().toEpochMilli();
      ...
}
```

```
public void update(@Observes AfterControllerEvent
    afterController) {
 long controllerElapseMillis =
   Instant.now().toEpochMilli()
   - controllerStarted;
 ...
 }
 ...
}
```

It is important that we have only one instance of the observer class spanning several invocations, and using the session scope ensures this is the case. If you don't need that, the @SessionScoped annotation can be removed (this is the same as using the @Dependent scope annotation).

Note   The Serializable marker interface is necessary for the session scope CDI bean to work correctly. If you omit it, you will get a runtime error message.

Configuration

Since Java MVC sits on top of JAX-RS, we can use a class inheriting from javax.ws.rs.core.Application to add an entry to the URL context path:

```
package any.project.package;

import javax.ws.rs.ApplicationPath;
import javax.ws.rs.core.Application;

@ApplicationPath("/mvc")
public class App extends Application {
}
```

This class is empty by intention. The context path element /mvc is added by the annotation alone. The resulting URL then is a server-dependent path, plus /mvc, plus whatever is specified in the controller's @Path annotation. We have used this kind of application configuration quite often in this book.

Note   For GlassFish, this server-dependent path by default reads `http://ser.`
`ver.addr:8080/WarName/`, where `WarName` needs to be replaced with the
name of the deployed WAR file, minus the `.war` file suffix.

You can specify a few more configuration items in the `Application` class. This time,
we overwrite the `getProperties()` method and write the following:

```
package any.project.package;

import javax.ws.rs.ApplicationPath;
import javax.ws.rs.core.Application;
import javax.mvc.engine.ViewEngine;
import javax.mvc.security.Csrf;
...

@ApplicationPath("/mvc")
public class App extends Application {
  @Override
  public Map<String,Object>getProperties(){
    final Map<String,Object> map = new HashMap<>();
    // This setting makes sure view files
    // will be looked up at some specified location
    // (default is /WEB-INF/views)
    map.put(ViewEngine.VIEW_FOLDER,"/jsp/");

    // Set a CSRF (cross site request forgery)
    // security mode. See Chapter 4 of the
    // specification
    map.put(Csrf.CSRF_PROTECTION, Csrf.CsrfOptions.OFF);   // default
    // ...or...
    map.put(Csrf.CSRF_PROTECTION, Csrf.CsrfOptions.EXPLICIT);
    // ...or...
    map.put(Csrf.CSRF_PROTECTION, Csrf.CsrfOptions.IMPLICIT);

    // Set CSRF header name. See Chapter 4 of the
    // specification. Default is "X-CSRF-TOKEN".
```

```
    map.put(Csrf.CSRF_HEADER_NAME,
      "CSRF-HDR");

    return map;
  }
}
```

To add a welcome file (a landing page), again avoiding a web.xml XML configuration file to simplify development, you can use an HTTP filter as follows:

```
package any.project.package;

import javax.servlet.FilterChain;
import javax.servlet.annotation.WebFilter;
import javax.servlet.http.HttpFilter;
import javax.servlet.http.HttpServletRequest;
import javax.servlet.http.HttpServletResponse;
import java.io.IOException;

@WebFilter(urlPatterns = "/")
public class RootRedirector extends HttpFilter {
    private static final long serialVersionUID =
        7332909156163673868L;
    @Override
    protected void doFilter(final HttpServletRequest req,
        final HttpServletResponse res,
        final FilterChain chain) throws IOException {
      res.sendRedirect("mvc/facelets");
    }
}
```

If it's used this way, an URL http://my.server:8080/TheWAR/ (on GlassFish, this corresponds to /, because this is the base URL) will send a REDIRECT to http://my.server:8080/TheWAR/mvc/facelets, which in turn is supposed to trigger, for example, a @GET annotated method of a Java MVC controller. In this example, the @Path from the controller class plus the @Path from the controller method must concatenate to /facelets (remember, the leading mvc/ is from the previous application configuration).

Exercises

Exercise 1: In the `HelloWorld` application from Chapter 4, first ensure that a model class `UserData` is used, then add a new integer field called `age`. Update the form in the view and add an input field labeled "What is your age?". Update the controller, and apply a bean validation constraint, making sure the users enter an age greater than zero. Add error handling, as described in Chapter 6. Also update the response page by adding the age.

Exercise 2: In the `HelloWorld` application from Chapter 4, inject the session into the controller. In the controller's `showIndex()` method, write the session ID into `System.err`.

Exercise 3: In the `HelloWorld` application from Chapter 4, inject the headers into the `greeting()` method. Write all request headers into `System.err`.

Exercise 4: From the previous exercise, extract the age input field into a new form and use AJAX to react to user input from that field (add a button). Write a page fragment using JSON as the AJAX response (`{"Text" : "Your age is ... " }`) and let it pass the response into an area `<div id = "ajax-response"> </div>`. Use jQuery as a JavaScript AJAX library.

Exercise 5: In the `HelloWorld` application from Chapter 4, write an observer calculating the controller response time. Output the result to `System.err`.

Summary

Bean validation (version 2.0) is described by the JSR 380 specification. This technology is about constraints defined by annotations. You can check whether a field or method parameter is null, whether a number exceeds some lower or upper bound, whether a string's size is within a certain range, whether a date is in the past or future, and more. You even can define your own custom annotations to check certain parameters or fields.

You can easily use bean validation in Java MVC next to form and query parameters inside controllers. If you have constraints, such as @CONSTRAINT1, @CONSTRAINT2, and so on, you can add them to fields and method parameters of controllers. Any violation will be forwarded as an error inside an injected `BindingResult`.

We can use a couple of context objects inside a Java MVC controller class. There are basically two methods to access them. First, we can use the `@Inject` annotation provided by CDI on a class instance level. Second, and as an additional feature of Java MVC, it is also possible to inject `javax.ws.rs.core.Request` and `javax.ws.rs.core.HttpHeaders` directly into controller methods. It does not matter where in the method's parameter list you add such `@Context` parameters. The `httpHeaders` parameter then enables access to HTTP header values, the language, cookie values, and more. The `request` parameter provides helper methods for preconditions and variants (we don't talk about preconditions and variants in this book).

For more details about such injected types, consult the API documentation (Jakarta EE, JAX-RS, and Java MVC).

If you need to persist state between several requests, the `HttpSession` class from the `javax.servlet.http` package is your friend. Whenever a user starts a web application on a browser, an instance of `HttpSession` is created. Once it exists, the very same session object is transparently assigned to subsequent HTTP request/response cycles, provided all the following are met:

- The user stays inside the same web application on the same server

- The user uses the same browser instance (the browser wasn't restarted)

- The session was not destroyed by the container because of a timeout

- The session was not destroyed explicitly by the web application

From your web application, you usually don't have to take any precautions in order to use sessions. All you have to do is register sessions-scoped CDI beans via the `@SessionScoped` annotation. The container automatically ensures that exactly one instance of each session-scoped CDI bean is used inside the same browser session.

Session data can be important for your web application to work properly, but bear in mind that, for many concurrently working web users, you also have many concurrently active sessions. Therefore, if you store many data items in the session storage, the memory footprint of your web application will rise, possibly destabilizing the application.

We learned that verbatim output from JSP view pages is not checked for syntactical correctness. So a file can be a correct JSP page, even though it does not produce valid HTML. If, for example, the output complies to the `text/plain` media type, a corresponding controller method return could read as follows:

```
return Response.ok("fragm1.jsp" ).type( MediaType.TEXT_PLAIN ).build();
```

You can even send this `text/plain` response to a browser client, which typically produces simple text output. Such `text/plain` pages neither contain any formatting instructions nor do they possibly present any input fields, so the question is how an application can take advantage of this fragmentary output.

When MVC was invented, the usual paradigm was to reload the *whole* page after any user submit, or to load a *complete* new page if the navigation demands it. Web developers felt uncomfortable from the very beginning about even very small changes to the resulting page leading to a full page being passed over the network. It seemed to be an unnecessary waste of network resources. For this reason, in the mid-2000s, AJAX started to become more and more popular. AJAX (Asynchronous JavaScript and XML) allowed browsers to request data from the server using JavaScript and work the result into the page, again using JavaScript. To ensure maximum frontend usability, this happens in the background (asynchronously) and the user can operate the browser while the AJAX process is still active.

Modern and highly dynamic web applications use AJAX quite often, so this begs the question as to whether we can also use AJAX from inside Java MVC. The answer is yes, because we learned that we can ask the server for page snippets. All that is missing are a couple of JavaScript functions to initiate an AJAX server request and later work in the result from the server into corresponding page parts. You could use plain JavaScript for this purpose, but using a JavaScript library like jQuery comes handy to even out browser differences and to simplify AJAX handling. You then add a new AJAX-related method to the controller class.

Java MVC, by virtue of CDI, provides an elegant observer mechanism, which you can use for cross-cutting concerns like logging, monitoring, and performance measurement, or for just diagnostic purposes. All you have to do is provide a CDI bean class with one or more methods with a parameter of an event type from the `javax.mvc.event` package. It must be marked with `@Observes` (in the `javax.enterprise.event` package). Java MVC then takes care of calling the appropriate observer methods during its processing requests.

Since Java MVC sits on top of JAX-RS, we can use a class inheriting from `javax.ws.rs.core.Application` to add an entry to the URL context path. This class is empty by intention. The context path element /mvc is added by the annotation alone. You can specify a few more configuration items in the `Application` class. You can, for example, overwrite the `getProperties()` method to add properties.

To add a welcome file (a landing page), again avoiding a `web.xml` XML configuration file to simplify development, you can use an HTTP filter.

In the next chapter, we talk about the internationalization of Java MVC applications.

CHAPTER 8

Internationalization

Java provides built-in internationalization support via *resource bundles*. It is possible to save text snippets in different languages in different language-related property files. Using tags, it is also possible to output numbers and dates in locale-specific formats, and Java MVC can handle user input based on the locale.

Language Resources

In standard JSP, language-related resources are addressed by the `fmt:setBundle` and `fmt:bundle` tags, and by the `fmt:message` tag, which uses the key attribute to refer to text from the bundle. You can, for example, write the following:

```
<%@ taglib uri="http://java.sun.com/jsp/jstl/core"
    prefix="c" %>
<%@ taglib prefix="fmt"
    uri="http://java.sun.com/jsp/jstl/fmt" %>
<html>
<head>
    <title>JSTL Bundles</title>
</head>
<body>
  <fmt:bundle
    basename="book.javamvc.helloworld.messages.Messages">
  <fmt:message key="msg.first"/><br/>
  <fmt:message key="msg.second"/><br/>
  <fmt:message key="msg.third"/><br/>
  </fmt:bundle>
</body>
</html>
```

223

© Peter Späth 2021
P. Späth, *Beginning Java MVC 1.0*, https://doi.org/10.1007/978-1-4842-6280-1_8

The basename attribute specifies where in the file system the language files exist.

For Facelets, you normally use JSF methodologies to access language resources. In the JSF configuration file faces-config.xml, you write the following:

```
<?xml version="1.0" encoding="UTF-8"?>
<faces-config xmlns="http://java.sun.com/xml/ns/javaee"
xmlns:xsi="http://www.w3.org/2001/XMLSchema-instance"
xsi:schemaLocation="http://java.sun.com/xml/ns/javaee http://java.sun.com/
xml/ns/javaee/web-facesconfig_2_0.xsd" version="2.0">
  <application>
    <resource-bundle>
      <base-name>
          book.javamvc.helloworld.messages.Messages
      </base-name>
      <var>msg</var>
    </resource-bundle>
...
  </application>
</faces-config>
```

In JSF/Facelets pages, you can then simply write ${msg.MSG_KEY} to refer to messages.

For the book.javamvc.helloworld.messages.Messages base name (and for both JSPs and Facelets), in the src/main/resources/book/javamvc/helloworld/messages folder, you now add these properties files: Messages.properties (default), Messages_en.properties (English), Messages_en_US.properties (English variant), Messages_de.properties (German), and so on:

```
-- File 'Messages.properties':
msg.first = First Message
msg.second = Second Message
msg.third = Third Message

-- File 'Messages_en.properties':
msg.first = First Message
msg.second = Second Message
msg.third = Third Message
```

```
-- File 'Messages_de.properties':
msg.first = Erste Nachricht
msg.second = Zweite Nachricht
msg.third = Dritte Nachricht
```

These approaches might suit your needs and you are free to use them. There are a couple of downsides, though:

- For JSPs, messages depend on the `fmt:` tag library. We cannot write something like `${msg.first}` to access a message.

- For JSPs, you have to use the rather awkward syntax `<input title = "<fmt:message key = "msg.first" />" />` to place a message in an attribute. Editors with syntax highlighting might not be able to cope with that.

- For JSPs, the view needs to know about some internal stuff, like the file position of the language properties files. Usually, the view shouldn't have to deal with such internals.

- For Facelets, we have to mix JSF and Java MVC, which, because of architecture paradigm mismatches, we rather want to avoid.

In the next section of this chapter, we work out an alternative message-access method.

Adding Localized Messages to the Session

It would be nice if we could just write `${msg.KEY}` to access a localized message anywhere on the page, for both JSPs and Facelets, *without* further JSF configuration. To achieve that, we let a `@WebFilter` register a localized resource bundle as a session attribute:

```
package book.javamvc.i18n;

import java.io.IOException;

import javax.servlet.Filter;
import javax.servlet.FilterChain;
import javax.servlet.FilterConfig;
import javax.servlet.ServletException;
```

```
import javax.servlet.ServletRequest;
import javax.servlet.ServletResponse;
import javax.servlet.annotation.WebFilter;
import javax.servlet.http.HttpServletRequest;

@WebFilter("/*")
public class SetBundleFilter implements Filter {

    @Override
    public void init(FilterConfig filterConfig)
      throws ServletException {
    }

    @Override
    public void doFilter(ServletRequest request,
                         ServletResponse response,
                         FilterChain chain)
      throws IOException, ServletException {
    BundleForEL.setFor((HttpServletRequest) request);
      chain.doFilter(request, response);
    }

    @Override
    public void destroy() {
    }
}
```

The doFilter() method is invoked for any request (the "/*" is an URL pattern matching any request), and it sends the request to the BundleForEL class.

The customized bundle class extracts the session and locale from the request and registers itself in the session's attribute store. The code reads as follows:

```
package book.javamvc.i18n;

import java.util.Enumeration;
import java.util.Locale;
import java.util.ResourceBundle;

import javax.servlet.http.HttpServletRequest;
```

```java
public class BundleForEL extends ResourceBundle {
  // This is the variable name used in JSPs
  private static final String TEXT_ATTRIBUTE_NAME =
    "msg";

  // This is the base name (including package) of
  // the properties files:
  // TEXT_BASE_NAME + ".properties"     -> default
  // TEXT_BASE_NAME + "_en.properties"      -> English
  // TEXT_BASE_NAME + "_en_US.properties"
  // TEXT_BASE_NAME + "_fr.properties"      -> Fench
  // ...
  private static final String TEXT_BASE_NAME =
    "book.javamvc.helloworld.messages.Messages";

  private BundleForEL(Locale locale) {
    setLocale(locale);
  }

  public static void setFor(
      HttpServletRequest request) {
   if (request.getSession().
        getAttribute(TEXT_ATTRIBUTE_NAME) == null) {
      request.getSession().
        setAttribute(TEXT_ATTRIBUTE_NAME,
          new BundleForEL(request.getLocale()));
    }
  }

  public static BundleForEL getCurrentInstance(
      HttpServletRequest request) {
    return (BundleForEL) request.getSession().
      getAttribute(TEXT_ATTRIBUTE_NAME);
  }

  public void setLocale(Locale locale) {
    if (parent == null ||
        !parent.getLocale().equals(locale)) {
```

```
        setParent(getBundle(TEXT_BASE_NAME, locale));
    }
  }

  @Override
  public Enumeration<String> getKeys() {
    return parent.getKeys();
  }

  @Override
  protected Object handleGetObject(String key) {
    return parent.getObject(key);
  }
}
```

The API documentation for ResourceBundle contains detailed information about the overridden methods. Important for our purposes is the setFor() method, which registers the localized bundle as a session attribute. The EL from JSTL (and Facelets) out-of-the-box knows how to handle Resource-Bundle objects, so we can write the following:

```
${msg.MSG_KEY}
<someTag someAttr="${msg.MSG_KEY}" />
```

To access localized messages from inside JSPs or Facelets, replace MSG_KEY with the message key used inside the properties files.

Because it is very hard for a new developer to understand what msg refers to, you should add a comment in each JSP or Facelets page, describing where msg comes from:

```
<%-- ${msg} is the localized bundle variable,
     registered by class SetBundleFilter      --%>
```

Use this with Facelets:

```
<ui:remove> ${msg} is the localized bundle variable,
     registered by class SetBundleFilter      </ui:remove>
```

> **Note**   The `<ui:remove>` ... `</ui:remove>` at first sight looks strange.
> However, if you use HTML comments `<!- ->`, they *will* be written to the output.
> The `<ui:remove>` tag actually makes sure everything inside will be discarded for
> rendering.

Formatting Data in the View

If, on a view page, you write `${dbl}` and `dbl` refers to a double valued number, the
`toString()` representation of this number is printed. This is acceptable only if your
frontend user expects numbers formatted in the English locale. To make sure all other
users get the expected number format according to their country rules, JSTL provides
an `http://java.sun.com/jsp/jstl/fmt` tag library, which gathers tags for object
formatting using the locale information.

The full specification of this tag library can be examined at `https://docs.oracle.`
`com/javaee/5/jstl/1.1/docs/tlddocs/fmt/tld-frame.html`(one line), but the
two most important tags are `<fmt:formatNumber>` and `<fmt:formatDate>`. You use
`<fmt:formatNumber>` in JSP pages as follows:

```
<%@ page contentType="text/html;charset=UTF-8"
    language="java" %>
<%@ taglib prefix="c"
    uri="http://java.sun.com/jsp/jstl/core" %>
<%@ taglib prefix="fmt"
    uri="http://java.sun.com/jsp/jstl/fmt" %>
<html>
...

   <%-- Supposing ${dbl1} refers to a float or double --%>

   <fmt:formatNumber value="${dbl1}" type="number" var="n1" />
   <%-- <= Use Java's DecimalFormat class to format    --%>
   <%-- the number. Store as string in variable n1     --%>

   <fmt:formatNumber value="${dbl1}" type="currency" var="n1" />
   <%-- <= Format as currency     --%>
```

```
<fmt:formatNumber value="${dbl1}" type="percent" var="n1" />
<%-- <= Format as percentage  --%>

<fmt:formatNumber value="${dbl1}" type="number"
   maxFractionDigits="6"
   minFractionDigits="2"
  var="n1" />
<%-- <= We can set the minimum and maximum    --%>
<%-- number of fraction digits    --%>

<fmt:formatNumber value="${dbl1}" type="number"
    pattern="#,##0.00;(#,##0.00)"
    var="n1" />
<%-- <= Set the pattern according to the    --%>
<%-- DecimalFormat API documentation    --%>

The number reads: ${n1}
...
</html>
```

On Facelets pages, you write the same code, but with a different header (and the <%edertscomments removed):

```
<!DOCTYPE html>
<html lang="en"
   xmlns="http://www.w3.org/1999/xhtml"
   xmlns:ui="http://java.sun.com/jsf/facelets"
   xmlns:c="http://java.sun.com/jsp/jstl/core"
   xmlns:fmt="http://java.sun.com/jsp/jstl/fmt">
...
   <fmt:formatNumber value="${dbl1}" type="number"
      var="n1" />
...
</html>
```

The complete set of attributes for <fmt:formatNumber> are explained in Table 8-1.

Table 8-1. *FormatNumber Tag*

Attribute	Required	Description
value	x	The value. Use EL syntax, such as `${someBean.someField}`
type	-	The type. One of `number`, `currency`, or `percent`. Default is number.
pattern	-	Formatting pattern, as described for the `DecimalFormat` class.
currencyCode	-	ISO 4217 currency code. Only if `type` = `"currency"`.
currencySymbol	-	The currency symbol. Only if `type` = `"currency"`.
groupingUsed	-	Whether or not grouping is used (e.g., the thousands separator). True or false.
minFractionDigits	-	Minimum number of fraction digits.
maxFractionDigits	-	Maximum number of fraction digits.
minIntegerDigits	-	Minimum number of integer digits.
maxIntegerDigits	-	Maximum number of integer digits.
var	-	Name of the variable where the formatting result will be written to. If you use this attribute, the direct output of the number will be suppressed.
scope	-	Scope of the variable where the formatting result will be written to. One of `page` (default), `application`, `session`, or `request`.

With `fmt:formatDate`, it is possible to format a `java.util.Date` object. Using various attributes, it is possible to output only the day part, or only the time-of-day part, or both given some pattern:

```
<%@ page contentType="text/html;charset=UTF-8"
    language="java" %>
<%@ taglib prefix="c"
    uri="http://java.sun.com/jsp/jstl/core" %>
<%@ taglib prefix="fmt"
    uri="http://java.sun.com/jsp/jstl/fmt" %>
```

231

```
<html>
...
   <%-- Supposing ${date1} refers to a java.util.Date --%>

   <fmt:formatDate value="${date1}" type="date" var="d1" />
   <%-- <= Use Java's DateFormat class to format a    --%>
   <%-- day (ignore the time-of-day) in the user's    --%>
   <%-- locale default format.    --%>
   <%-- Store the result in page scope variable "d1" --%>

   <fmt:formatDate value="${date1}" type="date"
      dateStyle="long"
      var="d1" />
   <%-- <= Use Java's DateFormat class to format a    --%>
   <%-- day in the user's locale "long" format    --%>
   <%-- Instead of "long" you can also write    --%>
   <%-- "default", "short", "medium", "long" or    --%>
   <%-- "full"    --%>

   <fmt:formatDate value="${date1}" type="time"
      var="d1" />
<%-- <= Use Java's DateFormat class to format a    --%>
<%-- time-of-day (ignore the day) in the user's    --%>
<%-- locale default format.    --%>
   <%-- Store the result in page scope variable "d1" --%>

   <fmt:formatDate value="${date1}" type="time" timeStyle="long"
      var="d1" />
   <%-- Time-of-day in long format.    --%>
   <%-- Instead of "long" you can also write    --%>
   <%-- "default", "short", "medium", "long" or    --%>
   <%-- "full"    --%>

   <fmt:formatDate value="${date1}" type="both"
      var="d1" />
   <%-- Write both day and time-of day. Use    --%>
   <%-- "dateStyle" and "timeStyle" to control the    --%>
   <%-- day and time-of-day styling as described    --%>
```

```
<%-- above.    --%>

<fmt:formatDate value="${date1}"
   pattern="yyyy-MM-dd hh:mm:ss"
   var="d1" />
<%-- Write day and/or time, as described by the   --%>
<%-- pattern (see class SimpleDateFormat for a    --%>
<%-- pattern description).    --%>

The date reads: ${d1}
...
</html>
```

The complete synopsis of fmt:formatDate is described in Table 8-2

Table 8-2. *FormatDate Tag*

Attribute	Required	Description
value	x	The value. Use EL syntax, such as ${someBean.someField}.
type	-	Which part to format. One of date, time, or both.
dateStyle	-	Specify the day style. One of default, short, medium, long, or full. Use Java's DateFormat class to specify the detail grade. Type must be date or both.
timeStyle	-	Specify the time-of-day style. One of default, short, medium, long, or full. Use JavaefaDateFormat class to specify the detail grade. Type must be date or both.
pattern	-	Write day and/or time, as described by the pattern. See the SimpleDateFormat class for a pattern description.
timeZone	-	Set the time zone. The format is described in the API documentation of java.util.TimeZone, method getTimeZone(). Directly passing a TimeZone object is also possible.
var	-	Name of the variable where the formatting result will be written to. If you use this attribute, the direct output will be suppressed.
scope	-	Scope of the variable where the formatting result will be written to. One of page (default), application, session, or request.

Using JSF for Formatting

If you use Facelets as a view engine and decide to disregard my warning about mixing Java MVC and JSF, the construct to declare number converters reads as follows:

```
<?xml version='1.0' encoding='UTF-8' ?>

<!DOCTYPE html>
<html xmlns="http://www.w3.org/1999/xhtml"
    xmlns:ui="http://java.sun.com/jsf/facelets"
    xmlns:h="http://java.sun.com/jsf/html"
    xmlns:f="http://java.sun.com/jsf/core">
<body>
...
<h:outputText value="${someBean.someField}">
   <f:convertNumber type="number"
       maxIntegerDigits="5"
       maxFractionDigits="5"
       groupingUsed="false"/>
</h:outputText>
...
</body>
</html>
```

So you have to put `<f:convertNumber>` *inside* the text output tag.

The various attributes of `<f:convertNumber>` do not differ much from the JSTL equivalent and are shown in Table 8-3.

Table 8-3. *ConvertNumber Tag*

Attribute	Required	Description
type	-	The type. One of number, currency, or percent. Default is number.
pattern	-	Formatting pattern, as described for the DecimalFormat class.
currencyCode	-	ISO 4217 currency code. Only if type = "currency".
currencySymbol	-	The currency symbol. Only if type = "currency".
groupingUsed	-	Whether or not grouping is used (e.g., the thousands separator). Use true or false.
minFractionDigits	-	Minimum number of fraction digits.
maxFractionDigits	-	Maximum number of fraction digits.
minIntegerDigits	-	Minimum number of integer digits.
maxIntegerDigits	-	Maximum number of integer digits.
integerOnly	-	If true, fractional digits are ignored. Either true or false.
locale	-	The locale to be used for displaying the number. Either directly a java.util.-Locale object, or a string suitable as the first argument to the Locale constructor.

In order to convert java.util.Date objects to string representations, you write the following in JSF:

```
<?xml version='1.0' encoding='UTF-8' ?>
<!DOCTYPE html>
<html xmlns="http://www.w3.org/1999/xhtml"
    xmlns:ui="http://java.sun.com/jsf/facelets"
    xmlns:h="http://java.sun.com/jsf/html"
    xmlns:f="http://java.sun.com/jsf/core">
<body>
...
<h:outputText value="${someBean.someField}">
  <f:convertDateTime type="both"
    dateStyle="full"
```

```
        timeStyle="medium" />
</h:outputText>
...
</body>
</html>
```

Not surprisingly, the set of possible attributes for f:convertDateTime very much resembles the attributes from the JSTL equivalent <fmt:formatDate>; see Table 8-4.

Table 8-4. *ConvertDateTime Tag*

Attribute	Required	Description
type	-	Which part to format. One of date, time, both, localDate, localTime, localDateTime, offsetTime, offset- DateTime, or zonedDateTime. Default is date.
dateStyle	-	Specify the day style. One of default, short, medium, long, or full. Use Java's DateFormat class to specify the detail grade.
timeStyle	-	Specify the time-of-day style. One of default, short, medium, long, or full. Use Java's DateFormat class to specify the detail grade.
pattern	-	Write day and/or time, as described by the pattern. See the SimpleDateFormat class for a pattern description.
timeZone	-	Set the time zone. The format is described in the API documentation of java.util.TimeZone, method getTimeZone(). Directly passing a TimeZone object also is possible.
locale	-	The locale to be used for displaying the date/time. Either directly via a java.- util.Locale object, or a string suitable as first argument to the Locale constructor.

Localized Data Conversion

We already used non-string types for form parameters in our MVC controllers:

```
@POST
@Path("/response")
public Response response(
```

```
@MvcBinding @FormParam("name") String name,
@MvcBinding @FormParam("userId") int userId) {
@MvcBinding @FormParam("rs") long timeStamp,
@MvcBinding @FormParam("rank") double rank) {

    // Handle form input, set model data, ...,
    // return response
}
```

For the parameter type, you can choose among String, int, long, float, double, BigDecimal, BigInteger, and boolean (true or false). Java MVC makes sure that user input is appropriately converted if you choose any type other than string. This conversion happens in a locale-specific manner. In an English locale, a user input of 0.45 has the correct format for a double parameter. In a German locale, for example, the same number has to be entered as 0,45. Correct conversion happens behind the scenes.

There is currently no reliable way to define custom converters. Also, there are no converters for times and dates. As a workaround, you can always pass values as Strings to the controller and then perform conversions programmatically.

```
@POST
@Path("/response")
public Response response(
 @MvcBinding @FormParam("day") String day,
 @Context HttpHeaders httpHeaders) {

    Locale loc = httpHeaders.getLanguage();
    // <- You could use this for locale specific
    // conversion rules.

    DateTimeFormatter formatter1 =
      DateTimeFormatter.ofPattern("yyyy-MM-dd");
    LocalDate ld = LocalDate.parse(day,
      formatter1);

    ...
}
```

Exercises

Exercise 1: In the HelloWorld application from Chapter 4, put the messages from the view files into a resource bundle and use the method described in the section entitled"Adding Localized Messages to the Session" to access the messages. Put the resource files in the src/main/resources/book/javamvc/helloworld/-messages folder.

Exercise 2: Continuing from the previous exercise, use the App class to move the constants from the BundleForEL class to application properties. Inject the application object into SetBundleFilter and update BundleForEL.setFor() to receive a bundle variable name and a bundle resources package name from the application object.

Exercise 3: Continuing from the previous exercise, add a double-valued rank field to the model class UserData. Add a Rank: labeled input field to the index.jsp view, and add formatted output for the same value to greeting.jsp. Update the controller class and add a method parameter called double rank to the @POST method.

Exercise 4: Continuing from the previous exercise, add a dateOfBirth field to the model class called UserData. Add a Date of Birth: labeled input field to the index.jsp view, and add a formatted output for the same value to greeting.jsp. Update the controller class and add a method parameter called String dateOfBirth to the @POST method.

Summary

Java provides built-in internationalization support via *resource bundles*. It is possible to save text snippets in different languages in different language-related property files. Using tags, it is also possible to output numbers and dates in locale-specific formats, and Java MVC can handle user input based on the locale.

In standard JSP, language-related resources are addressed by the `fmt:setBundle` and `fmt:bundle` tags, and by the `fmt:message` tag, which uses the key attribute to refer to text from the bundle.

For Facelets, you normally use JSF methodologies to access language resources, In the JSF configuration file `faces-config.xml`, you specify a resource bundle that can henceforth be used inside the views.

Although these approaches might suit your needs, there are a couple of downsides. By using a web filter and a `ResourceBundle` custom class, a simplified access to language resources can be provided.

If on a view page you write `${dbl}` and `dbl` refers to a double valued number, the `toString()` representation of this number is printed. This is acceptable only if your frontend user expects numbers formatted in the English locale. To make sure all other users get the expected number format according to their country rules, JSTL provides an `http://java.sun.com/jsp/jstl/fmt` tag library, which gathers tags for object formatting using the locale information.

In Facelets pages, you write the same code as for JSPs, but with a different header.

We already used non-string types for form parameters in our MVC controllers. For the parameter type, you can choose among `String`, `int`, `long`, `float`, `double`, `BigDecimal`, `BigInteger`, and `boolean` (true or false). Java MVC makes sure that the user input is appropriately converted if you choose any type other than `string`. This conversion happens in a locale-specific manner. In an English locale, a user input `0.45` has the correct format for a double parameter. In a German locale, for example, the same number has to be entered as `0,45`. Correct conversion happens behind the scenes.

There is currently no reliable way to define custom converters. Also, there are no converters for times and dates. As a workaround, you can always pass values as `Strings` to the controller and then perform conversions programmatically.

In the next chapter, we talk about Java MVC addressing EJBs, which is a standardized way to communicate with backend components.

CHAPTER 9

Java MVC and EJBs

Enterprise Java Beans (EJBs) are classes that encapsulate business functionalities, each of a certain kind. Unlike normal Java classes, however, EJBs run in a *container* environment, which means the server adds system-level services to them. These services include lifecycle management (instantiating and destroying, when and how), transactionality (building logical, atomic, rollback-enabled units of work), and security (which users can invoke which methods). Because Java MVC runs inside such a container, namely Jakarta EE, EJBs are a good way for Java MVC applications to encapsulate their business functionalities.

The EJB technology includes *session* beans and *message driven beans*. However, the latter go beyond the scope of this book, so here we will talk about *session* EJBs only.

About Session EJBs

Session EJBs can be accessed locally (in the same application), remotely (over the network, via method invocation), or via some web service interface (distributed applications across heterogeneous networks, HTML, XML, or JSON data formats).

Concerning the creation and destruction of session EJBs, there are three types of session EJBs:

- **Singleton:** With a singleton session EJB, the container instantiates only one instance and all clients share this single instance. You can do this if the EJB does not have a state that discriminates clients, and concurrent access does not impose problems.

- **Stateless:** EJBs of the "stateless" kind do not maintain a state, so a particular client can have different instances assigned to subsequent EJB invocations (the container handles this; the client doesn't know about this assignment).

241

© Peter Späth 2021
P. Späth, *Beginning Java MVC 1.0*, https://doi.org/10.1007/978-1-4842-6280-1_9

- **Stateful:** Stateful EJBs maintain a state and a client can be sure it will receive the same session EJB instance from the container for subsequent uses of the same EJB. You will often hear that stateful EJB clients maintain a *conversational* state concerning using stateful EJBs. Stateful session EJBs cannot implement web services, because web services are not allowed to have state and no session information is communicated.

Defining EJBs

To define a singleton EJB, a stateless EJB, or a stateful EJB, you add one of these annotations—@Singleton, @Stateless, or @Stateful, respectively—to the EJB implementation.

Consider three examples. An EJB called Configuration for the encapsulated access to application-wide configuration settings. Another EJB called Invoice, which handles invoice registration and inquiry given some invoice ID. A third EJB called TicTacToe for a simple tic-tac-toe game implementation. Obviously, for the configuration EJB we can use a singleton EJB, since neither local state nor concurrency matter. Similarly, for the invoice EJB, we can use a stateless EJB, since the state is mediated by the ID, which does not access an EJB state but rather a database state. The last one, the tic-tac-toe EJB, needs to maintain the game board for each client and we thus must use a stateful EJB for it.

```
import javax.ejb.Singleton;
import javax.ejb.Stateless;
import javax.ejb.Stateful;
...
@Singleton
public class Configuration {
    ... configuration access methods
}

@Stateless
public class Invoice {
    ... invoice access methods
}
```

```
@Stateful
public class TicTacToe {
    ... tic-tac-toe methods
}
```

Of course, all those classes must go to different files. We put them together for illustration purposes only.

Concerning their accessibility from client code, session EJBs can use one or a combination of three methods (all annotations shown are from the `javax.ejb` package):

- **No-interface:** You use this method if you don't want to describe the EJB access via an interface. This is only possible with local clients running inside the same application. While the separation into interfaces (describing *what* gets done in `interfaces`) and the implementation (the how, implemented in non-abstract `classes`) is generally a good idea for clean code, a no-interface view can make sense for simple EJBs. For no-interface EJBs, you just declare the implementation, as follows:

  ```
  @Stateless public class Invoice {
      ... implementation
  }
  ```

  The EJB clients can then of course only access the implementation class directly, without mediating interfaces.

- **Local:** If you want to define local access to session EJBs (EJBs and EJB clients running in the same application) and want to use an interface view for that, you can mark the interface with `@Local` and let the EJB implementation class implement the interface:

  ```
  @Local public interface InvoiceInterface {
      ... abstract interface methods
  }

  @Stateless public class Invoice
        implements InvoiceInterface {
      ... implementation
  }
  ```

Or you use the @Local annotation in the implementation class:

```
public interface InvoiceInterface {
    ... abstract interface methods
}

@Stateless
@Local(InvoiceInterface.class)
public class Invoice implements InvoiceInterface {
    ... implementation
}
```

You can even omit the implementation, as follows:

```
public interface InvoiceInterface {
    ... abstract interface methods
}

@Stateless
@Local(InvoiceInterface.class)
public class Invoice {
    ... implementation
}
```

This last method will further reduce the coupling of the interface, although this is in general not recommended.

- **@Remote:** Use the @Remote annotation for this session EJB to be accessible from outside the application. You can simply replace @Local with @Remote and everything that was said for the local access and concerning the interfaces is true unaltered for remote access. So you write the following, for example:

```
public interface InvoiceInterface {
    ... abstract interface methods
}

@Stateless
@Remote(InvoiceInterface.class)
public Invoice
```

```
        implements InvoiceInterface {
    ... implementation
}
```

EJBs can have a local *and* a remote interface; just use both annotations together:

```
public interface InvoiceLocal {
    ... abstract interface methods
}
public interface InvoiceRemote {
    ... abstract interface methods
}

@Stateless
@Local(InvoiceLocal.class)
@Remote(InvoiceRemote.class)
public Invoice
        implements InvoiceLocal,
                    InvoiceRemote {
    ... implementation
}
```

Also, nobody hinders us from using the same interface for both local and remote access:

```
public interface InvoiceInterface {
    ... abstract interface methods
}

@Stateless
@Local(InvoiceInterface.class)
@Remote(InvoiceInterface.class)
public Invoice implements InvoiceInterface {
    ... implementation
}
```

> **Caution**   Remote access means parameters in method calls are passed by value, not by reference! So, although local and remote interfaces are declared co-natural to each other, you must be careful with method parameters under certain circumstances.

Accessing EJBs

Accessing local EJBs from a Java MVC controller is easy: you just use the @EJB injection to let CDI assign an instance access to an EJB:

```
public class SomeController {
    ...
    @EJB
    private SomeEjbInterface theEjb;

    // or, for no-interface EJBs
    @EJB
    private SomeEjbClass theEjb;
    ...
}
```

Addressing remote EJBs is considerably more complicated compared to local-access EJBs. You have to set up a JNDI context and then use it to do a lookup of a remote instance:

```
...
String remoteServerHost = "localhost";
// or "192.168.1.111" or something
String remoteServerPort = "3700";
// Port 3700 is part of the GlassFish conf

Properties props = new Properties();
props.setProperty("java.naming.factory.initial",
  "com.sun.enterprise.naming."+
  "SerialInitContextFactory");
props.setProperty("java.naming.factory.url.pkgs",
```

```
  "com.sun.enterprise.naming");
props.setProperty("java.naming.factory.state",
  "com.sun.corba.ee.impl.presentation.rmi."+
  "JNDIStateFactoryImpl");
props.setProperty("org.omg.CORBA.ORBInitialHost",
  remoteServerHost);
props.setProperty("org.omg.CORBA.ORBInitialPort",
  remoteServerPort);

try {
  InitialContext ic = new InitialContext(props);

  // Use this to see what EJBs are available
  // and how to name them
  //NamingEnumeration<NameClassPair> list =
  //        ic.list("");
  //while (list.hasMore()) {
  //  System.out.println(list.next().getName());
  //}

  // Looking up a remote EJB
    SomeEjbRemote testEJB = (SomeEjbRemote)
        ic.lookup(
          "book.jakarta8.testEjbServer.SomeEjbRemote");

  // Invoking some EJB method
  System.out.println(testEJB.tellMe());
}catch(Exception e) {
  e.printStackTrace(System.err);
}
```

This example assumes that, on the remote server side, you created a session EJB with a remote interface:

```
package book.jakarta8.testEjbServer;

public interface SomeEjbRemote {
    String tellMe();
}
```

And an implementation like this one:

```
package book.jakarta8.testEjbServer;

import javax.ejb.Remote;
import javax.ejb.Stateless;

@Stateless
@Remote(SomeEjbRemote.class)
public class SomeEjb implements SomeEjbRemote {
  @Override
    public String tellMe() {
      return "Hello World";
    }
}
```

Obviously, for this to work, the Java MVC application must have access to the compiled remote interfaces. That means in the EJB server build, you must have somehow included a step to extract the interfaces from the generated classes. We'll talk about that in detail later.

If the remote EJB server is a GlassFish server, you can also use its `asadmin` command to see which EJBs are eligible for remote access and how they are named:

```
cd [GLASSFISH_INST]
cd bin
./asadmin list-jndi-entries
```

Other Java Enterprise Edition (JEE or Jakarta EE) application servers probably apply other naming schemes for remotely accessible EJBs. So you must consult their documentation and/or get the remotely visible JNDI entry listing. For the latter, you can try programmatic access (commented out in the previous listing), or use some administration features implemented for the remote EJB server.

EJB Projects

Jakarta EE projects don't have to be web projects; they can also just expose services to clients accessing their remote EJB interfaces. Web interfaces, like REST or web service interfaces, are your first choice for interoperability with web browsers and non-Jakarta

EE servers. But for faster communication among Jakarta EE participants in a larger system with different network nodes, using Component-to-EJB communication might be a better choice.

Web projects can also expose remote EJBs to appropriate clients. If you want to have a streamlined project without web capabilities, the procedure to do that inside Eclipse is described in the following paragraphs.

Start a new Gradle project similar to the web projects we created so far, but change the plugin declaration to the following:

```
plugins {
    id 'java-library'
}
```

From there on, create the EJBs and their remote interfaces as described, with the following additional constraint: move the EJB interfaces to their own package. For example:

```
book.javamvc.ejbproj.ejb              <- Implementation
book.javamvc.ejbproj.ejb.interfaces   <- Interfaces
```

Inside the build file, we add a task that automates the EJB stub generation:

```
task extractStubs (type: Jar, dependsOn:classes) {
  archiveClassifier = 'ejb-stubs'
  from "$buildDir/classes/java/main"
  include "**/interfaces/*.class"
}
jar.finalizedBy(extractStubs)
```

This ensures that, after each jar task execution, the stubs are created. You can then run the jar task to create the full EJB jar *and* the stubs. You'll find both in the build/libs folder. You may have to press F5 on that folder to update the view. Any client wishing to communicate with the EJBs must include the interface JAR as a dependency. Of course, the EJB project itself must be deployed on the server for the EJBs to work.

EJBs with Dependencies

Until now, we developed only very simple EJBs without the need to use libraries included as JARs. Once you need to add libraries to an EJB, you'll run into trouble. The reason for this is that there is no standard way to add dependencies to isolated EJB modules. If you need to add library JARs, the best way is to pack the EJB module into an Enterprise Archive (EAR).

EARs are archives that bundle EJBs, web applications (WARs), and library JARs. Dealing with EARs instead of isolated EJBs somewhat increases the complexity of the administration activities. But adding library JARs to EARs is the best way of including dependencies with non-web applications.

In order to add EAR functionality to an application inside Eclipse, you basically have to do the following:

1. Build a new Gradle project. Go to New ➤ Other... ➤ Gradle ➤ Gradle Project.

2. Choose any name you like. It's a good idea to add "ear" to the end of the name.

3. Inside `build.gradle`, change the `plugins { }` section to `plugins { id 'ear' }`.

4. Inside `build.gradle`, use as the `dependencies { }` section:

```
dependencies {
  deploy project(path: ':war',
      configuration: 'archives')
  deploy project(path: ':ejb1',
      configuration: 'archives')
  earlib "org.apache.commons:"+
      "commons-math3:3.6.1"
}
```

5. Create the `war` and `ejb1` folders in the project root.

6. Open the `settings.gradle` file and add the following:

    ```
    include 'war', 'ejb1'
    ```

7. Invoke Gradle ➤ Refresh Gradle Project. Eclipse might throw an error message; you can ignore it for now.

8. The two subprojects `war` and `ejb1` show up in the Project Explorer. You may have to update the working set if you are using one.

9. Convert both subprojects to a Faceted form (choose Configure ➤ Convert to Faceted Form...), and in the settings, add Java 1.8 capabilities.

We now have an EAR project with two subprojects. What is left to do is to add Gradle capabilities to each of the subprojects. The WAR project needs a build file like one of the many `build.gradle` files we used for Java MVC projects. What is different, though, is that we add a dependency to the sibling EJB project:

```
dependencies {
    implementation project(":ejb1")
    // Other dependencies...
}
```

Note   This is for the Gradle dependencies. In order for Eclipse to recognize the dependency, you have to add the EJB project as a dependency in the Java Build Path (choose Project Settings ➤ Java Build Path ➤ Projects tab).

For the EJB project, you probably use a `build.gradle` file like the following:

```
plugins {
    id 'java-library'
}

java {
    sourceCompatibility = JavaVersion.VERSION_1_8
    targetCompatibility = JavaVersion.VERSION_1_8
}
```

```
repositories {
    jcenter()
}

dependencies {
    implementation 'javax:javaee-api:8.0'
    // Add dependencies here...
}
```

If you run the ear task, the subprojects and the EAR file will be built. The latter can be found in the build/libs folder.

Asynchronous EJB Invocation

EJB clients call EJB methods asynchronously. This means the client invokes an EJB method that was marked eligible for asynchronous invocation, immediately regains control of the program execution, and handles the result from the EJB invocation later, when it is available.

To mark an EJB method for asynchronous invocation, you add the @Asynchronous annotation from the javax.ejb package to the method:

```
import java.util.concurrent.Future;
import javax.ejb.AsyncResult;
import javax.ejb.Asynchronous;
import javax.ejb.Singleton;

@Singleton // Example only, all EJB types work!
public class SomeEjb {
  @Asynchronous
  public Future<String> tellMeLater() {

    // Simulate some long running calculation
    try {
      Thread.sleep(2000);
    } catch (InterruptedException e) {
    }
```

```
    return new AsyncResult<String>(
        "Hi from tellMeLater()");
    }
}
```

This example EJB uses the no-interface method, but asynchronous invocation works for local and remote interfaces as well. `AsyncResult` is a convenience class that allows for the easy creation of a `Future`. This `Future` object will not be exposed to the client; its main purpose is to obey the method signature. The `Future` returned to the client will instead be transparently created by the EJB container.

On the EJB client side, you invoke the EJB as usual, and handle the `Future` you received from the EJB invocation as used from the JRE concurrency API:

```
...
@EJB
private SomeEjb someEjb;
...
Future<String> f = someEjb.tellMeLater();
try {
    // Example only: block until the result
    // is available:
    String s = f.get();
    System.err.println(s);
} catch (Exception e) {
    e.printStackTrace(System.err);
}
```

Timer EJBs

EJBs can be equipped with timer facilities, such as for delayed execution of some task or recurring automatic method invocations. You have two options: automatic timers and programmatic timers.

For automatic timers, you add a `@Schedule` or `@Schedules` annotation (from the `javax.ejb` package) to any `void` method (the visibility doesn't matter) either without a parameter, or with a `javax.ejb.Timer` parameter. The parameters of the `@Schedule` annotation describe the frequency, as follows:

```
@Stateless
public class SomeEjb {
  @Schedule(minute="*", hour="0", persistent=false)
  // every minute during the hour between 00:00 and 01:00
  public void timeout1() {
    System.err.println("Timeout-1 from " + getClass());
  }
}
```

A delayed execution like "Do something once ten seconds after the server has started" is not possible with automatic timers.

The following is a listing of some example schedules you can use inside automatic timers:

```
@Schedule(second="10", minute="0", hour="0")
  // <- at 00:00:10 every day

@Schedule(minute="30", hour="0",
      dayOfWeek="Tue")
  // <- at 00:30:00 on Tuesdays (second defaults to 00)

@Schedule(minute="11", hour="15",
      dayOfWeek="Mon,Tue,Fri")
  // <- at 15:11:00 on mondays, Tuesdays and Fridays

@Schedule(minute="*/10", hour="*")
  // <- every 10 minutes, every hour

@Schedule(minute="25/10", hour="1")
  // <- 01:25, 01:35, 01:45 and 01:55

@Schedule(hour="*", dayOfMonth="1,2,3")
  // <- every hour at 1st, 2nd and 3rd each month
  // (minute defaults to 00)

@Schedule(hour="*/10")
  // <- every 10 hours
```

```
@Schedule(month="Feb,Aug")
  // <- 00:00:00 each February and August
  // (hour defaults to 00)

@Schedule(dayOfMonth="1", year="2020")
  // <- 00:00:00 each 1st each month during 2020

@Schedule(dayOfMonth="1-10")
  // <- 00:00:00 each 1st to 10th each month
```

The @Schedules annotation can be used to apply several @Schedule specifications to a timer callback:

```
@Schedules({
  @Schedule(hour="*"),
  @Schedule(hour="0", minute="30")
})
private void someMethod(Timer tm) {
    ...
}
```

This means every x:00:00 (x = 00 through 23), but also at 00:30:00. Unless you also give a persistent=false to the @Schedule annotation, a timer survives an application and a server restart.

Timers can also be defined programmatically. Here it is also possible to define a one-time shot, such as this:

```
@Singleton
@Startup
public class Timer1 {
  @Resource
  private SessionContext context;

  @PostConstruct
  public void go() {
    context.getTimerService().
        createSingleActionTimer(5000, new TimerConfig());
  }
```

```
@Timeout
public void timeout(Timer timer) {
  System.err.println("Hello from " + getClass());
}
}
```

The method annotated with @Timeout is called every time the timer fires. For this example, this will be 5000 milliseconds after EJB creation, because of the createSingleActionTimer() invocation. The timer service you get with context.getTimerService() enables various scheduling options; see the API documentation for details.

Exercises

Exercise 1

Which of the following is/are true?

- EJBs must have a local *and* a remote interface.

- Not providing interfaces means EJBs are automatically assigned to local and remote interfaces by the EJB container (the part of the Jakarta EE server that handles EJBs).

- A remote EJB means the EJB can be accessed from other applications on the same server. Access from other Jakarta EE servers is not possible.

- EJBs cannot have a state.

- If a client accesses an EJB, a new instance of the EJB is created on the server side.

- To access any EJB from a client, you must use do a lookup in a JNDI context.

- In order to use an EJB from a client, the EJB's interfaces and its implementation must be imported into the client project.

Exercise 2

Create four projects:

- A JSE project (no Jakarta EE capabilities) with a single `MyDateTime` class and a method called `date( String format )`, which returns the `LocalDateTime` as a string, according to the format string specified as a parameter. Make it a Gradle project.

- An EJB project with a single EJB `MyDateTimeEjb` and local and remote interfaces. Have it use the JAR file generated from the JRE project above. Hint: You can use something like `implementation files( '../../- SimpleNoJEE/build/libs/SimpleNoJEE.jar' )` to specify a local dependency.

- An EAR project that contains the EJB project and adds the necessary JAR dependency.

- A simple no-Jakarta-EE EJB client project that tests the remote interface from the `MyDateTimeEjb` EJB. Hint: Include `gf-client.jar` from GlassFish's `lib` folder as a library dependency.

Summary

Enterprise Java Beans (EJBs) are classes that encapsulate business functionalities, each of a certain kind. Unlike normal Java classes, however, EJBs run in a *container* environment, which means the server adds system-level services to them. These include lifecycle management (instantiating and destroying, when and how), transactionality (building logical, atomic, rollback-enabled units of work), and security (which users can invoke which methods). Because Java MVC runs inside such a container, namely Jakarta EE, EJBs are a good way for Java MVC applications to encapsulate their business functionalities.

The EJB technology includes *session* beans and *message driven beans*. Session EJBs can be accessed locally (in the same application), remotely (over the network, via method invocation), or via some web service interface (distributed applications across heterogeneous networks, HTML, XML or JSON data formats).

Concerning the creation and destruction of session EJBs, there are three types of session EJBs. Singleton EJBs, stateless EJBs, and stateful EJBS. To define any of them, you add the appropriate annotation—@Singleton, @Stateless, or @Stateful—to the EJB implementation.

Concerning their accessibility from client code, session EJBs can use one or a combination of three methods: no-interface access, local access, or remote access.

Accessing local EJBs from a Java MVC controller is easy: you just use the @EJB injection to let CDI assign instance access to an EJB: @EJB private SomeEjbInterface theEjb.

Addressing remote EJBs is considerably more complicated compared to l ocal-access EJBs. You have to set up a JNDI context and then use it to do a lookup of a remote instance.

For this to work, the Java MVC application must have access to the compiled remote interfaces. That means, in the EJB server build, you must have somehow included a step to extract the interfaces from the generated classes.

Jakarta EE projects don't have to be web projects; they can also just expose services to clients accessing their remote EJB interfaces. Web interfaces, like REST or web service interfaces, are your first choice for interoperability with web browsers and non-Jakarta EE servers. For faster communication among Jakarta EE participants in a larger system with different network nodes, using Component-to-EJB communication might be a better choice. Web projects also can expose remote EJBs to appropriate clients.

Once you need to add libraries to an EJB, the best way is to pack the EJB module into an Enterprise Archive (EAR). EARs are archives that bundle EJBs, web applications (WARs), and library JARs. Dealing with EARs instead of isolated EJBs somewhat increases the complexity of the administration activities. But once you're finished, if you run the ear task, the subprojects and the EAR file will be built. The latter can be found in the build/libs folder.

EJB clients call EJB methods asynchronously. This means the client invokes an EJB method that was marked eligible for asynchronous invocation, immediately regains control of the program execution, and handles the result from the EJB invocation later, when it is available.

To mark an EJB method for asynchronous invocation, you add the @Asynchronous annotation from the javax.ejb package to the method.

EJBs can be equipped with timer facilities, such as for delayed execution of some task or reoccurring automatic method invocations. You have two options: automatic timers and programmatic timers.

With automatic timers, you add a @Schedule or @Schedules annotation (from the javax.ejb package) to any void method (the visibility doesn't matter), either without a parameter or with a javax.ejb.Timer parameter. The parameters of the @Schedule annotation describe the frequency.

Timers can also be defined programmatically. It is also possible to define a one-time invocation.

In the next chapter, we learn how to connect Java MVC to databases.

## CHAPTER 10

Connecting Java MVC to a Database

Databases are needed if you want to persist data for a longer period of time, or if data must consistently be accessible from different sessions (different users). This chapter refers to SQL (Structured Query Language) databases. For an introduction, see for example the article at `https://en.wikipedia.org/wiki/Database`.

JPA (Java Persistence API) is the dedicated technology used to access relational databases from inside Jakarta EE. Its aim is to provide a bridge between SQL tables and Java objects. This task is much more complex than in other basic data schemes. The reason for this is that, in relational database schemes, we have associations between different tables: One row in one table may refer to one or many rows in another table or the other way round, and there could be references spanning three or more tables. And think of column-type conversions—a database may have different ideas about numbers, boolean indicators, and dates and times compared to Java. In addition, `null` values in database tables require increased attention if they're used in table references and while converting to Java values.

In this chapter, we talk about basic issues when using JPA inside Java MVC. For a complete and deep overview of JPA, covering more complex issues than we do in this chapter, consult the online JPA documentation and specification on the web. A good starting URL is `https://docs.oracle.com/javaee/6/tutorial/doc/bnbpy.html`.

Abstracting Away Database Access with JPA

One of the primary purposes of JPA is to abstract away database access and map database objects to Java classes. In the end, we want to be able to query the database and get Java objects, or to put Java objects in the database. JPA hides the details of how

261

P. Späth, *Beginning Java MVC 1.0*, https://doi.org/10.1007/978-1-4842-6280-1_10

this can be done, including connection properties like usernames and passwords, and including handling connection lifecycles.

The central JPA class for this purpose is `EntityManager`, which uses a single configuration file called `persistence.xml`, together with some settings inside the Jakarta EE application server. On the Java side, the classes that correspond to table rows are called *entity* classes. See Figure 10-1 for an overview of JPA.

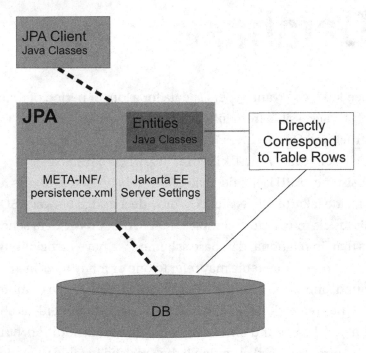

Figure 10-1. JPA inside Jakarta EE at work

Setting Up a SQL Database

SQL databases come in two flavors—you can have fully fledged client-server databases and embedded databases (possibly using some in-memory storage). In this book, we use the Apache Derby database included in the GlassFish server distribution. This database runs independent from GlassFish, but the GlassFish administrative tools also provide some commands for handling the Apache Derby instance. As a client, we use JPA from inside the Java MVC application.

Note   In the GlassFish documentation, you'll frequently see the name "JavaDB" as the product name for the database. JavaDB actually was the name of Derby while it was included in the JDK versions 6 through 8. Now it's kind of obsolete, so we don't use the name "JavaDB" in this book.

Switching to a different database product is a non-intrusive operation, so you can start learning JPA with Apache Derby and only later switch to some other database management system.

Note   From an architectural point of view, database access is best included in an EJB or EAR module. For simplicity, we include JPA directly in a Java MVC project, but the procedures to do that in an EJB or EAR module are very similar.

If you start a GlassFish server, the Apache Derby database does not automatically start as well. Instead, you must run it inside the console:

```
cd [GLASSFISH_INST]
bin/asadmin start-database
```

where [GLASSFISH_INST] is your GlassFish server's installation directory.

Caution   Although they are both administered by asadmin, the GlassFish Jakarta EE server and the Apache Derby database management system are independent of each other. If you stop either of them, the other one continues running.

To stop a running Apache Derby, enter this inside the console:

```
cd [GLASSFISH_INST]
bin/asadmin stop-database
```

Creating a Datasource

In order for JPA to work, we need to add an *object relational mapping* (ORM) library to the project. There are several options here, but we choose EclipseLink as an ORM library, since EclipseLink is the reference implementation of JPA 2.2 (this is the version of JPA used in Jakarta EE 8 and Java MVC 1.0).

ORMs do not directly connect to databases but instead connect to *datasources* that abstract away the database access. This indirection allows for establishing connection pools, caches, transactionality, and administration of data handling using server-side administrative tools.

In order to create a suitable datasource for GlassFish, enter the following in the same terminal you used to start the database:

```
cd [GLASSFISH_INST]
cd javadb/bin
# start the DB client
./ij
```

(Or use ij for Windows.) We are now inside the ij database client, which you can see since the ij> prompt appears in the terminal. Enter the following to create a database named hello (enter this in one line without spaces in front of the create=):

```
ij> connect 'jdbc:derby://localhost:1527/hello;
    create=true;user=user0';
```

The database is now created with an owner named user0. We also add a password for the user:

```
ij> call SYSCS_UTIL.SYSCS_CREATE_USER('user0','pw715');
```

Note   Apache Derby by default does not enable authentication for new databases. This normally does not cause problems if you're using the database only for development, because network access is restricted to local users only. Many Java applications and database tools, however, behave strangely if you try to access the database without authentication, so we add a password.

Next, restart the database for the authentication to start working:

```
cd [GLASSFISH_INST]
cd bin
./asadmin stop-database
./asadmin start-database
```

This needs to be done only once. Quit and reopen the connection inside the ij tool (or quit ij altogether by pressing Ctrl+D; then restart ij and connect again):

```
ij> disconnect;
ij> connect 'jdbc:derby://localhost:1527/hello;
    user=user0;password=pw715';
```

(Enter the last ij command in one line.) You can check the authentication mechanism: if you omit the username or password, or both, you'll get an appropriate error message.

For transparent and simple connection to the database, we create two resources in the GlassFish server configuration:

```
cd [GLASSFISH_INST]
cd bin
./asadmin create-jdbc-connection-pool \
  --datasourceclassname \
    org.apache.derby.jdbc.ClientXADataSource \
  --restype javax.sql.XADataSource \
  --property \
    portNumber=1527:password=pw715:user=user0:
    serverName=localhost:databaseName=hello:
    securityMechanism=3 \
  HelloPool

./asadmin create-jdbc-resource \
  --connectionpoolid HelloPool jdbc/Hello
```

(No line break and no spaces after user=user0: or databaseName = hello:.) This creates a connection pool and a JDBC resource connecting to it. We will later be using the jdbc/Hello identifier to allow JPA to connect to the database.

You can see both configuration items if you enter the administration console in your web browser at http://localhost:4848. Navigate to Resources ➤ JDBC ➤ JDBC Resources and Resources ➤ JDBC ➤ JDBC Connection Pools. See Figure 10-2.

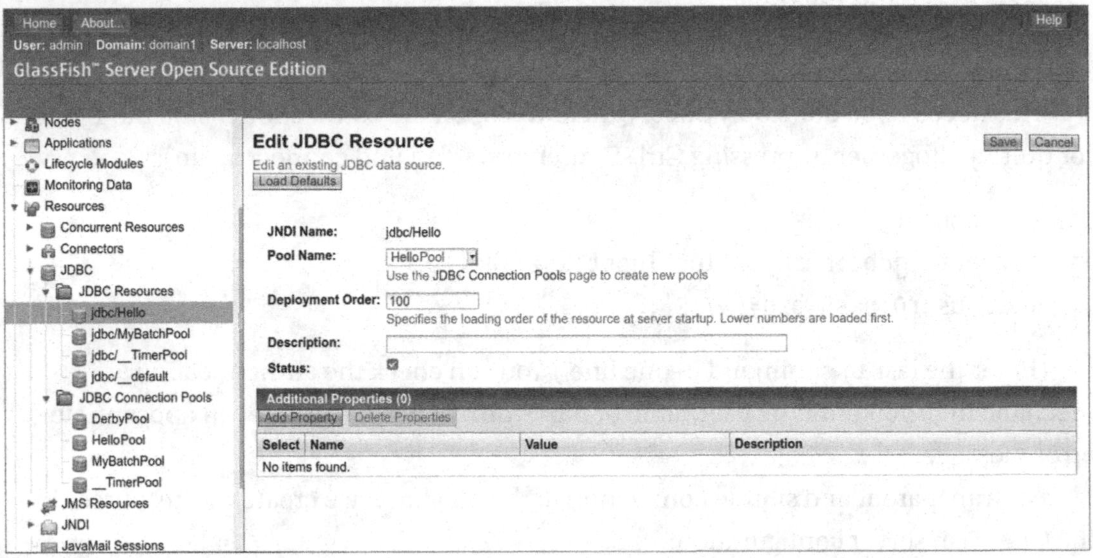

Figure 10-2. *JDBC resources*

In the rest of this chapter, we assume you know how to enter database commands. Either use the ij tool (don't forget to connect after you start it), or use any other database client, such as the open source tool called *Squirrel*.

Preparing the Member Registration Application

In this chapter, we develop a basic member administration application for Java MVC. The members are stored in a database table called MEMBER. The SQL commands to create the table and a sequence generator for the unique ID generation are as follows:

```
CREATE TABLE MEMBER (
    ID      INT             NOT NULL,
    NAME    VARCHAR(128)    NOT NULL,
    PRIMARY KEY (ID));

INSERT INTO MEMBER (ID, NAME)
```

```
VALUES (-3, 'John'),
       (-2, 'Linda'),
       (-1, 'Pat');

CREATE SEQUENCE MEMBER_SEQ start with 1 increment by 50;
```

We also added a couple of example entries.

Note   Apache Derby knows how to auto-generate unique IDs. We however let EclipseLink take care of that. For this reason, the ID field is left as a simple integer value field without any additional semantics. EclipseLink needs the sequence to take care of generating such unique IDs (at least if it's used the way we are going to use it).

The project structure for the new database project is as follows:

```
Project HelloJpa
 src/main/java
   book.javamvc.jpa
     data
       User.java
     db
       Member.java
       MemberDAO.java
     i18n
       BundleForEL.java
       SetBundleFilter.java
     model
       UserEntering.java
       UserList.java
     AjaxController.java
     App.java
     HelloJpaController.java
     RootRedirector.java
  src/main/resources
    book.javamvc.jpa.messages
```

```
      Messages.properties
    META-INF
      persistence.xml
  src/main/webapp
    js
      jquery-3.5.1.min.js
    WEB-INF
      views
        index.jsp
    beans.xml
    glassfish-web.xml
  build.gradle
  gradle.properties
  settings.gradle
```

We don't want to mix Java MVC model classes and database model classes, so in the User.java class, we abstract away any user data:

```java
package book.javamvc.jpa.data;

public class User {
    private int id;
    private String name;

    public User() {
    }

    public User(int id, String name) {
        this.id = id;
        this.name = name;
    }

    // Getters and setters...
}
```

The BundleForEL and SetBundleFilter classes are exactly the same as in the
HelloWorld application, but with the addition to factor out configuration values (made
in one of the exercises). For clarity, I repeat the code here:

```
package book.javamvc.jpa.i18n;

import java.util.Enumeration;
import java.util.Locale;
import java.util.ResourceBundle;
import javax.servlet.http.HttpServletRequest;

public class BundleForEL extends ResourceBundle {
    private BundleForEL(Locale locale, String baseName) {
        setLocale(locale, baseName);
    }

    public static void setFor(HttpServletRequest request,
        String i18nAttributeName, String i18nBaseName) {
      if (request.getSession().
          getAttribute(i18nAttributeName) == null) {
        request.getSession().setAttribute(
          i18nAttributeName,
          new BundleForEL(request.getLocale(),
                       i18nBaseName));
        }
    }

    public void setLocale(Locale locale,
         String baseName) {
      if (parent == null ||
            !parent.getLocale().equals(locale)) {
          setParent(getBundle(baseName, locale));
      }
    }

    @Override
    public Enumeration<String> getKeys() {
        return parent.getKeys();
    }
```

```
    @Override
    protected Object handleGetObject(String key) {
        return parent.getObject(key);
    }
}
```

and

```
package book.javamvc.jpa.i18n;

import java.io.IOException;
import java.util.Map;

import javax.inject.Inject;
import javax.servlet.Filter;
import javax.servlet.FilterChain;
import javax.servlet.FilterConfig;
import javax.servlet.ServletException;
import javax.servlet.ServletRequest;
import javax.servlet.ServletResponse;
import javax.servlet.annotation.WebFilter;
import javax.servlet.http.HttpServletRequest;
import javax.ws.rs.core.Application;

@WebFilter("/*")
public class SetBundleFilter implements Filter {
    @Inject private Application appl;
    private String i18nAttributeName;
    private String i18nBaseName;

    @Override
    public void init(FilterConfig filterConfig)
            throws ServletException {
      Map<String,Object> applProps = appl.getProperties();
      i18nAttributeName = (String) applProps.get(
          "I18N_TEXT_ATTRIBUTE_NAME");
      i18nBaseName = (String) applProps.get(
          "I18N_TEXT_BASE_NAME");
    }
```

```java
@Override
public void doFilter(ServletRequest request,
    ServletResponse response, FilterChain chain)
    throws IOException, ServletException {
  BundleForEL.setFor((HttpServletRequest) request,
    i18nAttributeName, i18nBaseName);
  chain.doFilter(request, response);
}

@Override
public void destroy() {
}
}
```

We place the two Java MVC model classes for the new member entry and the member list into the book.javamvc.jpa.model package. The code reads as follows:

```java
package book.javamvc.jpa.model;

import javax.enterprise.context.RequestScoped;
import javax.inject.Named;
import book.javamvc.jpa.data.User;

@Named
@RequestScoped
public class UserEntering extends User {
}
```

and

```java
package book.javamvc.jpa.model;

import java.util.ArrayList;
import javax.enterprise.context.RequestScoped;

import javax.inject.Named;
import book.javamvc.jpa.data.User;

@Named
@RequestScoped
```

```java
public class UserList extends ArrayList<User>{
    private static final long serialVersionUID =
            8570272213112459191L;
}
```

The App and RootRedirector classes are the same as in the HelloWorld application, but with the refactoring done in one of the exercises:

```java
package book.javamvc.jpa;

import java.util.HashMap;
import java.util.Map;

import javax.annotation.PostConstruct; import javax.ws.rs.ApplicationPath;
import javax.ws.rs.core.Application;

@ApplicationPath("/mvc")
public class App extends Application {
    @PostConstruct
    public void init() {
    }

    @Override
    public Map<String, Object> getProperties() {
      Map<String, Object> res = new HashMap<>();
      res.put("I18N_TEXT_ATTRIBUTE_NAME",
        "msg");
      res.put("I18N_TEXT_BASE_NAME",
        "book.javamvc.jpa.messages.Messages");
      return res;
    }
}
```

and

```java
package book.javamvc.jpa;

import javax.servlet.FilterChain;
import javax.servlet.annotation.WebFilter;
import javax.servlet.http.HttpFilter;
```

```java
import javax.servlet.http.HttpServletRequest;
import javax.servlet.http.HttpServletResponse;
import java.io.IOException;

/**
 * Redirecting http://localhost:8080/HelloJpa/
 * This way we don't need a <welcome-file-list> in web.xml
 */
@WebFilter(urlPatterns = "/")
public class RootRedirector extends HttpFilter {
    private static final long serialVersionUID =
            7332909156163673868L;

    @Override
    protected void doFilter(final HttpServletRequest req,
            final HttpServletResponse res,
            final FilterChain chain) throws IOException {
        res.sendRedirect("mvc/hello");
    }
}
```

`build.gradle` takes the following code:

```gradle
plugins {
  id 'war'
}

java {
  sourceCompatibility = JavaVersion.VERSION_1_8
  targetCompatibility = JavaVersion.VERSION_1_8
}

repositories {
  jcenter()
}

dependencies {
  testImplementation 'junit:junit:4.12'
  implementation 'javax:javaee-api:8.0'
```

```
implementation 'javax.mvc:javax.mvc-api:1.0.0'
implementation 'org.eclipse.krazo:krazo-jersey:1.1.0-M1'
implementation 'jstl:jstl:1.2'
implementation 'org.eclipse.persistence:'+
    'eclipselink:2.7.7'
}

task localDeploy(dependsOn: war,
   description:">>> Local deploy task") {
  // Take the code from the HelloWorld example
}

task localUndeploy(
   description:">>> Local undeploy task") {
  // Take the code from the HelloWorld example
}
```

The settings.gradle file is prepared by the project generator wizard, and the gradle.properties file can directly be taken from Chapter 4.

All other files are described in the subsequent sections.

Adding EclipseLink as ORM

To add the EclipseLink ORM to the project, add the following to the dependencies { } section of the build.gradle file:

```
dependencies {
    ...
    implementation 'org.eclipse.persistence:'+
        'eclipselink:2.7.7'
}
```

Next, create a src/main/resources/META-INF/persistence.xml file with the following contents:

```
<persistence
    xmlns=
        "http://java.sun.com/xml/ns/persistence"
```

```
xmlns:xsi=
    "http://www.w3.org/2001/XMLSchema-instance"
xsi:schemaLocation=
    "http://java.sun.com/xml/ns/persistence persistence_1_0.xsd"
version="1.0">
<persistence-unit name="default"
    transaction-type="JTA">
    <jta-data-source>jdbc/Hello</jta-data-source>
    <exclude-unlisted-classes>
      false
    </exclude-unlisted-classes>
    <properties />
</persistence-unit>
</persistence>
```

This is the central configuration file for JPA. Here, we indicate how to connect to the database. Note that we refer to the datasource resources we configured previously.

Note   The Eclipse IDE has a few helper wizards for JPA-related development, and it also has a JPA facet you can add to projects. I decided against using these in this introductory level chapter, to avoid a vendor lock-in and to show the basics needed while following the JPA specification. You are free to try the JPA facet of Eclipse.

Controllers

The controller for the member registration application closely resembles the HelloWorld controller from previous chapters—we again have a landing page that this time lists all the members, and an input form for new members. Adding a member leads to a database INSERT operation, and in contrast to HelloWorld, we don't show a response page but reload the index page with the updated member list. The code reads as follows:

```
package book.javamvc.jpa;

import java.util.ArrayList;
import java.util.List;
```

```java
import java.util.stream.Collectors;

import javax.ejb.EJB;
import javax.enterprise.context.RequestScoped;
import javax.inject.Inject;
import javax.inject.Named;
import javax.mvc.Controller;
import javax.mvc.binding.BindingResult;
import javax.mvc.binding.MvcBinding;
import javax.mvc.binding.ParamError;
import javax.ws.rs.FormParam;
import javax.ws.rs.GET;
import javax.ws.rs.POST;
import javax.ws.rs.Path;
import javax.ws.rs.core.Response;

import book.javamvc.jpa.data.User;
import book.javamvc.jpa.db.MemberDAO;
import book.javamvc.jpa.model.UserEntering;
import book.javamvc.jpa.model.UserList;

@Path("/hello")
@Controller
public class HelloJpaController {
  @Named
  @RequestScoped
  public static class ErrorMessages {
    private List<String> msgs = new ArrayList<>();

    public List<String> getMsgs() {
      return msgs;
    }

    public void setMsgs(List<String> msgs) {
      this.msgs = msgs;
    }

    public void addMessage(String msg) {
```

```java
      msgs.add(msg);
  }
}

@Inject private ErrorMessages errorMessages;
@Inject private BindingResult br;

@Inject private UserEntering userEntering;
@Inject private UserList userList;

@EJB private MemberDAO memberDao;


@GET
public String showIndex() {
  addUserList();
  return "index.jsp";
}

@POST
@Path("/add")
public Response addMember(
      @MvcBinding @FormParam("name") String name) {
  if(br.isFailed()) {
    br.getAllErrors().stream().
        forEach((ParamError pe) -> {
      errorMessages.addMessage(pe.getParamName() +
          ": " + pe.getMessage());
    });
  }

  userEntering.setName(name);

  memberDao.addMember(userEntering.getName());

  addUserList();
  return Response.ok("index.jsp").build();
}
```

```
//////////////////////////////////////////////////////
//////////////////////////////////////////////////////
private void addUserList() {
  userList.addAll(
    memberDao.allMembers().stream().map(member -> {
        return new User(member.getId(),
                          member.getName());
    }).collect(Collectors.toList())
  );
}
}
```

An important distinction in the HelloWorld example application is the inclusion
of the MemberDAO data access object for database operations it gets referred to from the
member addition and listing methods. We'll talk about the DAO in the next sections.

A member deletion is handled by an AJAX request. In contrast to what we did in
previous chapters, we don't let the Java MVC controller deal with AJAX requests. Instead,
we add an additional JAX-RS controller, as follows:

just for AJAX:

```
package book.javamvc.jpa;

import javax.ejb.EJB;
import javax.ws.rs.DELETE;
import javax.ws.rs.Path;
import javax.ws.rs.PathParam;
import javax.ws.rs.core.Response;

import book.javamvc.jpa.db.MemberDAO;

@Path("/ajax")
public class AjaxController {
  @EJB private MemberDAO memberDao;

  @DELETE
  @Path("/delete/{id}")
  public Response delete(@PathParam("id") int id) {
```

```
        memberDao.deleteMember(id);
        return Response.ok("{}").build();
    }
}
```

Adding Data Access Objects

A data access object, or DAO, is a Java class that encapsulates database operations like CRUD (create, read, update, and delete). A client of the DAO then doesn't have to know *how* the DAO works and only needs to take care of the business functionality.

Inside the controllers, a DAO class called MemberDAO is injected via the @EJB annotation. This class goes to the book.javamvc.jpa.db package. Create the package and the class, and then write the following class code:

```
package book.javamvc.jpa.db;

import java.util.List;

import javax.ejb.Stateless;
import javax.persistence.EntityManager;
import javax.persistence.PersistenceContext;
import javax.persistence.TypedQuery;

@Stateless
public class MemberDAO {
    @PersistenceContext
    private EntityManager em;

    public int addMember(String name) {
      List<?> l = em.createQuery(
            "SELECT m FROM Member m WHERE m.name=:name").
         setParameter("name",  name).
         getResultList();
      int id = 0;
      if(l.isEmpty()) {
        Member member = new Member();
        member.setName(name);
```

```
      em.persist(member);
      em.flush(); // needed to get the ID
      id = member.getId();
    } else {
      id = ((Member)l.get(0)).getId();
    }
    return id;
  }

  public List<Member> allMembers() {
    TypedQuery<Member> q = em.createQuery(
      "SELECT m FROM Member m", Member.class);
    List<Member> l = q.getResultList();
    return l;
  }

  public void deleteMember(int id) {
    Member member = em.find(Member.class, id);
    em.remove(member);
  }
}
```

We provide methods to add members (avoiding duplicates), to list all members, and to delete members. Update and search methods are left for future improvements. You can see that database operations are exclusively handled by an `EntityManager`, which is injected by the `@PersistenceContext` annotation. By the configuration file `persistence.xml`, JPA knows which database the entity manager needs to access. For most operations currently needed, we can use the methods from the `EntityManager` class. The only exception is the complete list for which we use the JPA query language expression `SELECT m FROM Member m`.

The application knows that this DAO is an EJB by the `@Stateless` class annotation. Because of this, the container (the part of the server that handles EJB objects) knows that instances of this class don't have a state.

Updating the View

For the basic member registration application, as a view, we only need the index.jsp file:

```jsp
<%@ page contentType="text/html;charset=UTF-8"
    language="java" %>
<%@ taglib prefix="c"
    uri="http://java.sun.com/jsp/jstl/core" %>
<%@ taglib prefix="fmt"
    uri="http://java.sun.com/jsp/jstl/fmt" %>
<html>
<head>
    <meta charset="UTF-8">
    <script type="text/javascript"
      src="${mvc.basePath}/../js/jquery-3.5.1.min.js">
    </script>
    <title>${msg.title}</title>
    <script type="text/javascript">
      function deleteItm(id) {
        var url =
          "${pageContext.servletContext.contextPath}" +
              "/mvc/ajax/delete/" + id;
        jQuery.ajax({
          url : url,
          method: "DELETE",
          dataType: 'json',
          success: function(data, textStatus, jqXHR) {
              jQuery('#itm-'+id).remove();
          },
          error: function (jqXHR, textStatus,
                           errorThrown) {
            console.log(errorThrown);
          }
        });
        return false;
      }
```

```
      </script>
  </head>
  <body>
    <form method="post"
        action="${mvc.uriBuilder(
            'HelloJpaController#greeting').build()}">
      ${msg.enter_name}
      <input type="text" name="name" />
      <input type="submit" value="${msg.btn_submit}" />
    </form>

    <table>
      <thead>
        <tr>
          <th>${msg.tblhdr_id}</th>
          <th>${msg.tblhdr_name}</th>
          <th></th>
        </tr>
      <thead>
      <tbody>
        <c:forEach    items="${userList}" var="itm">
          <tr id="itm-${itm.id}">
            <td>${itm.id}</td>
            <td>${itm.name}</td>
            <td><button onclick="deleteItm(${itm.id})">
                ${msg.btn_delete}</button></td>
          </tr>
        </c:forEach>
      </tbody>
    </table>
  </body>
</html>
```

This page shows the form for entering a new member and the full member list.
Because of the itm-[ID] we add to each table row, the AJAX code to remove an item can
remove a table row without having to reload the full page.

The view refers to the jQuery library. Download it and copy it to `src/main/webapp/js`. Adapt versions accordingly.

A language resource goes to `src/main/resources/book/javamvc/jpa/messages/Messages.properties`:

```
title = Hello Jpa
enter_name = Enter your name:
btn_delete = Delete
btn_submit = Submit
tblhdr_id = ID
tblhdr_name = Name
```

You can copy the `beans.xml` and `glassfish-web.xml` files from Chapter 4.

Adding Entities

An entity is a representation of a table row as an object. If we think of the MEMBER table, an entity is something that has a name and a single ID. Obviously, this corresponds to a Java class with the `name` and `id` fields. So we create such a class and put it in the `book.javamvc.jpa.db` package:

```
public class Member {
    private int id; // + getter/setter
    private String name; // + getter/setter
}
```

To complete the database-interfacing process, we need to add meta-information though. The information that this is an entity class, the table name, column names, a dedicated ID column name, a unique ID generator specification, and database field value constraints. As is usually the case with Java, we use annotations for such meta-information. Our class, with all those amendments, reads as follows:

```
package book.javamvc.jpa.db;

import javax.persistence.Column;
import javax.persistence.Entity;
import javax.persistence.GeneratedValue;
```

```java
import javax.persistence.GenerationType;
import javax.persistence.Id;
import javax.persistence.SequenceGenerator;
import javax.persistence.Table;
import javax.validation.constraints.NotNull;

@Entity
@Table(name="MEMBER")
@SequenceGenerator(name="HELLO_SEQ",
                   initialValue=1, allocationSize = 50)
public class Member {
  @Id
  @GeneratedValue(strategy = GenerationType.IDENTITY,
       generator = "HELLO_SEQ")
  @Column(name = "id")
  private int id;

  @NotNull
  @Column(name = "name")
  private String name;

  public int getId() {
    return id;
  }

  public void setId(int id) {
    this.id = id;
  }

  public String getName() {
    return name;
  }

  public void setName(String name) {
    this.name = name;
  }
}
```

In detail, the annotations we added are:

- @Entity: Marks this as an entity so JPA knows this is an entity class.

- @Table: Used to specify the table name. If omitted, the class name (without package) will be used as a table name.

- @SequenceGenerator: Used to specify a sequence generator for unique IDs.

- @Id: Indicates that the corresponding field refers to the unique ID of the entity.

- @GeneratedValue: Indicates that new entities will auto-generate values for this field.

- @Column: Used to specify the column name corresponding to this field. If unspecified, the field name will be used as the column name.

- @NotNull: A constraint indicating that neither the field nor the database field can be null.

Given the entity classes, JPA now knows how to map database entry fields to Java classes. With the Java MVC controller adapted and the DAO and entity classes added, the application has a fully functional JPA support engaged and you can deploy and try it at http://localhost:8080/HelloJpa. Also try restarting the server and verify that the entries were persisted and survive a server restart. You can also directly check the database using a database client tool and investigate the table rows that were added there.

Adding Relations

Relational data is about relationships like one table entry referring to entries from other tables. JPA provides a solution to such relationships, again by special annotations you can add to entity classes.

Consider the following example: In our membership application, we add another table called STATUS that contains membership status entries, such as Gold, Platinum, Senior, or whatever you might think of. Each member may have 0 to N status entries, so we talk about a "one-to-many" relationship between members and status entries.

To achieve this, we first create the STATUS table and a STATUS_SEQ sequence for it:

```
CREATE TABLE STATUS (
    ID          INT           NOT NULL,
    MEMBER_ID   INT           NOT NULL,
    NAME        VARCHAR(128)  NOT NULL,
  PRIMARY KEY (ID));

CREATE SEQUENCE STATUS_SEQ start with 1 increment by 50;
```

Next, we create a new entity class called Status inside the book.javamvc.jpa.db package with the following contents:

```java
package book.jakarta8.calypsojpa.jpa;

import javax.persistence.*;
import javax.validation.constraints.*;

@Entity
@Table(name="STATUS")
@SequenceGenerator(name="STATUS_SEQ",
                   initialValue=1, allocationSize = 50)
public class Status implements Comparable<Status> {
    @Id
    @GeneratedValue(strategy = GenerationType.IDENTITY,
                    generator="STATUS_SEQ")

    @Column(name = "ID")
    private int id;

    @NotNull
    @Column(name = "MEMBER_ID")
    private int memberId;

    @NotNull
    @Column(name = "NAME")
    private String name;

    public Status() {
    }

    public Status(String name) {
```

```
    this.name = name;
  }

  @Override
  public int compareTo(Status o) {
    return -o.name.compareTo(name);
  }

  // + getters and setters
}
```

We added a constructor for easy construction using the name. It is important to know that the JPA specification requires that there be a public no-argument constructor.

Inside the entity class Member, we add a field that corresponds to the actual relationship between member and status:

```
...
@JoinColumn(name = "MEMBER_ID")
@OneToMany(cascade = CascadeType.ALL, orphanRemoval= true)
private Set<Status> status; // + getter / setters
...
```

Everything else is untouched. The @JoinColumn field refers to a member in the *associated* class or table, so we don't have to update the member table for this new field.

Because the two entity classes' relationship is announced via @OneToMany, any entity manager operations will automatically take care of correctly cascading database operations to related entities. For example, to create a new member, you can write the following:

```
...
Member m = new Member();
m.setName(...);

Set<Status> status = new HashSet<>();
status.add(new Status("Platinum"));
status.add(new Status("Priority"));
m.setStatus(status);

em.persist(m);
...
```

So you don't have to explicitly tell the entity manager to persist the related Status entities.

In the frontend code, you can add a text field with a comma-separated list of status values, or a select listbox or menu to reflect the relationship. The same holds for UPDATE and DELETE operations. Because of the cascade = CascadeType.ALL inside the @OneToMany annotation, JPA will even delete related Status entries from the STATUS table if members are deleted.

There are other association types in a relational data model. The possible association types you can declare for entities in JPA are as follows:

- **@OneToMany**

  For entities of entity class A, zero to many related entries of entity class B exist. Inside class A, you define a field of type Set with the OneToMany annotation. Inside entity B's table, you then have a foreign key called ID_A (or whatever name you like), and inside the entity class B is a field called aId (or whatever name you like) pointing to A IDs. To tell A how it is related to B, you then add another annotation called @JoinColumn, as in:

  ```
  @OneToMany
  @JoinColumn(name="ID_A")   // In table B!
  private Set<B> b;
  ```

  Or you add an attribute to @OneToMany, as in:

  ```
  @OneToMany(mappedBy = "aId") // Field in class B!
  private Set<B> b;
  ```

- **@ManyToOne**

  For zero or many entities of entity class A, one related entry of entity class B exists. Inside class A, you add a field of type B with the @ManyToOne and @JoinColumn annotations, where for the latter, you provide a column name (inside A's table) for the join:

  ```
  @ManyToOne
  @JoinColumn(name="ID_B") // In table A
  private B b;
  ```

- **@OneToOne**

  For one entity of entity class A, one related entry of entity class B
  exists. Inside class A, you add a field of type B with the @OneToOne
  and @JoinColumn annotations, where for the latter, you provide a
  column name (inside A's table) for the join:

  ```
  @OneToOne
  @JoinColumn(name="ID_B") // In table A
  private B b;
  ```

- **@ManyToMany**

  For zero or many entities of entity class A, zero or many related
  entries of entity class B exist. Here, we need a third table serving as an
  intermediate join table; for example MTM_A_B, with columns ID_A and
  ID_B. The annotations in entity class A (with ID column "ID") then
  read as follows:

  ```
  @ManyToMany
  @JoinTable(
    name = "MTM_A_B",
    joinColumns = @JoinColumn(
      name = "ID_A",
      referencedColumnName="ID"),
    inverseJoinColumns = @JoinColumn(
      name = "ID_B",
      referencedColumnName="ID"))
  private Set<B> b;
  ```

Exercises

Exercise 1: Which of the following are true?

1. JPA connects to a database via some datasource, which is a server-
   managed resource.

2. JPA connects to a database via some datasource, which JPA itself
   provides.

3. JPA connects to a database via JDBC.

4. JPA connects to a database via EJB.

Exercise 2: Which component of JPA (or *concept,* if you like) translates between database tables and Java objects (three letter acronym)?

Exercise 3: Which of the following is true:

1. DAOs are needed to connect to databases via JPA.

2. DAOs are needed to provide the database username and password.

3. In DAOs, database column names have to be specified.

4. DAOs are used to avoid using database table details in JPA client classes.

5. To use DAOs, they must be injected as EJBs.

Exercise 4: Which of the following are true?

1. One entity class corresponds to one database table.

2. An entity class must have the same name as the database table.

3. Properties (fields) of entity classes must have the same names as the columns in the database table.

4. Properties of entity classes can have restrictions.

Exercise 5: Add the STATUS table to the database and update the member entry application's code to reflect the status of members. For simplicity, use a text field whereby you can enter a comma-separated list of status values.

Exercise 6: Name the four annotations used inside JPA for relationships between tables.

Summary

JPA (Java Persistence API) is the dedicated technology used to accessing relational databases from inside Jakarta EE. Its aim is to provide a bridge between SQL tables and Java objects.

One of the primary purposes of JPA is to abstract away database access and map database objects to Java classes. In the end, we want to be able to query the database and get Java objects, or to put Java objects in the database. JPA helps to hide the details of how this can be done, including connection properties like usernames and passwords, and including handling connection lifecycles.

The central JPA class for this purpose is the `EntityManager` class, which uses a single configuration file called `persistence.xml`, together with some settings inside the Jakarta EE application server. On the Java side, the classes that correspond to table rows are called *entity* classes.

In order for JPA to work, we need to add an *object relational mapping* (ORM) library to the project. There are several options here, but we choose EclipseLink as an ORM library, since EclipseLink is the reference implementation of JPA 2.2 (this is the version of JPA used in Jakarta EE 8 and Java MVC 1.0).

ORMs do not directly connect to databases, but instead connect to datasources that abstract away the database access. This indirection allows for establishing connection pools, caches, transactionality, and administration of data handling using server-side administrative tools. Datasources are installed in a server product specific manner.

A data access object, or DAO, is a Java class that encapsulates database operations like CRUD (create, read, update, and delete). A client of the DAO then doesn't have to know *how* the DAO works and only needs to take care of the business functionality.

An entity is a representation of a table row as an object. To complete the database-interfacing process, we need to add meta-information. The information that this is an entity class, the table name, column names, a dedicated ID column name, a unique ID generator specification, and database field value constraints. As is usually the case with Java, we use annotations for such meta-information.

Given the entity classes, JPA now knows how to map database entry fields to Java classes. With the Java MVC controller adapted and the DAO and entity classes added, the application has fully functional JPA support engaged.

Relational data is about relationships, such as one table entry referring to entries from other tables. JPA provides a solution to such relations, again by special annotations you can add to entity classes.

The possible association types you can declare for entities in JPA are as follows:

- **@OneToMany**

  For entities of entity class A, zero to many related entries of entity class B exist. Inside class A, you define a field of type Set with the OneToMany annotation. Inside entity B's table, you then have a foreign key called ID_A (or whatever name you like), and inside the entity class B is a aId field (or whatever name you like) pointing to A IDs. To tell A how it is related to B, you then add another annotation called @JoinColumn, as in:

  ```
  @OneToMany
  @JoinColumn(name="ID_A")   // In table B!
  private Set<B> b;
  ```

  Or you add an attribute to @OneToMany, as in:

  ```
  @OneToMany(mappedBy = "aId") // Field in class B!
  private Set<B> b;
  ```

- **@ManyToOne**

  For zero or many entities of entity class A, one related entry of entity class B exists. Inside class A, you add a field of type B with the @ManyToOne and @JoinColumn annotations, where for the latter you provide a column name (inside A's table) for the join:

  ```
  @ManyToOne
  @JoinColumn(name="ID_B") // In table A
  private B b;
  ```

- **@OneToOne**

  For one entity of entity class A, one related entry of entity class B exists. Inside class A, you add a field of type B with the @OneToOne and @JoinColumn annotations, where for the latter, you provide a column name (inside A's table) for the join:

  ```
  @OneToOne
  @JoinColumn(name="ID_B") // In table A
  private B b;
  ```

– **@ManyToMany**

For zero or many entities of entity class A, zero or many related entries of entity class B exist. Here, we need a third table serving as an intermediate join table; for example, MTM_A_B, with columns ID_A and ID_B. The annotations in entity class A (with ID column "ID") then read as follows:

```
@ManyToMany
@JoinTable(
  name = "MTM_A_B",
  joinColumns = @JoinColumn(
    name = "ID_A",
    referencedColumnName="ID"),
  inverseJoinColumns = @JoinColumn(
    name = "ID_B",
    referencedColumnName="ID"))
private Set<B> b;
```

In the next chapter, we talk about logging in Java MVC.

CHAPTER 11

Logging Java MVC Applications

Logging is a vital part of any application of mid- to high-level complexity. While the program runs through its execution paths, several logging statements describe what the program is doing, which parameters are passed to method calls, what values local variables and class fields have and how they change, which decisions are made, and so on. This logging information is collected and sent to a file, a database, a message queue, or whatever, and the developer and the operations team can investigate program flows for bug-fixing or auditing purposes.

This chapter is about the various options you have to add logging to your programs or to investigate existing server logging.

System Streams

The Java Standard Environment (JSE) on which Jakarta EE builds its server technologies provides the well-known standard output and error output streams you address as follows:

```
System.out.println("Some information: ...");
System.err.println("Some error: ...");
```

While at first sight, it seems easy to generate diagnostic information using these streams, it is not recommended that you use this procedure. The primary reason is that method is highly operating system and server product dependent. We will introduce superior methods shortly, but in case you are temporarily tempted to use the system streams for diagnostic output, it is important to know that most Jakarta EE servers fetch the streams and redirect them to some file.

© Peter Späth 2021
P. Späth, *Beginning Java MVC 1.0*, https://doi.org/10.1007/978-1-4842-6280-1_11

Note   Up until now, we used the output and error output streams for diagnostic output. We did that for simplicity. In any serious project, you should not do that, and the subsequent sections show you how to avoid it.

The Jakarta EE 8 GlassFish server version 5.1 adds the output and error output stream to the `server.log` file you will find at

`GLASSFISH_INST/glassfish/domains/domain1/logs`

In this usually verbose listing, you will recognize the `System.out` and `System.err` output as lines containing an [`SEVERE`] (for `System.err`) and [`INFO`] (for `System.out`):

```
...
[2019-05-20T14:42:03.791+0200] [glassfish 5.1] [SEVERE]
    [] [] [tid: _ThreadID=28 _ThreadName=Thread-9]
    [timeMillis: 1558356123791] [levelValue: 1000] [[
    The System.err message ]]
...
[2019-05-20T14:42:03.796+0200] [glassfish 5.1] [INFO]
    [NCLS-CORE-00022] [javax.enterprise.system.core]
    [tid: _ThreadID=28
    _ThreadName=RunLevelControllerThread-1558356114688]
    [timeMillis: 1558356123796] [levelValue: 800] [[
    The System.out message ]]
...
```

We will later learn how to change the verbosity level and the format of these logging lines.

JDK Logging in GlassFish

The logging API specification JSR 47 is part of Java and can be used by any Java program, including Jakarta EE server applications and of course Java MVC programs. You can download the specification from `https://jcp.org/en/jsr/detail?id=47`.

GlassFish Log Files

GlassFish uses this platform standard API JSR 47 for logging. Unless you change the configuration, you can find the logging file at

`GLASSFISH_INST/glassfish/domains/domain1/logs/server.log`

In the same folder, you will also find archived logs called `server.log_TS`, were TS is a timestamp, such as `2019-05-08T15-45-58`.

The standard logging format is defined as a combination of various information snippets, of course including the actual logging message:

```
[Timestamp] [Product-ID]
    [Message-Type] [Message-ID] [Logger-Name] [Thread-ID]
    [Raw-Timestamp] [Log-Level]
    [[Message]]
```

For example:

```
[2019-05-20T14:42:03.796+0200] [glassfish 5.1] [INFO]
    [NCLS-CORE-00022] [javax.enterprise.system.core]
    [tid: _ThreadID=28
    _ThreadName=RunLevelControllerThread-1558356114688]
    [timeMillis: 1558356123796]
    [levelValue: 800]
    [[Loading application xmlProcessing done in 742 ms]]
```

Adding Logging Output to the Console

If you want to have the logging output also appear in the terminal where your start the GlassFish server, use the following:

```
cd GLASSFISH_INST
bin/asadmin start-domain --verbose
```

This will show the complete logging output. It will also not place the server process in the background, as a `asadmin start-domain` without –verbose does, so the server will be stopped when you close the terminal. You will not be able to enter more commands into the terminal after the server started (for new commands you can of course enter a second terminal). To stop this foreground server process, press Ctrl+C.

Using the Standard Logging API for Your Own Projects

To add diagnostic output to your own classes using the JSR 47 methodology, you write something like the following in your classes:

```
...
import java.util.logging.Logger;

public class MyClass {
  private final static Logger LOG =
      Logger.getLogger(MyClass.class.toString());

  public void someMethod() {
    LOG.entering(this.getClass().toString(),"someMethod");
    ...
    // different logging levels:
    LOG.finest("Finest: ...");
    LOG.finer("Finer: ...");
    LOG.fine("Fine: ...");
    LOG.info("Some info: ...");
    LOG.warning("Some warning: ...");
    LOG.severe("Severe: ...");
    ...
    LOG.exiting(this.getClass().toString(),"someMethod");
  }
  ...
}
```

For LOG.entering(), there is also a variant where you can add method parameters to the logging statement. Likewise, for LOG.exiting(), a variant allows you to add a returned value to the logging statement:

```
  ...
  public String someMethod(String p1, int p2) {
    LOG.entering(this.getClass().toString(),"someMethod",
```

```
        new Object[]{ p1, p2 });
    ...
    String res = ...;
    LOG.exiting(this.getClass().toString(),"someMethod",
        res);
    return res;
  }
  ...
}
```

Logging Levels

From these examples, you can see there are several levels you can use to indicate the severity of logging output. For standard logging, the levels are, in order, *severe* ➤ *warning* ➤ *info* ➤ *fine* ➤ *finer* ➤ *finest*. This greatly improves the usability of logging. At an early stage of a project, you can set the logging threshold to a low value, for example `fine`, and you will see all the `fine`-level logging and all higher levels up to `severe` in the logging file.

If you lower the threshold (to `finest`, for example), the logging shows more detail, but the logging file will be larger of course. This is why you do this for bug-fixing purposes; having more detail helps you more easily identify problematic code. Later in the project, when the maturity rises, you apply a higher threshold (such as `warning` for example). This way, the logging file does not get too big, but you still see important issues in the logging.

The special `Logger` methods called `entering()` and `exiting()` belong to the log level `finer`. All the other methods we showed here match the equally named level, so a `LOG.severe()` belongs to level `severe`, a `LOG.warning()` belongs to level `warning`, and so on.

The Logger Hierarchy and Thresholds

If you create a logger like this:

```
Logger.getLogger("com.example.projxyz.domain.Person");
```

You can span up a hierarchy com ➤ com.example ➤com.example.projxyz ➤ com. example.projxyz.domain ➤ com.example.projxyz.domain.Person.

This plays a role if you assign logging thresholds. This assignment happens in the configuration, via asadmin, or in the web administration console. We will see shortly how to do that. It is important to know that the threshold setting follows the logger hierarchy. If you assign a level LEV1 (severe, warning, info, and so on) to com, this means the complete subtree at com gets the LEV1 threshold., unless you also specify levels for elements deeper in the hierarchy. So if you also assign a LEV2 level to com.example, LEV2 takes precedence over LEV1 for com.example and all elements deeper in that hierarchy. More precisely, the rules are shown in Table 11-1.

Table 11-1. *Logging Hierarchy Rules*

Hierarchy	Level	Logger	Description
com	FINE	com.ClassA	FINE applies, because com.ClassA is inside the com hierarchy.
com	FINE	org.ClassA	FINE does not apply, because org.ClassA is not inside the com hierarchy.
com.ClassA	FINER	com.ClassA	FINER applies, because com.ClassA is inside the com.ClassA hierarchy. FINE no longer applies, because the hierarchy specification com.ClassA is more specific compared to just com.
com.example	WARNING	com.ClassA	WARNING does not apply, because com.ClassA is not inside the com.example hierarchy.
com.example	WARNING	com.example.ClassA	WARNING applies, because com.example.ClassA is inside the com.example hierarchy. The level specified for com no longer applies, because com.example is more specific compared to com.
com.example	WARNING	org.example.ClassA	WARNING does not apply, because org. is not inside the com.example hierarchy.

The Logging Configuration

The logging configuration of a JSR 47 standard logging relies on a configuration file called logging.properties. Normally, this file resides in the JDK installation directory, but the GlassFish server overrules the standard logging configuration and uses this file instead:

```
GLASSFISH_INST/glassfish/domains/domain1/
     config/logging.properties
```

Here, the various logging properties are specified. We don't talk about all of them—the specification for JSR 47 and the GlassFish server documentation will give you more ideas. The most important settings are the level thresholds. You will find them under the #All log level details line:

```
...
#All log level details
com.sun.enterprise.server.logging.GFFileHandler.level=ALL
javax.enterprise.system.tools.admin.level=INFO
org.apache.jasper.level=INFO
javax.enterprise.system.core.level=INFO
javax.enterprise.system.core.classloading.level=INFO
java.util.logging.ConsoleHandler.level=FINEST
javax.enterprise.system.tools.deployment.level=INFO
javax.enterprise.system.core.transaction.level=INFO
org.apache.catalina.level=INFO
org.apache.coyote.level=INFO
javax.level=INFO
...
```

Here, we already have an example for the hierarchic level assignment: if you change the level at javax.enterprise.system.core.level to FINE, any javax. logger will use the threshold INFO because of the javax.level = INFO line, but a javax.enterprise.system.core.Main logger will use FINE, because it matches the level we just entered and is more specific.

A setting of the form .level=INFO later in the logging.properties file ensures that all loggers not dedicatedly specified in the logging properties will use the INFO threshold.

That is why, in the standard configuration variant of GlassFish, no `fine`, `finer`, or `finest` messages appear.

Instead of changing the file, you can also use the web administration console at `http://localhost:4848`. Navigate to Configurations ➤ Server-Config ➤ Logger Settings. Changes will be directly written to the `logging.properties` file.

As a third way to change the logging configuration, the `asadmin` command-line utility provides us with various logging related subcommands. The following shows you some examples:

```
./asadmin list-log-levels
# -> A list of all log levels, like
# javax                           <INFO>
# javax.mail                      <INFO>
# javax.org.glassfish.persistence <INFO>
# org.apache.catalina             <INFO>
# org.apache.coyote               <INFO>
# org.apache.jasper               <INFO>
# ...

./asadmin delete-log-levels javax.mail
# -> Deletes a level specification

./asadmin set-log-levels javax.mail=WARNING
# -> Setting a specific log level

./asadmin list-log-attributes
# -> Shows all log attributes (not the levels)

./asadmin set-log-attributes \
    com.sun.enterprise.server.logging.
    GFFileHandler.rotationLimitInBytes=2000000
# (discard the line break after "logging.")
# -> Sets an attribute. Attribute names are the same
# as in the logging.properties file

./asadmin rotate-log
# -> Manually rotates the log file. Takes the current
# server.log file, archives it and starts a fresh
# empty server.log file.
```

Logging level changes are dynamic, so you can change logging levels while the server is running.

The Logging Format

For the JSR 47 standard logging, the logging format is prescribed by the logging handler. In order to change the logging format, you have to develop a new logging handler. This is not particularly hard to achieve, but we leave it to your discretion if you need to change the format and want to stick to the Java platform logging.

Otherwise, you can easily switch to using a logging library. Most of the candidates for such a choice allow you to change the logging format by adjusting a configuration property. We will shortly talk about the Log4j logging framework and also discuss the logging formatting options that Log4j provides.

Using JDK Standard Logging for Other Servers

Although most developers prefer to use a logging library like Apache Commons Logging, Log4j, or Logback, you can use the JSR 47 logging for servers other than GlassFish as well. Just make sure you provide a customized `logging.properties` file. Do not change the `logging.properties` file in the JDK installation folder, though—changing the configuration there is highly discouraged.

Instead, provide your own `logging.properties` file and add the following to the server startup parameters (on one line, remove the line break and the spaces after =):

```
-Djava.util.logging.config.file=
    /path/to/logging.properties
```

Your server documentation will tell you how to do that.

Adding Log4j Logging to Your Application

Log4j is a logging framework often used for all kinds of Java applications. Its features include:

- Clear separation of API and implementation. In a server environment, you install the Log4j implementation on the server itself, while on the clients, you only refer to a small-footprint Log4j API library.

- High performance. Log4j includes lambda support, so message calculations can be avoided if a corresponding log level will not be logged. For example, in `LOG.info("Error", () -> expensiveOperation())`, the method call will not happen if `info`-level messages are disabled for the logger.

- Automatic configuration reloading. For Log4j, it is easy to enable automatic configuration reloading. Any change in the logging configuration will then be applied immediately without a server restart.

- The logging format and various other logging properties can be set in the configuration.

- The Log4 configuration files can be formatted in XML, Java properties, JSON, and YAML.

- Log4j can easily be extended by plugins.

Log4j can be downloaded from `http://logging.apache.org/log4j/2.x/`. The still widely used Log4j version 1.x is deprecated and we will not talk about Log4j in version 1.x in this book.

Log4j needs a couple of additional permissions in order to pass security checks. For this aim, open this file:

```
GLASSFISH_INST/glassfish/domains/domain1/
    config/server.policy
```

And add the following to the end:

```
// Added for Log4j2
grant {
    permission
        java.lang.reflect.ReflectPermission
        "suppressAccessChecks";
    permission
        javax.management.MBeanServerPermission "*";
    permission
        javax.management.MBeanPermission "*", "*";
    permission
        java.lang.RuntimePermission "getenv.*";
};
```

Caution   This requirement is specific to the GlassFish server. For other servers, different settings might be necessary.

Adding Log4j Server-Wide

Adding Log4j server-wide means you put the Log4j implementation into a common libraries folder, write one Log4j configuration file, which serves all Jakarta EE applications running on that server at once, and let all applications and application modules use the Log4j API. This setting needs to be configured only once and then all the current and future applications on a server can easily use Log4 for their logging purposes. Because it's simple, this way of including Log4j is probably used most often. You can instead add Log4j on a per-application basis, but you should do this only if you have important reasons to encapsulate Log4j with the applications, such as if you are also running legacy applications that use old Log4j 1.x versions. We describe this method a little bit later.

To add Log4j server-wide, you first download the Log4j distribution from `https://logging.apache.org/log4j/2.x/`. Then copy the `log4j-core-2.11.2.jar`, `log4j-api-2.11.2.jar`, and `log4j-appserver-2.11.2` files (or whatever version you downloaded) to the following folder:

```
GLASSFISH_INST/glassfish/domains/domain1/
    modules/autostart
```

Note   The Log4j JAR files are implemented as OSGi bundles. This is why we put them into the `modules` folder. If you don't know OSGi, consider it an advanced library management framework.

Then add a file called `log4j2.json` to the `GLASSFISH_INST/glassfish/domains/domain1/lib/classes` folder. As basic contents of this file, use:

```json
{
"configuration": {
  "name": "Default",
  "appenders": {
    "RollingFile": {
      "name":"File",
      "fileName":
          "${sys:com.sun.aas.instanceRoot}/logs/log4j.log",
      "filePattern":
          "${sys:com.sun.aas.instanceRoot}/
          logs/log4j-backup-%d{MM-dd-yy-HH-mm-ss}-%i.gz",
      "PatternLayout": {
          "pattern":
              "%d{yyyy-MM-dd HH:mm:ss} %-5p %c{1}:%L - %m%n"
      },
      "Policies": {
        "SizeBasedTriggeringPolicy": {
            "size":"10 MB"
        }
      },
```

```
        "DefaultRolloverStrategy": {
           "max":"10"
        }
      }
   },
   "loggers": {
     "logger" : [
        {
           "name" : "book.javamvc",
           "level":"debug",
           "appender-ref": {
              "ref":"File"
           }
        },{
           "name" : "some.other.logger",
           "level":"info",
           "appender-ref": {
              "ref":"File"
           }
        }
     ],
     "root": {
         "level":"error",
         "appender-ref": {
            "ref":"File"
         }
     }
   }
 }
}
```

This adds a root logger with the error level and two more loggers, called
book.javamvc and some.other.logger, with threshold levels set to debug and info,
respectively. The logger names inside the "logger" array correspond to logger hierarchy
specifications. They work the same way as described for the standard JDK logging
process (JSR 47). So the book.javamvc logger applies to logging statements

for book.javamvc.SomeClass and book.javamvc.pckg.OtherClass, but not to book.jakarta99.FooClass. The special "root" logger serves as the default and matches all loggers for which no explicit logger specification can be found.

This file gives you a starting point. You can add more appenders and loggers. See the latest Log4j2 documentation on the Internet to learn how to extend the configuration.

Note   Log4j allows configuration files to use different formats. We chose the JSON format because of its conciseness.

If the server is running, restart it. This needs to be done because of the global nature of adding Log4j this way. You can now start using Log4j in your applications, as described in the "Using Log4j in the Coding" section.

Note   Add -Dlog4j2.debug as a server startup JVM parameter to get more output about what Log4j is doing. This meta-diagnostic information is printed to the standard server.log file.

Changing the Logging Format

In the Log4j configuration file, we already specified a logging pattern:

```
...
"pattern":
    "%d{yyyy-MM-dd HH:mm:ss} %-5p %c{1}:%L - %m%n"
...
```

This prints a timestamp, as specified by %d{yyyy-MM-dd HH:mm:ss}, the logging level as specified by %p (the −5 adds a padding to the output), the last path element of the logger name as specified by %c{1}, the line number because of the %L, and the message because of the %m. The %n finally adds a line break at the end.

You can change this at will. The section entitled "Layouts" of online Log4j2 manual lists all the options. Table 11-2 shows the most important options.

Table 11-2. *Logging Patterns*

Pattern	Description
m	The message.
C	The name of the logger.
c[N]	Only the last *N* path parts of the logger name. So with a logger called org.example.memory.Main, a %c{1} creates Main as output, a %{2} creates memory.Main, and so on.
c[-N]	Remove the first N path parts of the logger name. So with a logger called org.example.memory.Main, a %c{-1} creates example.memory.Main, and so on.
c[1.]	Replaces all but the last part of the logger name with a dot ".". So with a logger called org.example.memory.Main, a %c{1.} creates o.e.m.Main.
p	The log level.
-5p	The log level, right-padded with spaces to five characters.
d	Outputs a timestamp like 2019-09-23 07:23:45,123.
d[DEFAULT_MICROS]	Same as plain %d, but adds the microseconds: 2019-09-23 07:23:45,123456.
d[ISO8601]	Output such as 2019-09-23T07:23:45,123.
d[UNIX_MILLIS]	Milliseconds since 1970-01-01 00:00:00 UTC.
highlight{p}	Adds ANSI colors to the enclosed pattern, p. For example: highlight{%d %-5p %c{1.}: %m}%n.
L	The line number. This is an expensive operation; use it with care.
M	The method name. This is an expensive operation; use it with care.
n	Line break.
t	The name of the thread.
T	The ID of the thread.

Log4j2 also creates logging output in CSV format, in GELF format, embedded in a HTML page, and as JSON, XML, or YAML. See the Log4j2 manual for details.

Adding Log4j to Jakarta EE Web Applications

If you think you should add Log4j on a per-application basis and leave other applications running on the server unaffected, you can add the Log4j implementation to your web application (WAR).

Note   Running Log4j in such an isolated way could be necessary if your server is also running legacy applications that use the the old Log4j 1.x .

To add the Log4j implementation, we update the dependencies in our Gradle build file. Open the `build.gradle` file and add the following to the `dependencies { }` section:

```
implementation 'org.apache.logging.log4j:log4j-core
  :2.11.2'
implementation 'com.fasterxml.jackson.core:jackson-core
  :2.7.4'
implementation 'com.fasterxml.jackson.core:jackson-
  databind:2.7.4'
implementation 'com.fasterxml.jackson.core:jackson-
  annotations:2.7.4'
```

Here, the central part is the dependency on `log4j-core`; the dependencies on `jackson` are needed because we will be using JSON-formatted configuration files and Log4j needs `jackson` to parse them.

The Log4j configuration file needs to be called `log4j2.json` and it must be placed in the `src/main/resources` folder for web applications (WARs). As a simple configuration, set the contents of `log4j2.json` to the following:

```
{
"configuration": {
  "name": "Default",
  "appenders": {
    "RollingFile": {
      "name":"File",
      "fileName":
          "${sys:com.sun.aas.instanceRoot}/logs/log4j.log",
      "filePattern":
```

```
            "${sys:com.sun.aas.instanceRoot}/
            logs/log4j-backup-%d{MM-dd-yy-HH-mm-ss}-%i.gz",
        "PatternLayout": {
            "pattern":
                "%d{yyyy-MM-dd HH:mm:ss} %-5p %c{1}:%L - %m%n"
        },
        "Policies": {
            "SizeBasedTriggeringPolicy": {
                "size":"10 MB"
            }
        },
        "DefaultRolloverStrategy": {
            "max":"10"
        }
    }
},
"loggers": {
    "logger" : [
        {
            "name" : "book.javamvc",
            "level":"debug",
            "appender-ref": {
            "ref":"File"
            }
        },{
            "name" : "some.other.logger",
            "level":"debug",
            "appender-ref": {
            "ref":"File"
            }
        }
    ],
    "root": {
        "level":"debug",
        "appender-ref": {
```

```
        "ref":"File"
      }
    }
  }
}
}
```

Using Log4j in the Coding

To use Log4 in your Java MVC application, make sure each project in question has the following Gradle dependency:

```
implementation 'org.apache.logging.log4j:log4j-api:2.11.2'
```

You then import Logger and LogManager into the classes and use a static logger field, as follows:

```
import org.apache.logging.log4j.*;

public class SomeClass {
  private final static Logger LOG =
      LogManager.getLogger(SomeClass.class);
  ...
  public void someMethod() {
    ...
    // different logging levels:
    LOG.trace("Trace: ...");
    LOG.debug("Debug: ...");
    LOG.info("Some info: ...");
    LOG.warn("Some warning: ...");
    LOG.error("Some error: ...");
    LOG.fatal("Some fatal error: ...");
    ...
    // Logging in try-catch clauses
    try {
      ...
    } catch(Exception e) {
      ...
```

```
        LOG.error("Some error", e);
    }
  }
}
```

Inside the `log4j2.json` configuration file, the `level` inside each logger then declares a logging threshold:

```
"loggers": {
  "logger": [
    {
        "name":"book.javamvc",
        "level":"debug",
        "appender-ref": {
          "ref":"appenderName"
        }
    }
    ...
  ]
  ...
}
```

The level can be set to `trace`, `debug`, `info`, `warn`, `error`, or `fatal`.

Exercises

Exercise 1: Add JSR 47 logging (in the `java.util.logging` package) to the `@PostConstruct public void init()` and `@Override public Map<String, Object> getProperties()` methods of the App class from Chapter 4 (the `HelloWorld` application). Tell how to enter each method, and also about the properties set in `getProperties()`.

Exercise 2: Add server-wide Log4j logging to your GlassFish server. Choose any of your projects and add Log4j logging to it.

Summary

Logging is a vital part of any application of mid- to high-level complexity. While the program runs through its execution paths, several logging statements describe what the program is doing, which parameters are passed to method calls, what values local variables and class fields have and how they change, which decisions are made, and so on. This logging information is collected and sent to a file, a database, a message queue, or whatever, and the developer and the operations team can investigate program flows for bug-fixing or auditing purposes.

The logging API specification JSR 47 is part of Java and can be used by any Java program, including Jakarta EE server applications and Java MVC programs. You can download the specification from https://jcp.org/en/jsr/detail?id=47.

GlassFish uses this platform standard API JSR 47 for logging. Unless you change the configuration, you can find the logging file here:

```
GLASSFISH_INST/glassfish/domains/domain1/logs/server.log
```

To add diagnostic output to your own classes using the JSR 47 methodology, you write the following in your classes:

```
...
import java.util.logging.Logger;

public class MyClass {
  private final static Logger LOG =
        Logger.getLogger(MyClass.class.toString());

  public void someMethod() {
    LOG.entering(this.getClass().toString(),"someMethod");
    ...
    // different logging levels:
    LOG.finest("Finest: ...");
    LOG.finer("Finer: ...");
    LOG.fine("Fine: ...");
    LOG.info("Some info: ...");
    LOG.warning("Some warning: ...");
    LOG.severe("Severe: ...");
    ...
```

```
    LOG.exiting(this.getClass().toString(),"someMethod");
  }
  ...
}
```

For standard logging, the levels are, in order, *severe* ➤ *warning* ➤ *info* ➤ *fine* ➤ *finer* ➤ *finest*. This greatly improves the usability of logging. At an early stage of a project, you can set the logging threshold to a low value, for example `fine`, and you will see all the `fine`-level logging and higher levels, up to `severe`, in the logging file.

The logging configuration of a JSR 47 standard logging relies on a configuration file called `logging.properties`. Normally, this file resides in the JDK installation directory, but the GlassFish server overrules the standard logging configuration and uses this file instead:

`GLASSFISH_INST/glassfish/domains/domain1/ config/logging.properties`

Log4j is a logging framework often used for all kinds of Java applications. Log4j can be downloaded from `http://logging.apache.org/log4j/2.x/`.

Adding Log4j server-wide means you put the Log4j implementation into a common libraries folder, write one Log4j configuration file, which serves all Jakarta EE applications running on that server at once, and let all applications and application modules use the Log4j API. Because this needs to be configured only once and then all the current and future applications on a server can easily use Log4 for their logging purposes, this way of including Log4j is probably most common. You can instead add Log4j on a per-application basis, but you should do this only if you have important reasons to encapsulate Log4j with the applications, such as if you are also running legacy applications that use old Log4j 1.x versions.

To add Log4j server-wide, you first download the Log4j distribution from `https://logging.apache.org/log4j/2.x/`. Then copy the `log4j-core-2.11.2.jar`, `log4j-api-2.11.2.jar`, and `log4j-appserver-2.11.2` files (or whatever version you downloaded) to this folder:

`GLASSFISH_INST/glassfish/domains/domain1/`
`        modules/autostart`

Then add the `log4j2.json` file to the GLASSFISH_INST/glassfish/domains/
domain1/lib/classes folder. The basic contents of this file are as follows:

```
{
"configuration": {
  "name": "Default",
  "appenders": {
    "RollingFile": {
      "name":"File",
      "fileName":
          "${sys:com.sun.aas.instanceRoot}/logs/log4j.log",
      "filePattern":
          "${sys:com.sun.aas.instanceRoot}/
          logs/log4j-backup-%d{MM-dd-yy-HH-mm-ss}-%i.gz",
          "PatternLayout": {
              "pattern":
                  "%d{yyyy-MM-dd HH:mm:ss} %-5p %c{1}:%L - %m%n"
          },
          "Policies": {
            "SizeBasedTriggeringPolicy": {
                "size":"10 MB"
            }
          },
          "DefaultRolloverStrategy": {
              "max":"10"
          }
      }
    },
    "loggers": {
      "logger" : [
          {
              "name" : "book.javamvc",
              "level":"debug",
              "appender-ref": {
                "ref":"File"
              }
```

```
        },{
            "name" : "some.other.logger",
            "level":"info",
            "appender-ref": {
                "ref":"File"
            }
        }
    ],
    "root": {
        "level":"error",
        "appender-ref": {
            "ref":"File"
        }
    }
  }
}
}
```

If you think you should add Log4j on a per-application basis and leave other applications running on the server unaffected, you can add the Log4j implementation to your web application (WAR).

To add the Log4j implementation, you update the dependencies in your Gradle build file. Open the build.gradle file and add this to the dependencies { } section:

```
implementation 'org.apache.logging.log4j:log4j-core
    :2.11.2'
implementation 'com.fasterxml.jackson.core:jackson-core
    :2.7.4'
implementation 'com.fasterxml.jackson.core:jackson-
    databind:2.7.4'
implementation 'com.fasterxml.jackson.core:jackson-
    annotations:2.7.4'
```

Here, the central part is the dependency on log4j-core; the dependencies on jackson are needed because we will be using JSON-formatted configuration files and Log4j needs jackson to parse them.

The configuration file for Log4j needs to be called `log4j2.json` and it must go in the `src/main/resources` folder for web applications (WARs). As a simple configuration, set the contents of `log4j2.json` to the following:

```json
{
"configuration": {
    "name": "Default",
    "appenders": {
      "RollingFile": {
        "name":"File",
        "fileName":
            "${sys:com.sun.aas.instanceRoot}/logs/log4j.log",
        "filePattern":
            "${sys:com.sun.aas.instanceRoot}/
            logs/log4j-backup-%d{MM-dd-yy-HH-mm-ss}-%i.gz",
        "PatternLayout": {
          "pattern":
              "%d{yyyy-MM-dd HH:mm:ss} %-5p %c{1}:%L - %m%n"
          },
          "Policies": {
            "SizeBasedTriggeringPolicy": {
                "size":"10 MB"
            }
          },
      "DefaultRolloverStrategy": {
          "max":"10"
          }
       }
    },
    "loggers": {
    "logger" : [
        {
            "name" : "book.javamvc",
            "level":"debug",
            "appender-ref": {
```

```
            "ref":"File"
          }
        },{
            "name" : "some.other.logger",
            "level":"debug",
            "appender-ref": {
            "ref":"File"
            }
        }
    ],
    "root": {
        "level":"debug",
        "appender-ref": {
        "ref":"File"
          }
        }
      }
    }
}
```

To use Log4 in your Java MVC application, make sure each project in question also has the following Gradle dependency:

```
implementation 'org.apache.logging.log4j:log4j-api:2.11.2'
```

You then import `Logger` and `LogManager` in the classes and use a static logger field, as follows:

```
import org.apache.logging.log4j.*;

public class SomeClass {
  private final static Logger LOG =
        LogManager.getLogger(SomeClass.class);
  ...
  public void someMethod() {
  ...
```

```
   // different logging levels:
   LOG.trace("Trace: ...");
   LOG.debug("Debug: ...");
   LOG.info("Some info: ...");
   LOG.warn("Some warning: ...");
   LOG.error("Some error: ...");
   LOG.fatal("Some fatal error: ...");
   ...
   // Logging in try-catch clauses
   try {
      ...
   } catch(Exception e) {
      ...
      LOG.error("Some error", e);
   }
 }
}
```

In the next chapter, which concludes the book, we work out a comprehensive example Java MVC application.

CHAPTER 12

A Java MVC Example Application

We finish the book with a comprehensive example application covering many of the aspects we talked about in previous chapters. The application in question is a book club administration that we call BooKlubb. We limit the domain to books and members, which only to some small extent supersedes the various examples we already talked about, but nevertheless can serve as a blueprint for many applications. You'll often encounter this kind of people-things combination.

The BooKlubb application concentrates on Java MVC capabilities; we do not spend much energy on frontend design and we also do not use AJAX, to keep the distraction at a minimum. Of course, you can work out the application to any extent you like.

The BooKlubb Database

We talked about using databases in Chapter 10. We use the same built-in Apache Derby database for BooKlubb. There are three tables: MEMBER for BooKlubb members, BOOK for the books, and BOOK_RENTAL for book rental information (assigning books to members).

Before you can use Apache Derby, remember you have to start it via bin/asadmin start-database from inside the GlassFish installation folder.

Next we connect to the new database via the ij client (use any other suitable DB client if you like), and add user credentials to it:

```
cd [GLASSFISH_INST]
cd javadb/bin
# start the DB client
./ij
ij> connect 'jdbc:derby://localhost:1527/booklubb;
```

© Peter Späth 2021
P. Späth, *Beginning Java MVC 1.0*, https://doi.org/10.1007/978-1-4842-6280-1_12

```
create=true;user=bk';
ij> call SYSCS_UTIL.SYSCS_CREATE_USER('bk','pw715');
```

Note   Next time you connect, you have to provide the password, as in `connect`
`'...;user=bk;password=pw715';`

To create the tables and ID sequences, you enter the following:

```
CREATE TABLE MEMBER (
    ID          INT          NOT NULL,
    FIRST_NAME  VARCHAR(128) NOT NULL,
    LAST_NAME   VARCHAR(128) NOT NULL,
    BIRTHDAY    DATE         NOT NULL,
    SSN         VARCHAR(16)  NOT NULL,
    PRIMARY KEY (ID));
CREATE SEQUENCE MEMBER_SEQ start with 1 increment by 1;

CREATE TABLE BOOK (
    ID          INT          NOT NULL,
    TITLE       VARCHAR(128) NOT NULL,
    AUTHOR_FIRST_NAME  VARCHAR(128)  NOT NULL,
    AUTHOR_LAST_NAME   VARCHAR(128)  NOT NULL,
    MAKE        DATE         NOT NULL,
    ISBN        VARCHAR(24)  NOT NULL,
    PRIMARY KEY (ID));
CREATE SEQUENCE BOOK_SEQ start with 1 increment by 1;

CREATE TABLE RENTAL (
    ID         INT   NOT NULL,
    MEMBER_ID  INT   NOT NULL,
    BOOK_ID    INT   NOT NULL,
    RENTAL_DAY DATE  NOT NULL,
    PRIMARY KEY (ID));
CREATE SEQUENCE RENTAL_SEQ start with 1 increment by 1;
```

In the GlassFish server, we need to create resources for the database connection. We can use the asadmin tool to achieve that:

```
cd [GLASSFISH_INST]
cd bin
./asadmin create-jdbc-connection-pool \
    --datasourceclassname \
      org.apache.derby.jdbc.ClientXADataSource \
    --restype javax.sql.XADataSource \
    --property \
      portNumber=1527:password=pw715:user=bk:
      serverName=localhost:databaseName=booklubb:
      securityMechanism=3 \
    BooKlubbPool

./asadmin create-jdbc-resource \
--connectionpoolid BooKlubbPool jdbc/BooKlubb
```

(There should be no line break and no spaces after bk: and booklubb:.). Because of these resources, JPA knows how to connect to the database. JPA needs a datasource and the commands create exactly such a datasource.

Caution   Datasource creation is specific to the server. If you use a server other than GlassFish, you have to consult the manual in order to learn how to crate datasources.

The BooKlubb Eclipse Project

Open Eclipse and select any suitable workspace. For example, choose the same workspace as in the book's examples.

Create a new Gradle project: choose File ➤ New ➤ Other... ➤ Gradle ➤ Gradle Project. Enter the name BooKlubb.

If a build path error appears (view Problems), right-click the project and choose Properties ➤ Java Build Path. Remove the false JRE System Library (marked unbound), then choose Add Library and select your Java 8 JDK. Click Apply and Close. Also see the section entitled "More About Gradle" in Chapter 3.

Replace the contents of the build.gradle file with the following:

```
plugins {
    id 'war'
}

java {
    sourceCompatibility = JavaVersion.VERSION_1_8
    targetCompatibility = JavaVersion.VERSION_1_8
}

repositories {
    jcenter()
}

dependencies {
  testImplementation 'junit:junit:4.12'
  implementation 'javax:javaee-api:8.0'
  implementation 'javax.mvc:javax.mvc-api:1.0.0'
  implementation 'org.eclipse.krazo:krazo-jersey:1.1.0-M1'
  implementation 'jstl:jstl:1.2'
}

task localDeploy(dependsOn: war,
            description:">>> Local deploy task") {
  doLast {
    def FS = File.separator
    def glassfish =
        project.properties['glassfish.inst.dir']
    def user = project.properties['glassfish.user']
    def passwd = project.properties['glassfish.passwd']

    File temp = File.createTempFile("asadmin-passwd",
      ".tmp")
    temp << "AS_ADMIN_${user}=${passwd}\n"

    def sout = new StringBuilder()
    def serr = new StringBuilder()
    def libsDir =
```

```
        "${project.projectDir}${FS}build${FS}libs"
      def proc = """"${glassfish}${FS}bin${FS}asadmin
        --user ${user} --passwordfile ${temp.absolutePath}
          deploy --force=true
          ${libsDir}/${project.name}.war""".execute()
    proc.waitForProcessOutput(sout, serr)
    println "out> ${sout}"
    if(serr.toString()) System.err.println(serr)

    temp.delete()
  }
}

task localUndeploy(
              description:">>> Local undeploy task") {
  doLast {
    def FS = File.separator
    def glassfish =
        project.properties['glassfish.inst.dir']
    def user = project.properties['glassfish.user']
    def passwd = project.properties['glassfish.passwd']

    File temp = File.createTempFile("asadmin-passwd",
        ".tmp")
    temp << "AS_ADMIN_${user}=${passwd}\n"

    def sout = new StringBuilder()
    def serr = new StringBuilder()
    def proc = """"${glassfish}${FS}bin${FS}asadmin
      --user ${user} --passwordfile ${temp.absolutePath}
      undeploy ${project.name}""".execute()
    proc.waitForProcessOutput(sout, serr)
    println "out> ${sout}"
    if(serr.toString()) System.err.println(serr)

    temp.delete()
  }
}
```

This is the same build file described in Chapter 4. Choose Gradle ➤ Refresh Gradle Project to make sure the dependencies are transported to the Java build path.

As a configuration for deployment and "un-deployment," add a `gradle.properties` file to the project, adapting the values according to your needs:

```
glassfish.inst.dir = /path/to/your/glassfish5.1
glassfish.user = admin
glassfish.passwd =
```

The BooKlubb Infrastructure Classes

Similar to the `HelloWorld` example in Chapter 4, we use the `App` and `RootRedirector` classes to tailor the context path and create the landing page:

```java
package book.javamvc.bk;

import java.util.HashMap;
import java.util.Map;
import java.util.logging.Logger;

import javax.annotation.PostConstruct;
import javax.inject.Inject;
import javax.ws.rs.ApplicationPath;
import javax.ws.rs.core.Application;

@ApplicationPath("/mvc")
public class App extends Application {
  @PostConstruct
  public void init() {
  }

  @Override
  public Map<String, Object> getProperties() {
  Map<String, Object> res = new HashMap<>();
  res.put("I18N_TEXT_ATTRIBUTE_NAME",
    "msg");
  res.put("I18N_TEXT_BASE_NAME",
    "book.javamvc.bk.messages.Messages");
```

```
  return res;
  }
}
```

and

```
package book.javamvc.bk;

import javax.servlet.FilterChain;
import javax.servlet.annotation.WebFilter;
import javax.servlet.http.HttpFilter;
import javax.servlet.http.HttpServletRequest;
import javax.servlet.http.HttpServletResponse;
import java.io.IOException;

/**
 * Redirecting http://localhost:8080/BooKlubb/
 * This way we don't need a <welcome-file-list> in web.xml
 */
@WebFilter(urlPatterns = "/")
public class RootRedirector extends HttpFilter {
  private static final long serialVersionUID =
      73329091561636673868L;
  @Override
  protected void doFilter(final HttpServletRequest req,
      final HttpServletResponse res,
      final FilterChain chain) throws IOException {
    res.sendRedirect("mvc/bk");
  }
}
```

Configuring BooKlubb Database Access

The application uses JPA to access the database. As described in Chapter 10, we need a persistence.xml file in src/main/resources/META-INF, as follows:

```
<persistence
    xmlns="http://java.sun.com/xml/ns/persistence"
    xmlns:xsi="http://www.w3.org/2001/XMLSchema-instance"
    xsi:schemaLocation=
      "http://java.sun.com/xml/ns/persistence
       persistence_1_0.xsd"
    version="1.0">
<persistence-unit name="default" transaction-type="JTA">
    <jta-data-source>jdbc/BooKlubb</jta-data-source>
    <exclude-unlisted-classes>
      false
    </exclude-unlisted-classes>
    <properties />
</persistence-unit>
</persistence>
```

This file's main responsibility is to describe which database to use for the application.

The BooKlubb Internationalization

As Chapter 8 described, we use two classes, called BundleForEL and SetBundleFilter, for internationalization purposes:

```
package book.javamvc.bk.i18n;

import java.util.Enumeration;
import java.util.Locale;
import java.util.ResourceBundle;
import javax.servlet.http.HttpServletRequest;

public class BundleForEL extends ResourceBundle {
    private BundleForEL(Locale locale, String baseName) {
```

```java
            setLocale(locale, baseName);
    }

    public static void setFor(HttpServletRequest request,
        String i18nAttributeName, String i18nBaseName) {
      if (request.getSession().
          getAttribute(i18nAttributeName) == null) {
        request.getSession().setAttribute(
          i18nAttributeName,
          new BundleForEL(request.getLocale(),
                          i18nBaseName));
      }
    }

    public void setLocale(Locale locale,
         String baseName) {
      if (parent == null ||
          !parent.getLocale().equals(locale)) {
         setParent(getBundle(baseName, locale));
      }
    }

    @Override
    public Enumeration<String> getKeys() {
       return parent.getKeys();
    }

    @Override
    protected Object handleGetObject(String key) {
       return parent.getObject(key);
    }
}
```

and

```java
package book.javamvc.bk.i18n;

import java.io.IOException;
import java.util.Map;
```

```java
import javax.inject.Inject;
import javax.servlet.Filter;
import javax.servlet.FilterChain;
import javax.servlet.FilterConfig;
import javax.servlet.ServletException;
import javax.servlet.ServletRequest;
import javax.servlet.ServletResponse;
import javax.servlet.annotation.WebFilter;
import javax.servlet.http.HttpServletRequest;
import javax.ws.rs.core.Application;

@WebFilter("/*")
public class SetBundleFilter implements Filter {
    @Inject private Application appl;
    private String i18nAttributeName;
    private String i18nBaseName;

    @Override
    public void init(FilterConfig filterConfig)
          throws ServletException {
      Map<String,Object> applProps = appl.getProperties();
      i18nAttributeName = (String) applProps.get(
          "I18N_TEXT_ATTRIBUTE_NAME");
      i18nBaseName = (String) applProps.get(
          "I18N_TEXT_BASE_NAME");
  }

    @Override
    public void doFilter(ServletRequest request,
        ServletResponse response, FilterChain chain)
        throws IOException, ServletException {
      BundleForEL.setFor((HttpServletRequest) request,
        i18nAttributeName, i18nBaseName);
      chain.doFilter(request, response);
  }
```

```
    @Override
    public void destroy() {
    }
}
```

In `src/main/resources/book/javamvc/bk/messages/Messages.properties`, we put a resources file with these contents:

```
title = BooKlubb

menu_search_member = Search Member
menu_new_member = New Member
menu_search_book = Search Book
menu_new_book = New Book

current_member = Current Member:

enter_memberFirstName = First Name:
enter_memberLastName = Last Name:
enter_memberBirthday = Birthday:
enter_memberSsn = SSN:

enter_authorFirstName = Author First Name:
enter_authorLastName = Author First Name:
enter_bookTitle = Title:
enter_bookMake = Make:
enter_isbn = ISBN:

hd_searchResult = Search Result
hd_searchMember = Search Member
hd_newMember = New Member
hd_searchBook = Search Book
hd_newBook = New Book
hd_memberDetails = Member Details
hd_booksAssigned = Books Assigned

tblhdr_id = ID
tblhdr_last_name = Last Name
tblhdr_first_name = First Name
```

```
tblhdr_birthday = Birthday
tblhdr_ssn = SSN
tblhdr_author_last_name = Last Name
tblhdr_author_first_name = First Name
tblhdr_book_title = Title
tblhdr_book_make = Make
tblhdr_isbn = ISBN

btn_search = Search
btn_new = New
btn_delete = Delete
btn_select = Select
btn_details = \u2190
btn_assign = Assign
btn_unassign = Unassign
no_result = ---- No result ----

new_member_added = New Member Added
new_book_added = New Book Added
member_deleted = Member Deleted
book_deleted = Book Deleted

memb_id = ID:
memb_firstName = First Name:
memb_lastName = Last Name:
memb_birthday = Birthday:
memb_ssn = SSN:
```

These key-value pairs are used exclusively by the view pages only.

The BooKlubb Entity Classes

With the database table definitions at hand, we can immediately write the JPA entity classes. This is possible without having defined any functionalities, since entity classes don't contain any programming logic. For BooKlubb, they read as follows:

```
package book.javamvc.bk.db;

import java.util.Date;
import java.util.Set;

import javax.persistence.CascadeType;
import javax.persistence.Column;
import javax.persistence.Entity;
import javax.persistence.GeneratedValue;
import javax.persistence.GenerationType;
import javax.persistence.Id;
import javax.persistence.JoinColumn;
import javax.persistence.OneToMany;
import javax.persistence.SequenceGenerator;
import javax.persistence.Table;
import javax.validation.constraints.NotNull;

@Entity
@Table(name = "MEMBER")
@SequenceGenerator(name = "MEMBER_SEQ", initialValue = 1,
      allocationSize = 1)
public class Member {
  @Id
  @GeneratedValue(strategy = GenerationType.IDENTITY,
      generator = "MEMBER_SEQ")
  @Column(name = "id")
  private int id;

  @NotNull
  @Column(name = "first_name")
  private String firstName;

  @NotNull
```

```java
@Column(name = "last_name")
private String lastName;

@NotNull
@Column(name = "birthday")
private Date birthday;

@NotNull
@Column(name = "ssn")
private String ssn;

@JoinColumn(name = "MEMBER_ID")
@OneToMany(cascade = CascadeType.ALL, orphanRemoval=true)
private Set<Rental> rental;

public int getId() {
  return id;
}

public void setId(int id) {
  this.id = id;
}

public String getFirstName() {
  return firstName;
}

public void setFirstName(String firstName) {
  this.firstName = firstName;
}

public String getLastName() {
  return lastName;
}

public void setLastName(String lastName) {
  this.lastName = lastName;
}
```

```java
  public Date getBirthday() {
    return birthday;
  }

  public void setBirthday(Date birthday) {
    this.birthday = birthday;
  }

  public String getSsn() {
    return ssn;
  }

  public void setSsn(String ssn) {
    this.ssn = ssn;
  }

  public Set<Rental> getRental() {
    return rental;
  }

  public void setRental(Set<Rental> rental) {
    this.rental = rental;
  }
}
```

and

```java
package book.javamvc.bk.db;

import java.util.Date;

import javax.persistence.CascadeType;
import javax.persistence.Column;
import javax.persistence.Entity;
import javax.persistence.GeneratedValue;
import javax.persistence.GenerationType;
import javax.persistence.Id;
import javax.persistence.OneToOne;
import javax.persistence.SequenceGenerator;
import javax.persistence.Table;
```

```java
import javax.validation.constraints.NotNull;

@Entity
@Table(name = "BOOK")
@SequenceGenerator(name = "BOOK_SEQ", initialValue = 1,
    allocationSize = 1)
public class Book {
  @Id
  @GeneratedValue(strategy = GenerationType.IDENTITY,
      generator = "BOOK_SEQ")
  @Column(name = "id")
  private int id;

  @NotNull
  @Column(name = "title")
  private String title;

  @NotNull
  @Column(name = "author_first_name")
  private String authorFirstName;

  @NotNull
  @Column(name = "author_last_name")
  private String authorLastName;

  @NotNull
  @Column(name = "make")
  private Date make;

  @NotNull
  @Column(name = "isbn")
  private String isbn;

  @OneToOne(cascade = CascadeType.ALL, orphanRemoval=true,
      mappedBy = "book")
  private Rental rental;

  public int getId() {
    return id;
  }
}
```

```java
public void setId(int id) {
  this.id = id;
}

public String getTitle() {
  return title;
}

public void setTitle(String title) {
  this.title = title;
}

public String getAuthorFirstName() {
  return authorFirstName;
}

public void setAuthorFirstName(String authorFirstName) {
  this.authorFirstName = authorFirstName;
}

public String getAuthorLastName() {
  return authorLastName;
}

public void setAuthorLastName(String authorLastName) {
  this.authorLastName = authorLastName;
}

public Date getMake() {
  return make;
}

public void setMake(Date make) {
  this.make = make;
}

public String getIsbn() {
  return isbn;
}
```

```java
  public void setIsbn(String isbn) {
    this.isbn = isbn;
  }

  public Rental getRental() {
    return rental;
  }

  public void setRental(Rental rental) {
    this.rental = rental;
  }
}
```

and

```java
package book.javamvc.bk.db;

import java.util.Date;

import javax.persistence.Column;
import javax.persistence.Entity;
import javax.persistence.GeneratedValue;
import javax.persistence.GenerationType;
import javax.persistence.Id;
import javax.persistence.JoinColumn;
import javax.persistence.OneToOne;
import javax.persistence.SequenceGenerator;
import javax.persistence.Table;
import javax.validation.constraints.NotNull;

@Entity
@Table(name = "RENTAL")
@SequenceGenerator(name = "RENTAL_SEQ", initialValue = 1,
    allocationSize = 1)
public class Rental {
  @Id
  @GeneratedValue(strategy = GenerationType.IDENTITY,
      generator = "RENTAL_SEQ")
  @Column(name = "id")
```

```java
private int id;

@NotNull
@Column(name = "member_id")
private int memberId;

@NotNull
@JoinColumn(name = "book_id")
@OneToOne
private Book book;

@NotNull
@Column(name = "rental_day")
private Date rentalDay;

public int getId() {
  return id;
}

public void setId(int id) {
  this.id = id;
}

public int getMemberId() {
  return memberId;
}

public void setMemberId(int memberId) {
  this.memberId = memberId;
}

public Book getBook() {
  return book;
}

public void setBook(Book book) {
  this.book = book;
}

public Date getRentalDay() {
```

```
    return rentalDay;
  }

  public void setRentalDay(Date rentalDay) {
    this.rentalDay = rentalDay;
  }
}
```

These classes reflect the database table fields and the relationships via the @OneToOne and @OneToMany annotations. The idea behind the latter is that a member may have zero, one, or more books rented (@OneToMany), and a book may or may not be rented (@OneToOne, with "not rented" reflected as a null value).

BooKlubb Database Access via DAOs

The DAOs encapsulate handling database access and deal with the entity classes. The DAOs provide methods to create, update, and delete entities, and to search inside the database. We put them in the book.javamvc.bk.db package.

```
package book.javamvc.bk.db;

import java.util.Date;
import java.util.List;
import java.util.Optional;

import javax.ejb.Stateless;
import javax.persistence.EntityManager;
import javax.persistence.PersistenceContext;
import javax.persistence.TypedQuery;

@Stateless
public class MemberDAO {
  @PersistenceContext
  private EntityManager em;

  public int addMember(String firstName, String lastName,
        Date birthday, String ssn) {
```

```
   // First check if there is already a member with the
   // same SSN. Create a new entry only if none found.
   List<?> l = em.createQuery("SELECT m FROM Member m "+
               "WHERE m.ssn=:ssn").
           setParameter("ssn",    ssn).
           getResultList();
   int id = 0;
   if(l.isEmpty()) {
     Member member = new Member();
     member.setFirstName(firstName);
     member.setLastName(lastName);
     member.setBirthday(birthday);
     member.setSsn(ssn);
     em.persist(member);
     em.flush(); // needed to get the ID
     id = member.getId();
   } else {
     id = ((Member)l.get(0)).getId();
   }
   return id;
}

public List<Member> allMembers() {
    TypedQuery<Member> q = em.createQuery(
        "SELECT m FROM Member m", Member.class);
    List<Member> l = q.getResultList();
    return l;
 }

public Member memberById(int id) {
  return em.find(Member.class, id);
}

public Optional<Member> memberBySsn(String ssn) {
  List<?> l = em.createQuery("SELECT m FROM Member m "+
          "WHERE m.ssn=:ssn").
      setParameter("ssn",    ssn).
```

```
        getResultList();
  if(l.isEmpty()) {
    return Optional.empty();
  } else {
    return Optional.of((Member)l.get(0));
  }
}

  @SuppressWarnings("unchecked")
  public List<Member> membersByName(String firstName,
      String lastName) {
  List<?> l = em.createQuery("SELECT m FROM Member m "+
        "WHERE m.firstName LIKE :fn AND "+
        "m.lastName LIKE :ln").
      setParameter("fn",  firstName.isEmpty() ?
        "%" : "%" + firstName + "%").
      setParameter("ln",  lastName.isEmpty() ?
        "%" : "%" + lastName + "%").
      getResultList();
  return (List<Member>) l;
}

public void deleteMember(int id) {
  Member member = em.find(Member.class, id);
  em.remove(member);
}
}
```

You can see that we inject an instance of EntityManager as an interface to JPA. From there, we can use its methods to access database tables. For example, in addMember(), we use the *JPA Query Language* (JQL) to search the member's table using the SSN given as a method parameter, and if we can't find one, we save a new entity via EntityManager. persist(). In memberById() instead we can directly use EntityManager.find(), since the argument is the entity class' primary key ID.

The other class, called BookDAO, primarily addresses the book table. Its code reads as follows:

```
package book.javamvc.bk.db;

import java.util.Date;
import java.util.List;
import java.util.Optional;
import java.util.Set;
import java.util.stream.Collectors;

import javax.ejb.Stateless;
import javax.persistence.EntityManager;
import javax.persistence.PersistenceContext;
import javax.persistence.TypedQuery;

@Stateless
public class BookDAO {
  @PersistenceContext
  private EntityManager em;

  public int addBook(String authorFirstName,
      String authorLastName, String title,
      Date make, String isbn) {

    // First check if there is already a book with the
    // same ISBN in the database. Create a new entry
    // only if none is found.
    List<?> l = em.createQuery("SELECT b FROM Book b "+
        "WHERE b.isbn=:isbn").
      setParameter("isbn",   isbn).
       getResultList();
    int id = 0;
    if(l.isEmpty()) {
      Book book = new Book();
      book.setAuthorFirstName(authorFirstName);
      book.setAuthorLastName(authorLastName);
      book.setTitle(title);
```

```
      book.setMake(make);
      book.setIsbn(isbn);
      em.persist(book);
      em.flush(); // needed to get the ID
      id = book.getId();
    } else {
      id = ((Book)l.get(0)).getId();
    }
    return id;
  }

  public List<Book> allBooks() {
    TypedQuery<Book> q = em.createQuery(
        "SELECT b FROM Book b", Book.class);
    List<Book> l = q.getResultList();
    return l;
  }

  public Book bookById(int id) {
    return em.find(Book.class, id);
  }

  public Optional<Book> bookByIsbn(String isbn) {
    List<?> l = em.createQuery("SELECT b FROM Book b "+
          "WHERE b.isbn=:isbn").
        setParameter("isbn",     isbn).
        getResultList();
    if(l.isEmpty()) {
     return Optional.empty();
    } else {
      return Optional.of((Book)l.get(0));
    }
  }

  @SuppressWarnings("unchecked")
  public List<Book> booksByName(String authorFirstName,
      String authorLastName, String bookTitle) {
```

```
    String afn = (authorFirstName == null ||
               authorFirstName.isEmpty() ) ?
       "%" : ("%"+authorFirstName+"%");
    String aln = (authorLastName == null ||
               authorLastName.isEmpty() ) ?
       "%" : ("%"+authorLastName+"%");
    String t = (bookTitle == null ||
               bookTitle.isEmpty() ) ?
       "%" : ("%"+bookTitle+"%");

    List<?> l = em.createQuery("SELECT b FROM Book b "+
         "WHERE b.title LIKE :title AND "+
         "b.authorLastName LIKE :aln AND "+
         "b.authorFirstName LIKE :afn").
       setParameter("title", t).
       setParameter("aln", aln).
       setParameter("afn", afn).
       getResultList();
    return (List<Book>) l;
  }

  public void deleteBook(int id) {
    Book book = em.find(Book.class, id);
    em.remove(book);
  }

}
```

The third DAO class, called RentalDAO, registers book rentals (assigns books to members):

```
package book.javamvc.bk.db;

import java.util.Date;
import java.util.Set;
import java.util.stream.Collectors;

import javax.ejb.Stateless;
import javax.persistence.EntityManager;
```

```java
import javax.persistence.PersistenceContext;

@Stateless
public class RentalDAO {
    @PersistenceContext
    private EntityManager em;

    public void rentBook(Book b, Member m, Date day) {
      Rental r = b.getRental();
      if(r == null) {
        r = new Rental();
      }

      // Update the BOOK table
      r.setBook(b);
      r.setMemberId(m.getId());
      r.setRentalDay(day);
      b.setRental(r);
      em.merge(b);

      // Update the MEMBER table
      Set<Rental> rs = m.getRental();
      if(rs.stream().allMatch(r1 -> {
          return r1.getBook().getId() != b.getId(); })) {
        rs.add(r);
        m.setRental(rs);
        em.merge(m);
      }
    }

  public void unrentBook(Book b, Member m) {
    Rental r = b.getRental();
    if(r == null) return;

    // Update the BOOK table
    b.setRental(null);
    em.merge(b);

    // Update the MEMBER table
```

```
    Set<Rental> newRental =
        m.getRental().stream().filter(rr -> {
            return rr.getBook().getId() != b.getId(); }).
        collect(Collectors.toSet());
    m.setRental(newRental);
    em.merge(m);
  }
}
```

The BooKlubb Model

The model part of the BooKlubb application (Java MVC model, not database model) consists of a couple of classes that transport data between the controller and the views:

- MemberModel: Contains a club member. We need it only as an item type for a member search result list. Request scoped.

- MemberSearchResult: A result list from a member search. Request scoped.

- BookModel: Contains book information. We need it as an item type for a book search result list, and for the book rentals listed in the current member's details view. Request scoped.

- BookSearchResult: A result list from a book search. Request scoped.

- CurrentMember: Contains information about the currently selected member. This is the only model bean that is session-scoped. We need this broader scope because a current member can be chosen from the member search result list and henceforth must be remembered in order to assign books to this member on a different page.

We put them all in the book.javamvc.bk.model package and the code reads as follows:

```
package book.javamvc.bk.model;

import java.util.Date;

public class MemberModel {
```

```java
  private int id;
  private String firstName;
  private String lastName;
  private Date birthday;
  private String ssn;

  public MemberModel(int id, String firstName,
      String lastName, Date birthday, String ssn) {
    this.id = id;
    this.firstName = firstName;
    this.lastName = lastName;
    this.birthday = birthday;
    this.ssn = ssn;
  }

  public int getId() {
    return id;
  }

  public void setId(int id) {
    this.id = id;
  }

  public String getFirstName() {
    return firstName;
  }

  public void setFirstName(String firstName) {
    this.firstName = firstName;
  }

  public String getLastName() {
    return lastName;
  }

  public void setLastName(String lastName) {
    this.lastName = lastName;
  }
```

```java
  public Date getBirthday() {
    return birthday;
  }

  public void setBirthday(Date birthday) {
    this.birthday = birthday;
  }

  public String getSsn() {
    return ssn;
  }

  public void setSsn(String ssn) {
    this.ssn = ssn;
  }
}
```

and

```java
package book.javamvc.bk.model;

import java.util.ArrayList;
import java.util.List;

import javax.enterprise.context.RequestScoped;
import javax.inject.Named;

import book.javamvc.bk.db.Member;

@Named
@RequestScoped
public class MemberSearchResult extends
      ArrayList<MemberModel>{
  private static final long serialVersionUID =
        -5926389915908884067L;
  public void addAll(List<Member> l) {
    l.forEach(m -> {
      add(new MemberModel(
        m.getId(),
        m.getFirstName(),
```

```
        m.getLastName(),
        m.getBirthday(),
        m.getSsn()
      ));
    });
  }
}
```

In this class, we added a convenience method called addAll(List < Member > l) with the Member class from the database layer. Normally we don't want to use database entities outside the DAOs, but Member is just a data holder and we don't need any functionalities for it. So mixing of layers doesn't impact the application architecture too much.

```
package book.javamvc.bk.model;

import java.util.Date;

public class BookModel {
  private int id;
  private String authorFirstName;
  private String authorLastName;
  private String title;
  private String isbn;
  private Date make;

  public BookModel(int id, String authorFirstName,
        String authorLastName, String title, String isbn,
        Date make) {
    this.id = id;
    this.authorFirstName = authorFirstName;
    this.authorLastName = authorLastName;
    this.title = title;
    this.isbn = isbn;
    this.make = make;
  }
```

```java
public int getId() {
  return id;
}

public void setId(int id) {
  this.id = id;
}

public String getAuthorFirstName() {
  return authorFirstName;
}

public void setAuthorFirstName(String authorFirstName) {
  this.authorFirstName = authorFirstName;
}

public String getAuthorLastName() {
  return authorLastName;
}

public void setAuthorLastName(String authorLastName) {
  this.authorLastName = authorLastName;
}

public String getTitle() {
  return title;
}

public void setTitle(String title) {
  this.title = title;
}

public String getIsbn() {
  return isbn;
}

public void setIsbn(String isbn) {
  this.isbn = isbn;
}
```

```java
  public Date getMake() {
    return make;
  }

  public void setMake(Date make) {
    this.make = make;
  }
}
```

and

```java
package book.javamvc.bk.model;

import java.util.ArrayList;
import java.util.List;

import javax.enterprise.context.RequestScoped;
import javax.inject.Named;

import book.javamvc.bk.db.Book;

@Named
@RequestScoped
public class BookSearchResult extends
      ArrayList<BookModel>{
  private static final long serialVersionUID =
      -5926389915908884067L;
  public void addAll(List<Book> l) {
    l.forEach(b -> {
      add(new BookModel(
        b.getId(),
        b.getAuthorFirstName(),
        b.getAuthorLastName(),
        b.getTitle(),
        b.getIsbn(),
        b.getMake()
      ));
    });
  }
}
```

and

```
package book.javamvc.bk.model;

import java.io.Serializable;
import java.util.Date;
import java.util.Set;

import javax.enterprise.context.SessionScoped;
import javax.inject.Named;

@Named
@SessionScoped
public class CurrentMember extends MemberModel
      implements Serializable {
  private static final long serialVersionUID =
      -7855133427774616033L;

  public CurrentMember(int id, String firstName,
      String lastName, Date birthday, String ssn) {
    super(id, firstName, lastName, birthday, ssn);
  }

  private boolean defined = false;
  private Set<BookModel> rentals;

  public boolean isDefined() {
    return defined;
  }

  public void setDefined(boolean defined) {
    this.defined = defined;
  }

  public void setRentals(Set<BookModel> rentals) {
    this.rentals = rentals;
  }
```

```
  public Set<BookModel> getRentals() {
    return rentals;
  }
}
```

The BooKlubb Controller

The controller is responsible for receiving all POST and GET actions from the views. In Java MVC and for the BooKlubb application, it looks like this:

```
package book.javamvc.bk;

import ...;

@Path("/bk")
@Controller
public class BooKlubbController {
  @Named
  @RequestScoped
  public static class ErrorMessages {
    private List<String> msgs = new ArrayList<>();
    public List<String> getMsgs() {
      return msgs;
    }
    public void setMsgs(List<String> msgs) {
      this.msgs = msgs;
    }
    public void addMessage(String msg) {
      msgs.add(msg);
    }
  }

  private @Inject ErrorMessages errorMessages;
  private @Inject BindingResult br;

  private @EJB MemberDAO memberDao;
  private @Inject MemberSearchResult memberSearchResult;
```

```
private @EJB BookDAO bookDao;
private @Inject BookSearchResult bookSearchResult;

private @EJB RentalDAO rentalDao;

private @Inject CurrentMember currentMember;

// action methods...
}
```

We use an inner class for the error messages, and we inject the various model classes and DAO EJBs needed to access the database.

The complete code reads as follows:

```
package book.javamvc.bk;

import java.time.LocalDate;
import java.time.ZoneId;
import java.time.format.DateTimeFormatter;
import java.util.ArrayList;
import java.util.Date;
import java.util.List;
import java.util.stream.Collectors;

import javax.ejb.EJB;
import javax.enterprise.context.RequestScoped;
import javax.inject.Inject;
import javax.inject.Named;
import javax.mvc.Controller;
import javax.mvc.binding.BindingResult;
import javax.mvc.binding.MvcBinding;
import javax.mvc.binding.ParamError;
import javax.validation.constraints.Pattern;
import javax.ws.rs.FormParam;
import javax.ws.rs.GET;
import javax.ws.rs.POST;
import javax.ws.rs.Path;
import javax.ws.rs.QueryParam;
import javax.ws.rs.core.Response;
```

```java
import book.javamvc.bk.db.Book;
import book.javamvc.bk.db.BookDAO;
import book.javamvc.bk.db.Member;
import book.javamvc.bk.db.MemberDAO;
import book.javamvc.bk.db.RentalDAO;
import book.javamvc.bk.model.BookModel;
import book.javamvc.bk.model.BookSearchResult;
import book.javamvc.bk.model.CurrentMember;
import book.javamvc.bk.model.MemberSearchResult;

@Path("/bk")
@Controller
public class BooKlubbController {
  @Named
  @RequestScoped
  public static class ErrorMessages {
    private List<String> msgs = new ArrayList<>();
    public List<String> getMsgs() {
      return msgs;
    }
    public void setMsgs(List<String> msgs) {
      this.msgs = msgs;
    }
    public void addMessage(String msg) {
      msgs.add(msg);
    }
  }

  private @Inject ErrorMessages errorMessages;
  private @Inject BindingResult br;

  private @EJB MemberDAO memberDao;
  private @Inject MemberSearchResult memberSearchResult;

  private @EJB BookDAO bookDao;
  private @Inject BookSearchResult bookSearchResult;
```

```
private @EJB RentalDAO rentalDao;

private @Inject CurrentMember currentMember;
```

We add a couple of methods that use @GET to retrieve pages without user input:

```
@GET
public String showIndex() {
  return "index.jsp";
}

@GET
@Path("/searchMember")
public Response searchMember() {
  return Response.ok("searchMember.jsp").build();
}

@GET
@Path("/newMember")
public Response newMember() {
  return Response.ok("newMember.jsp").build();
}

@GET
@Path("/searchBook")
public Response searchBook() {
  return Response.ok("searchBook.jsp").build();
}

@GET
@Path("/newBook")
public Response newBook() {
  return Response.ok("newBook.jsp").build();
}
```

The following are methods that relate to members: showing a list of searched-for members, reacting to creating a new member, deleting a member, showing member details, and selecting a member:

```java
@GET
@Path("/searchMemberSubmit")
public Response searchMemberSubmit(
    @MvcBinding @QueryParam("firstName")
        String firstName,
    @MvcBinding @QueryParam("lastName")
        String lastName,
    @MvcBinding @QueryParam("ssn")
        String ssn) {
  showErrors();

  String ssnNormal = ssn == null ?
      "" : ( ssn.replaceAll("\\D", "") );
  List<Member> l = new ArrayList<>();
  if(!ssnNormal.isEmpty()) {
    memberDao.memberBySsn(ssnNormal).ifPresent(
        m1 -> { l.add(m1); });
    } else {
      l.addAll( memberDao.membersByName(
          firstName, lastName) );
    }
    memberSearchResult.addAll(l);

    return Response.ok("searchMemberResult.jsp").build();
}

@POST
@Path("/newMemberSubmit")
public Response newMemberSubmit(
    @MvcBinding @FormParam("firstName")
        String firstName,
    @MvcBinding @FormParam("lastName")
        String lastName,
```

```
        @MvcBinding @FormParam("birthday")
            @Pattern(regexp = "\\d\\d/\\d\\d/\\d\\d\\d\\d")
            String birthday,
        @MvcBinding @FormParam("ssn")
            String ssn) {
    showErrors();

    DateTimeFormatter dtf = DateTimeFormatter.ofPattern(
            "MM/dd/yyyy");
    LocalDate ld = LocalDate.parse(birthday, dtf);
    Date date = Date.from(ld.atStartOfDay(
        ZoneId.systemDefault()).toInstant());

    memberDao.addMember(firstName, lastName, date, ssn);

    return Response.ok("newMemberResult.jsp").build();
}

@POST
@Path("/deleteMember")
public Response deleteMember(
    @MvcBinding @FormParam("memberId")
        int memberId) {
    showErrors();

    memberDao.deleteMember(memberId);

    return Response.ok("deleteMemberResult.jsp").build();
}

@POST
@Path("/selectMember")
public Response selectMember(
    @MvcBinding @FormParam("memberId")
        int memberId) {
    showErrors();
```

```
  Member m = memberDao.memberById(memberId);
  currentMember.setId(memberId);
  currentMember.setFirstName(m.getFirstName());
  currentMember.setLastName(m.getLastName());
  currentMember.setBirthday(m.getBirthday());
  currentMember.setSsn(m.getSsn());
  currentMember.setDefined(true);

  return Response.ok("index.jsp").build();
}

@POST
@Path("/memberDetails")
public Response memberDetails(
  @MvcBinding @FormParam("memberId")
      int memberId) {
  showErrors();

  Member m = memberDao.memberById(memberId);
  currentMember.setId(memberId);
  currentMember.setFirstName(m.getFirstName());
  currentMember.setLastName(m.getLastName());
  currentMember.setBirthday(m.getBirthday());
  currentMember.setSsn(m.getSsn());
  currentMember.setRentals(
    m.getRental().stream().map(r -> {
      Book b = r.getBook();
    return new BookModel(b.getId(),
        b.getAuthorFirstName(),
        b.getAuthorLastName(),
        b.getTitle(), b.getIsbn(), b.getMake());
    }).collect(Collectors.toSet())
  );
  currentMember.setDefined(true);

  return Response.ok("memberDetails.jsp").build();
}
```

We just need to add the book-related methods, which includes reacting to searching for books, adding or deleting a book, and assigning or "unassigning" a book:

```
@GET
@Path("/searchBookSubmit")
public Response searchBookSubmit(
    @MvcBinding @QueryParam("authorFirstName")
        String authorFirstName,
    @MvcBinding @QueryParam("authorLastName")
        String authorLastName,
    @MvcBinding @QueryParam("bookTitle")
        String bookTitle,
    @MvcBinding @QueryParam("isbn")
        String isbn) {
  showErrors();

  String isbnNormal = isbn == null ?
      "" : ( isbn.replaceAll("\\D", "") );
  List<Book> l = new ArrayList<>();
  if(!isbnNormal.isEmpty()) {
    bookDao.bookByIsbn(isbnNormal).ifPresent(m1 -> {
        l.add(m1); });
  } else {
    l.addAll( bookDao.booksByName(authorFirstName,
        authorLastName, bookTitle) );
  }
  bookSearchResult.addAll(l);

  return Response.ok("searchBookResult.jsp").build();
}

@POST
@Path("/newBookSubmit")
public Response newBookSubmit(
    @MvcBinding @FormParam("authorFirstName")
        String authorFirstName,
    @MvcBinding @FormParam("authorLastName")
        String authorLastName,
```

```java
    @MvcBinding @FormParam("title")
        String bookTitle,
    @MvcBinding @FormParam("make")
    @Pattern(regexp = "((\\d\\d/)?\\d\\d/)?\\d\\d\\d\\d")
        String make,
    @MvcBinding @FormParam("isbn")
        String isbn) {
  showErrors();

  String isbnNormal = isbn == null ?
      "" : ( isbn.replaceAll("\\D", "") );
  String makeNormal = make == null ? "" : (
    make.matches("\\d\\d\\d\\d") ?
        "01/01/" + make :
        (make.matches("\\d\\d/\\d\\d\\d\\d") ?
          make.substring(0,2) + "/01" +
        make.substring(2) : make)
  );
  DateTimeFormatter dtf = DateTimeFormatter.ofPattern(
      "MM/dd/yyyy");
  LocalDate ld = LocalDate.parse(makeNormal, dtf);
  Date date = Date.from(ld.atStartOfDay(
      ZoneId.systemDefault()).toInstant());
  bookDao.addBook(authorFirstName, authorLastName,
      bookTitle, date, isbnNormal);

  return Response.ok("newBookResult.jsp").build();
}

@POST
@Path("/deleteBook")
public Response deleteBook(
    @MvcBinding @FormParam("bookId")
        int bookId) {
  showErrors();
```

```java
    bookDao.deleteBook(bookId);

    return Response.ok("deleteBookResult.jsp").build();
}

@POST
@Path("/assignBook")
public Response assignBook(
    @MvcBinding @FormParam("bookId")
        int bookId,
    @MvcBinding @FormParam("userId")
        int userId) {
    showErrors();

    Book b = bookDao.bookById(bookId);
    Member m = memberDao.memberById(userId);
    Date now = new Date();
    rentalDao.rentBook(b, m, now);

    return Response.ok("index.jsp").build();
}

@POST
@Path("/unassignBook")
public Response unassignBook(
    @MvcBinding @FormParam("bookId")
        int bookId,
    @MvcBinding @FormParam("memberId")
        int userId) {
    showErrors();

    Book b = bookDao.bookById(bookId);
    Member m = memberDao.memberById(userId);
    rentalDao.unrentBook(b, m);

    currentMember.setRentals(
      m.getRental().stream().map(r -> {
        Book bb = r.getBook();
```

```
      return new BookModel(bb.getId(),
            bb.getAuthorFirstName(),
            bb.getAuthorLastName(),
            bb.getTitle(),
            bb.getIsbn(),
            bb.getMake());
    }).collect(Collectors.toSet())
    );

  return Response.ok("memberDetails.jsp").build();
}
```

We add one private method, which transports errors detected by Java MVC, and then close the class:

```
private void showErrors() {
  if(br.isFailed()) {
    br.getAllErrors().stream().forEach(
      (ParamError pe) -> {
        errorMessages.addMessage(pe.getParamName() +
        ": " + pe.getMessage());
    });
  }
}

} // closing the class
```

The BooKlubb View

As we did in the other Java MVC applications in this book, we add an empty file called beans.xml to src/main/webapp/WEB-INF. Also, add the usual glassfish-web.xml to the same folder:

```
<?xml version="1.0" encoding="UTF-8"?>
<glassfish-web-app error-url="">
    <class-loader delegate="true"/>
</glassfish-web-app>
```

Furthermore, download a jQuery distribution and put it in the src/main/webapp/js folder.

In the following section, we describe the view-related JSP files needed for BooKlubb.

Fragment Files

These elements are shown on every web page—a main menu, the currently selected member, and any error information. We therefore extract them as fragments to be included via the <%@ include ... %> directive.

The fragments are placed in the src/main/webapp/fragments folder; the code reads as follows:

```
<%-- File: currentMember.jsp ******************* --%>
<%@ page contentType="text/html;charset=UTF-8"
  language="java" %>
<%@ taglib prefix="c"
  uri="http://java.sun.com/jsp/jstl/core" %>
<%@ taglib prefix="fmt"
  uri="http://java.sun.com/jsp/jstl/fmt" %>

<div style="background-color:#AAA;margin-bottom:1em">
${msg.current_member}
<c:choose>
  <c:when test="${! currentMember.defined}">
    ----
  </c:when>
  <c:otherwise>
    <fmt:formatDate value="${currentMember.birthday}"
                    pattern="MM/dd/yyyy" var="cubd" />
    <span style="font-weight:bold">
      ${currentMember.firstName}
      ${currentMember.lastName}
      ${cubd} (${currentMember.ssn})
    </span>
  </c:otherwise>
</c:choose>
```

```
</div>

<%-- File: errors.jsp ***************************** --%>
<%@ page contentType="text/html;charset=UTF-8"
  language="java" %>
<%@ taglib prefix="c"
  uri="http://java.sun.com/jsp/jstl/core" %>
<%@ taglib prefix="fmt"
  uri="http://java.sun.com/jsp/jstl/fmt" %>

<div style="color:red">
  <c:forEach var="e" items="${errorMessages.msgs}">
    ${e}
  </c:forEach>
</div>

<%-- File: mainMenu.jsp *************************** --%>
<%@ page contentType="text/html;charset=UTF-8"
  language="java" %>
<%@ taglib prefix="c"
  uri="http://java.sun.com/jsp/jstl/core" %>
<%@ taglib prefix="fmt"
  uri="http://java.sun.com/jsp/jstl/fmt" %>

<div style="width:30%; float:left;">
  <ul>
    <li><a href="${mvc.uriBuilder(
        'BooKlubbController#searchMember').build()}">
      ${msg.menu_search_member}</a></li>
    <li><a href="${mvc.uriBuilder(
        'BooKlubbController#newMember').build()}">
      ${msg.menu_new_member}</a></li>
    <li><a href="${mvc.uriBuilder(
        'BooKlubbController#searchBook').build()}">
      ${msg.menu_search_book}</a></li>
    <li><a href="${mvc.uriBuilder(
        'BooKlubbController#newBook').build()}">
```

```
        ${msg.menu_new_book}</a></li>
    </ul>
</div>
```

Landing Page

The landing page, called index.jsp (in the src/main/webapp/WEB-INF/views folder), includes the aforementioned fragments and otherwise shows no content:

```jsp
<%@ page contentType="text/html;charset=UTF-8"
  language="java" %>
<%@ taglib prefix="c"
  uri="http://java.sun.com/jsp/jstl/core" %>
<%@ taglib prefix="fmt"
  uri="http://java.sun.com/jsp/jstl/fmt" %>
<html>
<head>
    <meta charset="UTF-8">
    <script type="text/javascript" src="${mvc.basePath}/../js/
    jquery-3.5.1.min.js">
    </script>
    <title>${msg.title}</title>
</head>
<body>
  <%@ include file="../../fragments/errors.jsp" %>

  <h1>${msg.title}</h1>
  <%@ include file="../../fragments/currentMember.jsp" %>

  <div>
    <%@ include file="../../fragments/mainMenu.jsp" %>
    <div style="float:left">
    </div>
  </div>

</body>
</html>
```

> **Caution**   Make sure you enter the correct version of the `jQuery` distribution you downloaded. The same holds true for all JSP files presented in subsequent sections.

All JSP files use the same overall structure:

```
<div style="float:left">
</div>
```

This empty tag will serve as a container for the actual page contents. Figure 12-1 shows the browser page when you're entering the application.

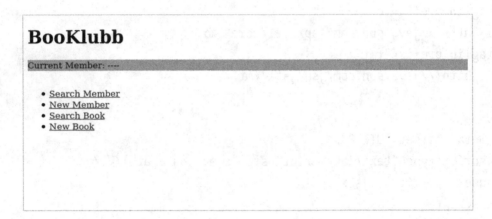

BooKlubb

Current Member: ----

- Search Member
- New Member
- Search Book
- New Book

Figure 12-1. *BooKlubb landing page*

Member-Related View Files

To create a new member, delete a member, search for a member, and show member details (including books assigned)—as well as for the action result pages for most of these—we need a separate JSP page. They all reside in the `src/main/webapp/WEB-INF/views` folder.

The code to create a new member and the resultant page are as follows:

```
<%-- File newMember.jsp **************************** --%>
<%@ page contentType="text/html;charset=UTF-8"
  language="java" %>
<%@ taglib prefix="c"
  uri="http://java.sun.com/jsp/jstl/core" %>
```

```
<%@ taglib prefix="fmt"
  uri="http://java.sun.com/jsp/jstl/fmt" %>
<html>
<head>
    <meta charset="UTF-8">
    <script type="text/javascript" src="${mvc.basePath}/../js/jquery--
      3.5.1.min.js">
    </script>
    <title>${msg.title}</title>
</head>
<body>
  <%@ include file="../../fragments/errors.jsp" %>

  <h1>${msg.hd_newMember}</h1>
  <%@ include file="../../fragments/currentMember.jsp" %>

  <div>
    <%@ include file="../../fragments/mainMenu.jsp" %>
    <div style="float:left">
      <form method="post"
          action="${mvc.uriBuilder(
              'BooKlubbController#newMemberSubmit').
              build()}">
    <table><tbody>
      <tr>
        <td>${msg.enter_memberFirstName}</td>
        <td><input type="text" name="firstName" /></td>
      </tr>
      <tr>
        <td>${msg.enter_memberLastName}</td>
        <td><input type="text" name="lastName" /></td>
      </tr>
      <tr>
        <td>${msg.enter_memberBirthday}</td>
        <td><input type="text" name="birthday" /></td>
      </tr>
```

```
      <tr>
        <td>${msg.enter_memberSsn}</td>
        <td><input type="text" name="ssn" /></td>
      </tr>
    </tbody></table>
    <input type="submit" value="${msg.btn_new}" />
  </form>
    </div>
    </div>

</body>
</html>

<%-- File newMemberResult.jsp ********************* --%>
<%@ page contentType="text/html;charset=UTF-8"
  language="java" %>
<%@ taglib prefix="c"
  uri="http://java.sun.com/jsp/jstl/core" %>
<%@ taglib prefix="fmt"
  uri="http://java.sun.com/jsp/jstl/fmt" %>
<html>
<head>
    <meta charset="UTF-8">
    <title>Member Search</title>
</head>
<body>
  <%@ include file="../../fragments/errors.jsp" %>

  <h1>${msg.new_member_added}</h1>
  <%@ include file="../../fragments/currentMember.jsp" %>

  <div>
    <%@ include file="../../fragments/mainMenu.jsp" %>
    <div style="float:left">
    </div>
  </div>

</body>
</html>
```

The newMember.jsp JSP shows the input form for a new member. See Figure 12-2. The resultant page just shows a corresponding success message.

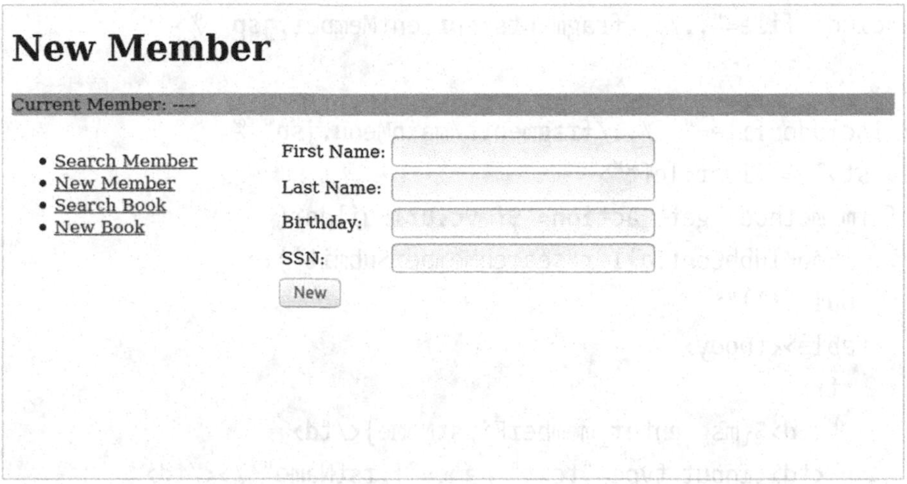

Figure 12-2. *BooKlubb New Member page*

The code to search in the member database and the page showing the resultant list are as follows:

```
<%-- File searchMember.jsp ************************* --%>
<%@ page contentType="text/html;charset=UTF-8"
  language="java" %>
<%@ taglib prefix="c"
  uri="http://java.sun.com/jsp/jstl/core" %>
<%@ taglib prefix="fmt"
  uri="http://java.sun.com/jsp/jstl/fmt" %>
<html>
<head>
    <meta charset="UTF-8">
    <script type="text/javascript" src="${mvc.basePath}/../js/
    jquery-3.5.1.min.js">
    </script>
    <title>${msg.title}</title>
</head>
```

```jsp
<body>
  <%@ include file="../../fragments/errors.jsp" %>

  <h1>${msg.hd_searchMember}</h1>
  <%@ include file="../../fragments/currentMember.jsp" %>

  <div>
    <%@ include file="../../fragments/mainMenu.jsp" %>
    <div style="float:left">
      <form method="get" action="${mvc.uriBuilder(
          'BooKlubbController#searchMemberSubmit').
          build()}">
        <table><tbody>
          <tr>
            <td>${msg.enter_memberFirstName}</td>
            <td><input type="text" name="firstName" /></td>
          </tr>
          <tr>
            <td>${msg.enter_memberLastName}</td>
            <td><input type="text" name="lastName" /> </td>
          </tr>
          <tr>
            <td>${msg.enter_memberSsn}</td>
            <td><input type="text" name="ssn" /> </td>
          </tr>
        </tbody></table>
        <input type="submit" value="${msg.btn_search}" />
      </form>
    </div>
  </div>

</body>
</html>

<%-- File searchMemberResult.jsp ******************* --%>
<%@ page contentType="text/html;charset=UTF-8"
  language="java" %>
```

```jsp
<%@ taglib prefix="c"
  uri="http://java.sun.com/jsp/jstl/core" %>
<%@ taglib prefix="fmt"
  uri="http://java.sun.com/jsp/jstl/fmt" %>
<html>
<head>
    <meta charset="UTF-8">
    <script type="text/javascript" src="${mvc.basePath}/../js/
    jquery-3.5.1.min.js">
    </script>
    <title>Member Search</title>
</head>
<body>
  <%@ include file="../../fragments/errors.jsp" %>

  <h1>${msg.hd_searchResult}</h1>
  <%@ include file="../../fragments/currentMember.jsp" %>

  <div>
    <%@ include file="../../fragments/mainMenu.jsp" %>

    <div style="float:left">
    <c:choose>
    <c:when test="${empty memberSearchResult}">
      ${msg.no_result}
    </c:when>
    <c:otherwise>
    <table>
    <thead>
      <tr>
        <th>${msg.tblhdr_id}</th>
        <th>${msg.tblhdr_last_name}</th>
        <th>${msg.tblhdr_first_name}</th>
        <th>${msg.tblhdr_birthday}</th>
        <th>${msg.tblhdr_ssn}</th>
        <th></th>
        <th></th>
```

```
      </tr>
    <thead>
    <tbody>
      <c:forEach items="${memberSearchResult}"
            var="itm">
        <tr id="itm-${itm.id}">
          <td>${itm.id}</td>
          <td>${itm.lastName}</td>
          <td>${itm.firstName}</td>
          <fmt:formatDate value="${itm.birthday}"
                 pattern="MM/dd/yyyy"
                 var="d1" />
          <td>${d1}</td>
          <td>${itm.ssn}</td>
          <td><button onclick="deleteItm(${itm.id})">
              ${msg.btn_delete}</button></td>
          <td><button onclick="selectMember(${itm.id})">
              ${msg.btn_select}</button></td>
          <td><button onclick="showDetails(${itm.id})">
              ${msg.btn_details}</button></td>
        </tr>
      </c:forEach>
    </tbody>
  </table>
  </c:otherwise>
  </c:choose>

  <script type="text/javascript">
    function deleteItm(id) {
      jQuery('#memberIdForDelete').val(id);
      jQuery('#deleteForm').submit();
    }
    function selectMember(id) {
      jQuery('#memberIdForSelect').val(id);
      jQuery('#selectForm').submit();
    }
```

```
  function showDetails(id) {
    jQuery('#memberIdForDetails').val(id);
    jQuery('#detailsForm').submit();
  }
</script>
<form id="deleteForm" method="post"
      action="${mvc.uriBuilder(
        'BooKlubbController#deleteMember').
        build()}">
  <input id="memberIdForDelete" type="hidden"
      name="memberId" />
</form>
<form id="selectForm" method="post"
      action="${mvc.uriBuilder(
        'BooKlubbController#selectMember').
        build()}">
  <input id="memberIdForSelect" type="hidden"
      name="memberId" />
</form>
<form id="detailsForm" method="post"
      action="${mvc.uriBuilder(
        'BooKlubbController#memberDetails').
        build()}">
  <input id="memberIdForDetails" type="hidden"
      name="memberId" />
</form>
</div>

</div>

</body>
</html>
```

The searchMember.jsp file shows an input form for a member search; see
Figure 12-3. The resultant page shows the corresponding member list, as shown in
Figure 12-4.

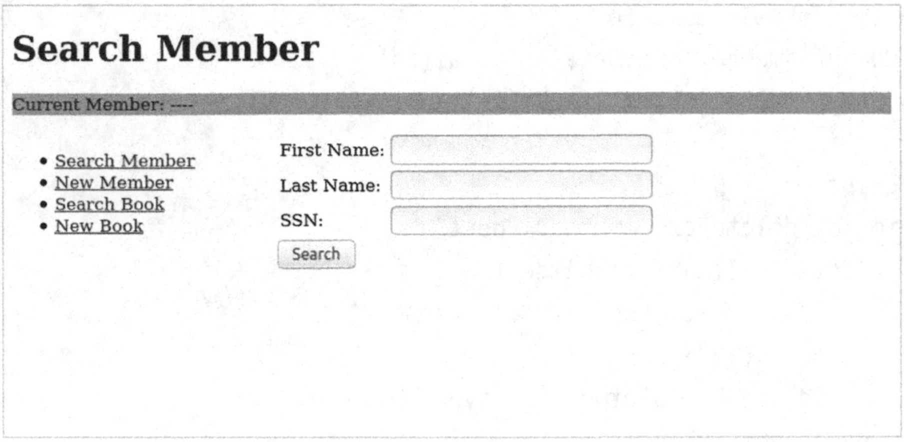

Figure 12-3. *BooKlubb Search Member page*

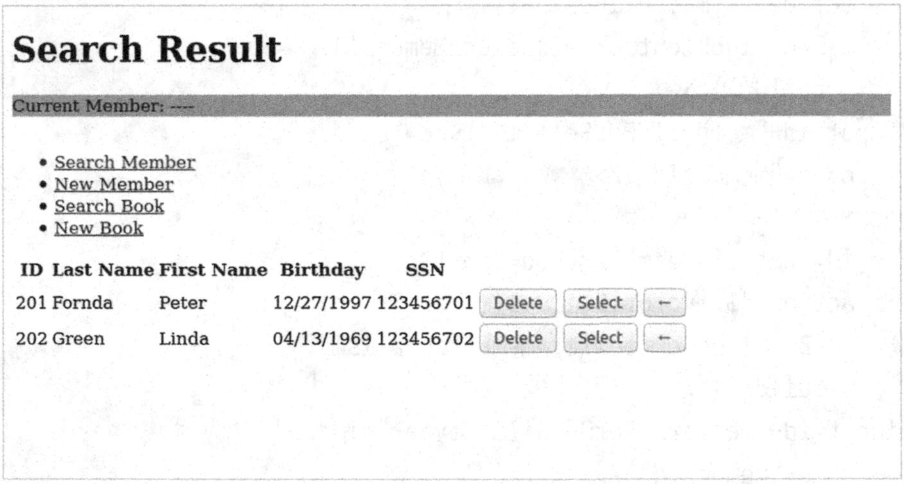

Figure 12-4. *BooKlubb search member result page*

You can see that each member item in the list has three buttons—one for deleting the member, one for making it the current member, one for showing member details. We use JavaScript to forward button clicks to one of the invisible forms added near the end of the file.

After member deletion, we just show a success message, which is defined in the deleteMemberResult.jsp file:

```
<%@ page contentType="text/html;charset=UTF-8"
  language="java" %>
<%@ taglib prefix="c"
  uri="http://java.sun.com/jsp/jstl/core" %>
<%@ taglib prefix="fmt"
  uri="http://java.sun.com/jsp/jstl/fmt" %>
<html>
<head>
    <meta charset="UTF-8">
    <title>Member Search</title>
</head>
<body>
  <%@ include file="../../fragments/errors.jsp" %>

  <h1>${msg.member_deleted}</h1>
  <%@ include file="../../fragments/currentMember.jsp" %>

  <div>
    <%@ include file="../../fragments/mainMenu.jsp" %>
    <div style="float:left">
    </div>
  </div>

</body>
</html>
```

On the details page, we show the member information and the books assigned. This is defined by the memberDetails.jsp file:

```
<%@ page contentType="text/html;charset=UTF-8"
  language="java" %>
<%@ taglib prefix="c"
  uri="http://java.sun.com/jsp/jstl/core" %>
<%@ taglib prefix="fmt"
  uri="http://java.sun.com/jsp/jstl/fmt" %>
```

```
<html>
<head>
    <meta charset="UTF-8">
    <script type="text/javascript"
        src="${mvc.basePath}/../js/jquery-3.5.1.min.js">
    </script>
    <title>${msg.title}</title>
</head>
<body>
  <%@ include file="../../fragments/errors.jsp" %>

  <h1>${msg.hd_memberDetails}</h1>
  <%@ include file="../../fragments/currentMember.jsp" %>

  <div>

      <%@ include file="../../fragments/mainMenu.jsp" %>
      <div style="float:left">
        <table>
          <tbody>
            <tr>
              <td>${msg.memb_id}</td>
              <td>${currentMember.id}</td>
            </tr>
            <tr>
              <td>${msg.memb_firstName}</td>
              <td>${currentMember.firstName}</td>
            </tr>
            <tr>
              <td>${msg.memb_lastName}</td>
              <td>${currentMember.lastName}</td>
            </tr>
            <fmt:formatDate value="${currentMember.birthday}"
                    pattern="MM/dd/yyyy"
                    var="bd" />
            <tr>
              <td>${msg.memb_birthday}</td>
```

```
        <td>${bd}</td>
      </tr>
      <tr>
        <td>${msg.memb_ssn}</td>
        <td>${currentMember.ssn}</td>
      </tr>
    </tbody>
</table>

<h2>${msg.hd_booksAssigned}</h2>
<c:choose>
  <c:when test="${empty currentMember.rentals}">
    ----
  </c:when>
  <c:otherwise>
    <table>
    <tbody>
      <c:forEach items="${currentMember.rentals}"
           var="r">
        <tr>
          <td>${r.authorFirstName}
              ${r.authorLastName}</td>
          <td>${r.title}</td>
          <fmt:formatDate value="${r.make}"
            pattern="MM/dd/yyyy"
            var="makeDay" />
          <td>${makeDay}</td>
          <td>
            <button onclick="unassign(
                ${currentMember.id},${r.id})">
              ${msg.btn_unassign}
            </button>
          </td>
        </tr>
      </c:forEach>
    </tbody>
```

```
                </table>
              </c:otherwise>
          </c:choose>
          <script type="text/javascript">
            function unassign(memberId,bookId) {
              jQuery('#memberIdForUnassign').val(memberId);
              jQuery('#bookIdForUnassign').val(bookId);
              jQuery('#unassignForm').submit();
            }
          </script>
          <form id="unassignForm" method="post"
              action="${mvc.uriBuilder(
                'BooKlubbController#unassignBook').build()}">
          <input id="memberIdForUnassign" type="hidden"
              name="memberId" />
          <input id="bookIdForUnassign" type="hidden"
              name="bookId" />
        </form>

    </div>
  </div>

</body>
</html>
```

In the books assigned list, we again use buttons to unassign books, and JavaScript to submit an invisible form. Figure 12-5 shows a details page example. Assigning books to members happens in the book search result list, discussed in a later section.

Member Details

Current Member: **Peter Fornda 12/27/1997 (123456701)**

- Search Member
- New Member
- Search Book
- New Book

ID: 201
First Name: Peter
Last Name: Fornda
Birthday: 12/27/1997
SSN: 123456701

Books Assigned

John Barda	The Midsummer	01/01/1968	Unassign
Grete Bostel	The Moon's Dream	01/01/2002	Unassign

Figure 12-5. BooKlubb Member Details page

Book-Related View Files

For books, we identify the following use cases: create a new book record, delete a book record, search for a book, and assign a book to a member (rental). We have JSP pages to create a book and to search for a book, plus action result pages. Just as with the members, they all reside in the src/main/webapp/WEB-INF/views folder. Book record deletion and assignment to the current member happens from inside the book search result list.

The code to create a book record and its corresponding submit result page is as follows:

```
<%-- File newBook.jsp ***************************** --%>
<%@ page contentType="text/html;charset=UTF-8"
  language="java" %>
<%@ taglib prefix="c"
  uri="http://java.sun.com/jsp/jstl/core" %>
<%@ taglib prefix="fmt"
  uri="http://java.sun.com/jsp/jstl/fmt" %>
<html>
<head>
    <meta charset="UTF-8">
```

```jsp
    <script type="text/javascript" src="${mvc.basePath}/../js/
    jquery-3.5.1.min.js">
    </script>
    <title>${msg.title}</title>
</head>
<body>
  <%@ include file="../../fragments/errors.jsp" %>

  <h1>${msg.hd_newBook}</h1>
  <%@ include file="../../fragments/currentMember.jsp" %>

  <div>
    <%@ include file="../../fragments/mainMenu.jsp" %>
    <div style="float:left">
      <form method="post"
          action="${mvc.uriBuilder(
          'BooKlubbController#newBookSubmit').build()}">
      <table><tbody>
        <tr>
          <td>${msg.enter_authorFirstName}</td>
          <td>
            <input type="text" name="authorFirstName" />
          </td>
        </tr>
        <tr>
          <td>${msg.enter_authorLastName}</td>
          <td>
            <input type="text" name="authorLastName" />
          </td>
        </tr>
        <tr>
          <td>${msg.enter_bookTitle}</td>
          <td>
            <input type="text" name="title" />
          </td>
        </tr>
```

```
        <tr>
          <td>${msg.enter_bookMake}</td>
          <td>
            <input type="text" name="make" />
          </td>
        </tr>
        <tr>
          <td>${msg.enter_isbn}</td>
          <td>
            <input type="text" name="isbn" />
          </td>
        </tr>
      </tbody></table>
    <input type="submit" value="${msg.btn_new}" />
    </form>
  </div>
  </div>

</body>
</html>

<%-- File newBookResult.jsp ************************ --%>
<%@ page contentType="text/html;charset=UTF-8"
  language="java" %>
<%@ taglib prefix="c"
  uri="http://java.sun.com/jsp/jstl/core" %>
<%@ taglib prefix="fmt"
  uri="http://java.sun.com/jsp/jstl/fmt" %>
<html>
<head>
  <meta charset="UTF-8">
  <title>Member Search</title>
</head>
<body>
  <%@ include file="../../fragments/errors.jsp" %>
```

```
<h1>${msg.new_book_added}</h1>
<%@ include file="../../fragments/currentMember.jsp" %>

<div>
    <%@ include file="../../fragments/mainMenu.jsp" %>
    <div style="float:left">
    </div>
</div>

</body>
</html>
```

The new book page is a form for entering the author's name, the book title, make, and the ISBN number. See Figure 12-6. The resultant page just shows an info message.

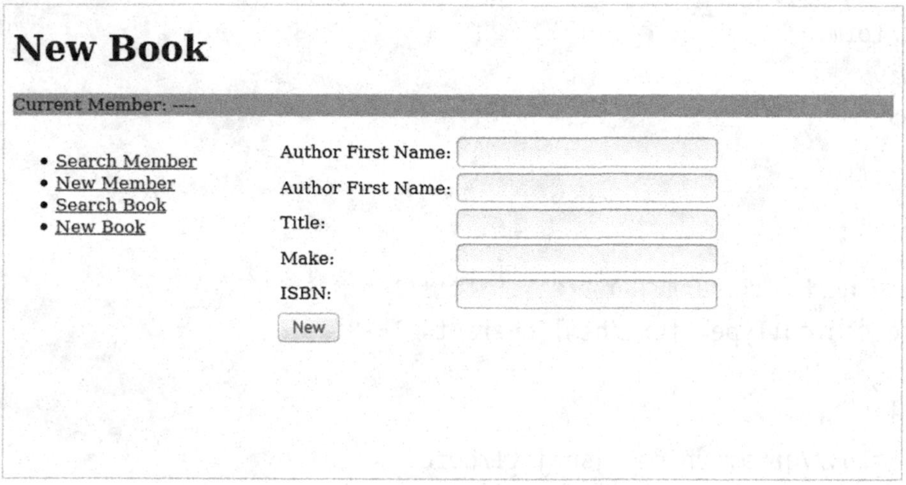

Figure 12-6. *BooKlubb New Book entry*

To search the database and present the search result list, the following two files are used:

```
<%-- File searchBook.jsp *************************** --%>
<%@ page contentType="text/html;charset=UTF-8"
  language="java" %>
<%@ taglib prefix="c"
  uri="http://java.sun.com/jsp/jstl/core" %>
```

```
<%@ taglib prefix="fmt"
  uri="http://java.sun.com/jsp/jstl/fmt" %>
<html>
<head>
    <meta charset="UTF-8">
    <script type="text/javascript" src="${mvc.basePath}/../js/
    jquery-3.5.1.min.js">
    </script>
    <title>${msg.title}</title>
</head>
<body>
  <%@ include file="../../fragments/errors.jsp" %>

  <h1>${msg.hd_searchBook}</h1>
  <%@ include file="../../fragments/currentMember.jsp" %>

  <div>
    <%@ include file="../../fragments/mainMenu.jsp" %>
    <div style="float:left">
    <form method="get"
        action="${mvc.uriBuilder(
        'BooKlubbController#searchBookSubmit').build()}">
    <table><tbody>
      <tr>
        <td>${msg.enter_authorFirstName}</td>
        <td>
          <input type="text" name="authorFirstName" />
        </td>
      </tr>
      <tr>
        <td>${msg.enter_authorLastName}</td>
        <td>
          <input type="text" name="authorLastName" />
        </td>
      </tr>
      <tr>
```

```
        <td>${msg.enter_bookTitle}</td>
        <td>
            <input type="text" name="bookTitle"/>
        </td>
      </tr>
      <tr>
        <td>${msg.enter_isbn}</td>
        <td>
          <input type="text" name="isbn"/>
        </td>
      </tr>
    </tbody></table>
    <input type="submit" value="${msg.btn_search}" />
    </form>
    </div>
  </div>

</body>
</html>

<%-- File searchBookResult.jsp ******************** --%>
<%@ page contentType="text/html;charset=UTF-8"
  language="java" %>
<%@ taglib prefix="c"
  uri="http://java.sun.com/jsp/jstl/core" %>
<%@ taglib prefix="fmt"
  uri="http://java.sun.com/jsp/jstl/fmt" %>
<html>
<head>
    <meta charset="UTF-8">
    <script type="text/javascript" src="${mvc.basePath}/../js/
    jquery-3.5.1.min.js">
    </script>
    <title>Book Search</title>
</head>
<body>
```

```
<%@ include file="../../fragments/errors.jsp" %>

<h1>${msg.hd_searchResult}</h1>
<%@ include file="../../fragments/currentMember.jsp" %>

<div>
  <%@ include file="../../fragments/mainMenu.jsp" %>
  <div style="float:left">
  <c:choose>
  <c:when test="${empty bookSearchResult}">
      ${msg.no_result}
  </c:when>
  <c:otherwise>
  <table>
    <thead>
      <tr>
        <th>${msg.tblhdr_id}</th>
        <th>${msg.tblhdr_author_last_name}</th>
        <th>${msg.tblhdr_author_first_name}</th>
        <th>${msg.tblhdr_book_title}</th>
        <th>${msg.tblhdr_book_make}</th>
        <th>${msg.tblhdr_isbn}</th>
        <th></th>
        <th></th>
      </tr>
    <thead>
    <tbody>
        <c:forEach    items="${bookSearchResult}"
             var="itm">
          <tr id="itm-${itm.id}">
            <td>${itm.id}</td>
            <td>${itm.authorLastName}</td>
            <td>${itm.authorFirstName}</td>
            <td>${itm.title}</td>
            <fmt:formatDate value="${itm.make}"
                  pattern="MM/dd/yyyy"
```

```
                        var="d1" />
          <td>${d1}</td>
          <td>${itm.isbn}</td>
          <td><button onclick="deleteItm(${itm.id})">
            ${msg.btn_delete}
            </button>
          </td>
          <td><button onclick="assignItm(${itm.id},
              ${currentMember.id})">
            ${msg.btn_assign}
            </button>
          </td>
        </tr>
      </c:forEach>
  </tbody>
</table>
</c:otherwise>
</c:choose>

<script type="text/javascript">
  function deleteItm(id) {
    jQuery('#bookIdForDelete').val(id);
    jQuery('#deleteForm').submit();
  }
  function assignItm(bookId, userId) {
    jQuery('#bookIdForAssign').val(bookId);
    jQuery('#userIdForAssign').val(userId);
    jQuery('#assignForm').submit();
  }
</script>
<form id="deleteForm" method="post"
    action="${mvc.uriBuilder(
    'BooKlubbController#deleteBook').build()}">
  <input id="bookIdForDelete" type="hidden"
    name="bookId" />
</form>
```

```
<form id="assignForm" method="post"
    action="${mvc.uriBuilder(
    'BooKlubbController#assignBook').build()}">
  <input id="bookIdForAssign" type="hidden"
      name="bookId" />
  <input id="userIdForAssign" type="hidden"
      name="userId" />
</form>
</div>
</div>

</body>
</html>
```

The book search result list is depicted in Figure 12-7. For each list item, we provide a Delete and an Assign button. JavaScript code takes care of forwarding button presses to one of the two invisible forms added near the end of the code.

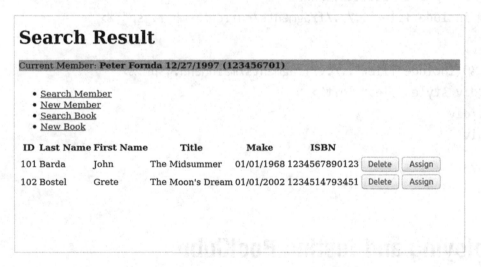

Figure 12-7. *BooKlubb book search result*

After clicking one of the Delete buttons, a simple success message is shown. The deleteBookResult.jsp file takes care of that:

```
<%@ page contentType="text/html;charset=UTF-8"
  language="java" %>
<%@ taglib prefix="c"
  uri="http://java.sun.com/jsp/jstl/core" %>
<%@ taglib prefix="fmt"
  uri="http://java.sun.com/jsp/jstl/fmt" %>
<html>
<head>
  <meta charset="UTF-8">
  <title>Book Search</title>
</head>
<body>
  <%@ include file="../../fragments/errors.jsp" %>

  <h1>${msg.book_deleted}</h1>
  <%@ include file="../../fragments/currentMember.jsp" %>

  <div>
    <%@ include file="../../fragments/mainMenu.jsp" %>
    <div style="float:left">
    </div>
  </div>

</body>
</html>
```

Deploying and Testing BooKlubb

To build and deploy the BooKlubb application, you enter the following inside the console:

```
./gradlew   localDeploy

# or, if you need to specify a certain JDK
JAVA_HOME=/path/to/jdk ./gradlew   localDeploy
```

For this to work, the GlassFish server must be running and the `gradle.properties` file must contain the correct connection properties for the GlassFish server. The WAR file that's built during this process is copied into the `build/libs` folder.

If everything works correctly, you can point your browser to the following URL to enter the application:

```
http://localhost:8080/BooKlubb
```

See Figure 12-1.

Summary

This chapter concluded the book with a comprehensive example application called `BooKlubb`, which illustrates many Java MVC features.

Appendix

Solutions to the Exercises

The following are the solutions to the exercises found in the chapters.

Chapter 1 Exercises

Exercise 1: Model, view, and controller.

Exercise 2: False. This is the controller's responsibility. Also, this is optional.

Exercise 3: No, this must be coded in the controller.

Exercise 4: True.

Exercise 5: None are true. Sessions are created by the framework, and they are passed through the HTTP transport as cookies, query parameters, or POST parameters. A session ID *might* be passed over as a model object, but the session itself is not part of the model.

Exercise 6: No, it became part of the Java EE/Jakarta EE specification in version 8.

© Peter Späth 2021
P. Späth, *Beginning Java MVC 1.0*, https://doi.org/10.1007/978-1-4842-6280-1

Chapter 2 Exercises

Exercise 1: JEE/Jakarta EE (Java/Jakarta Enterprise Edition) sits on top of JSE and extends it with enterprise features.

Exercise 2: No, Java MVC needs to be installed inside a Java EE/Jakarta EE server.

Exercise 3: No, Java MVC is *part* of Java EE/Jakarta EE.

Exercise 4: Not really. While Java EE and Jakarta EE version 8 coexist, Jakarta EE is considered the successor of Java EE.

Exercise 5: No, in order to use Oracle's JSE in a commercial product, you must pay for a subscription. OpenJDK is free also for commercial projects.

Exercise 6: True.

Exercise 7: Because it is free and the reference implementation.

Exercise 8: No. We have GET, POST, PUT, DELETE, HEAD, and TRACE.

Exercise 9: Java MVC sits on top of (uses) JAX-RS, and Java MVC and the REST controllers look similar.

Chapter 3 Exercises

Exercise 1: No, best practices indicate that for build scripts, declarative programming (indicating *what* a build script has to do, not *how* it should do it) is favorable over imperative programming (precise step-by-step instructions).

Exercise 2: No, you can use Groovy or Kotlin code.

Exercise 3: No, Eclipse allows different JREs for building (compiling) projects.

Exercise 4: Initialization, configuration, and execution.

Exercise 5: No, `src/main/java` is correct.

Exercise 6: No, you use the main build file called `build.gradle` for that.

Exercise 7: No, you use the `repositories { }` -section for that.

Exercise 8: A configuration in Gradle is a dependency scope. You have different scopes in a project, such as testing, compilation, inclusion into an archive, and so on.

Exercise 9: Start a Gradle project via File ➤ New ➤ Other... ➤ Gradle ➤ Gradle Project. Open `build.gradle` and replace its contents with the following:

```
plugins {
    id 'java-library'
}
java {
    sourceCompatibility = JavaVersion.VERSION_1_8
    targetCompatibility = JavaVersion.VERSION_1_8
}
repositories {
    jcenter()
}

dependencies {
    testImplementation 'junit:junit:4.12'
}
```

Fix any build path errors by right-clicking the project, then choosing Properties ➤ Java Build Path ➤ Libraries. Remove the erroneous JRE and add a correct JRE (JRE System Library) to the classpath. Right-click the project and then choose Gradle ➤ Refresh Gradle Project. Inside `src/main/java`, create a new package called `book.javamvc.graphicsprimitives`, and add two classes as follows:

```
// File Circle.java
package book.javamvc.graphicsprimitives;
public class Circle {
    private double cx, cy, r;
    // add consructor, getters, setters...

}
```

```
//File Rectangle.java
package book.javamvc.graphicsprimitives;
public class Rectangle {
    private double x, y, w, h;
    // add consructor, getters, setters...
}
```

Exercise 10: "Hi, I'm A" is printed unconditionally, even if task a is not explicitly invoked. This is because instructions directly inside task { } belong to the *configuration* phase, and the configuration phase always gets called for all tasks for any build. If you want to execute something during the execution phase, you must wrap it inside doFirst { } or doLast { }.

Exercise 11: No, the wrapper is a standalone Gradle installation. Java must be working, though.

Exercise 12: Do a export JAVA_HOME=/opt/jdk8 (in Linux) or a set JAVA_HOME=C:\jdk8 (in Windows).

Chapter 4 Exercises

Exercise 1: True. The wrapper supports both Windows and Linux.

Exercise 2: B and C are true.

Exercise 3: False. But we describe custom tasks for this purpose.

Exercise 4: Facelets and JSTL.

Exercise 5: It is possible to use dedicated Java bean classes. But no, you can also use a built-in container to hold model values (the javax.mvc.Models class).

Exercise 6: Inside a Jakarta EE server.

Exercise 7: False. We use Gradle in this book, but other build tools are possible as well.

Exercise 8: The UserData class reads as follows:

```
package book.javamvc.helloworld;

import javax.enterprise.context.RequestScoped;
import javax.inject.Named;

@Named
@RequestScoped
public class UserData {
  private String name;

  public String getName() {
    return name;
  }

  public void setName(String name) {
    this.name = name;
  }
}
```

In the controller, you write the following:

```
package book.javamvc.helloworld;

import javax.inject.Inject;
import javax.mvc.Controller;
import javax.mvc.binding.MvcBinding;
import javax.ws.rs.FormParam;
import javax.ws.rs.GET;
import javax.ws.rs.POST;
import javax.ws.rs.Path;
import javax.ws.rs.core.Response;

@Path("/hello")
@Controller
public class HelloWorldController {
  @Inject UserData userData;
```

```
    @GET
    public String showIndex() {
      return "index.jsp";
    }

    @POST
    @Path("/greet")
    public Response greeting(@MvcBinding
          @FormParam("name")
            String name) {
      userData.setName(name);
      return Response.ok("greeting.jsp").build();
    }
}
```

The greeting.jsp file reads as follows:

```
<%@ page contentType="text/html;charset=UTF-8"
  language="java" %>
<%@ taglib prefix="c"
  uri="http://java.sun.com/jsp/jstl/core" %>
<html>
<head>
    <meta charset="UTF-8">
    <title>Hello World</title>
</head>
<body>
  Hello ${userData.name}
</body>
</html>
```

Exercise 9: Replace the <body> of greeting.jsp with the following:

```
<body>
  Hello ${userData.name}
    <div>
```

```
    <a href="${mvc.uriBuilder(
        'HelloWorldController#showIndex'
      ).build()}">Back</a>
  </div>
</body>
```

Chapter 5 Exercises

Exercise 1: (B) is true.

Exercise 2: You at least need the @Controller class annotation.

Exercise 3: The controller classes are very similar, but Java MVC controllers must return page names, contrary to JAX-RS controllers, which return data.

Exercise 4: Placed next to the @FormParam and @QueryParam elements, the @MvcBinding annotation ensures conversion and validation errors don't automatically yield some error data being loaded (as dictated by JAX-RS). Instead, errors are passed over to an injected BindingResult instance (class instance level).

Exercise 5: Update the controller as follows:

```
package book.javamvc.helloworld;

import java.util.ArrayList;
import java.util.List;

import javax.enterprise.context.RequestScoped;
import javax.inject.Inject;
import javax.inject.Named;
import javax.mvc.Controller;
import javax.mvc.binding.BindingResult;
import javax.mvc.binding.MvcBinding;
import javax.mvc.binding.ParamError;
import javax.validation.constraints.*;
import javax.ws.rs.FormParam;
import javax.ws.rs.GET;
```

```
import javax.ws.rs.POST;
import javax.ws.rs.Path;
import javax.ws.rs.QueryParam;
import javax.ws.rs.core.Response;

@Path("/hello")
@Controller
public class HelloWorldController {
  @Named
  @RequestScoped
  public static class ErrorMessages {
    private List<String> msgs = new ArrayList<>();

    public List<String> getMsgs() {
      return msgs;
    }

    public void setMsgs(List<String> msgs) {
      this.msgs = msgs;
    }

    public void addMessage(String msg) {
      msgs.add(msg);
    }
  }

  private @Inject ErrorMessages errorMessages;
  private @Inject BindingResult br;
  ...

  @POST
  @Path("/greet")
  public Response greeting(
      @MvcBinding @FormParam("name")
      String name)
  {
    if(br.isFailed()) {
      br.getAllErrors().stream().forEach(
        (ParamError pe) -> {
```

```
        errorMessages.addMessage(pe.getParamName() +
        ": " + pe.getMessage());
    });
  }

  ...

  }
}
```

Inside `greeting.jsp`, add the following:

```
<div style="color:red">
<c:forEach var="e" items="${errorMessages.msgs}">
    ${e}
</c:forEach>
</div>
```

Exercise 6: Inside the controller class, add as annotation to the greeting() method's parameter, as follows:

```
import javax.validation.constraints.Pattern;
...
@POST
@Path("/greet")
public Response greeting(
    @MvcBinding @FormParam("name")
    @Pattern(regexp = "[A-Za-z]*")
    String name) {

    ...

}
```

Exercise 7: In the controller class, write the following for the showIndex() method:

```
@GET
public String showIndex(
    @MvcBinding @QueryParam("name")
    String name)
```

```
{
  if(name != null) {
    models.put("name", name);
  }
  return "index.jsp";
}
```

A missing name query parameter, for example when the start page
is loaded the first time, will lead to a null value. The code checks
that. Inside the index.jsp page, you can use ${ name } for the
input field's initial value, which will yield an empty string if the
model value doesn't exist:

```
...
<form method="post"
    action="${mvc.uriBuilder(
    'HelloWorldController#greeting').build()}">
  Enter your name:
  <input type="text" name="name" value="${name}" />
  <input type="submit" value="Submit" />
</form>
...
```

In the response page called greeting.jsp, you write the
following:

```
...
Hello ${name}
<div>
    <a href="${mvc.uriBuilder(
            'HelloWorldController#showIndex').
            queryParam('name', name).
            build()}">Back</a>
</div>
...
```

Chapter 6 Exercises

Exercise 1: The new model class reads as follows:

```
package book.javamvc.helloworld.model;

import javax.enterprise.context.RequestScoped;
import javax.inject.Named;

@Named
@RequestScoped
public class UserData {
  private String name;

  public String getName() {
    return name;
  }

  public void setName(String name) {
    this.name = name;
  }
}
```

In the controller class, you write the following:

```
...
@Controller
public class HelloWorldController {

  private @Inject UserData userData;
  //private @Inject Models models; REMOVE THIS

  ...

  @GET
  public String showIndex(@MvcBinding
        @QueryParam("name") String name) {
    if(name != null) {
      userData.setName(name);
    }
```

```
        return "index.jsp";
    }

    @POST
    @Path("/greet")
    public Response greeting(
        @MvcBinding @FormParam("name")
        @Pattern(regexp = "[A-Za-z]*")
        String name)
    {
        ...

        userData.setName(name);
        return Response.ok("greeting.jsp").build();
    }
}
```

In the index.jsp page, you must substitute ${ userData.name }
for ${ name }, as follows:

```
...
  <form method="post"
      action="${mvc.uriBuilder(
      'HelloWorldController#greeting').build()}">
    Enter your name:
    <input type="text" name="name" />
    <input type="submit" value="Submit" />
  </form>
...
```

Same for the greeting.jsp response page:

```
...
Hello ${userData.name}
<div>
    <a href="${mvc.uriBuilder(
      'HelloWorldController#showIndex').
```

```
        queryParam('name', userData.name).
          build()}">Back</a>
</div>
...
```

Exercise 2: The second option is true—each JSP gets its own servlet.

Exercise 3: Facelets are newer.

Exercise 4: No, you don't have to use JSF. In fact, it is better to avoid JSF features, since JSF is component-based and Java MVC does not use view components.

Chapter 7 Exercises

Exercise 1: As UserData, write the following:

```
package book.javamvc.helloworld;

import javax.enterprise.context.RequestScoped;
import javax.inject.Named;

@Named
@RequestScoped
public class UserData {
    private String name;
    private int age;
    // Getters and setters...
}
```

The updated (important) parts from the controller class HelloWorldController are as follows:

```
...
import javax.validation.constraints.Min;
...
@Path("/hello")
@Controller
```

```java
public class HelloWorldController {
  @Named
  @RequestScoped
 public static class ErrorMessages {
  private List<String> msgs = new ArrayList<>();
  public List<String> getMsgs() {
    return msgs;
  }
  public void setMsgs(List<String> msgs) {
    this.msgs = msgs;
  }
  public void addMessage(String msg) {
    msgs.add(msg);
  }
 }

 private @Inject UserData userData;
 private @Inject ErrorMessages errorMessages;
 private @Inject BindingResult br;
 ...

 @POST
 @Path("/greet")
 public Response greeting(
    @MvcBinding @FormParam("name")
    String name,
    @MvcBinding @FormParam("age")
    @Min(1)
    int age) {
 if(br.isFailed()) {
  br.getAllErrors().stream().forEach(
      (ParamError pe) -> {
        errorMessages.addMessage(
           pe.getParamName() + ": " +
            pe.getMessage());
    });
```

```
    }
    userData.setName(name);
    userData.setAge(age);
    return Response.ok("greeting.jsp").build();
    }
}
```

As the `index.jsp` view page, take the following:

```
<%@ page contentType="text/html;charset=UTF-8"
    language="java" %>
<%@ taglib prefix="c"
    uri="http://java.sun.com/jsp/jstl/core" %>
<html>
<head>
    <meta charset="UTF-8">
    <title>Hello World</title>
</head>
<body>
    <form method="post"
      action="${mvc.uriBuilder(
        'HelloWorldController#greeting').build()}">
     Enter your name:
        <input type="text" name="name" /> Enter your age:
        <input type="text" name="age" />
        <input type="submit" value="Submit" />
    </form>
</body>
</html>
```

As the response page `greeting.jsp`:

```
<%@ page contentType="text/html;charset=UTF-8"
    language="java" %>
<%@ taglib prefix="c"
    uri="http://java.sun.com/jsp/jstl/core" %>
<html>
```

```
<head>
   <meta charset="UTF-8">
   <title>Hello World</title>
</head>
<body>
   <div style="color:red">
    <c:forEach var="e"
        items="${errorMessages.msgs}">
      ${e}
    </c:forEach>
   </div>

   Hello ${userData.name}, your age is ${userData.age}
</body>
</html>
```

Exercise 2: The updated (important) parts of the controller class
HelloWorldController read as follows:

```
package book.javamvc.helloworld;

import javax.servlet.http.HttpSession;
...

@Path("/hello")
@Controller
public class HelloWorldController {
  ...
  private @Inject HttpSession httpSession;
  ...
  @GET
  public String showIndex() {
    System.err.println("Session ID: " +
        httpSession.getId());

    ...
  }
  ...
}
```

Exercise 3: The updated (important) parts of the controller class
`HelloWorldController` read as follows:

```java
import javax.ws.rs.core.HttpHeaders;
import javax.ws.rs.core.Context;
...

@POST
@Path("/greet")
public Response greeting(
    ...form parameters...,
    @Context HttpHeaders httpHeaders)
    {
        System.err.println("Headers: \n" +
        httpHeaders.getRequestHeaders().entrySet().
            stream().map( me -> {
        return me.getKey() + ": " +
                    me.getValue();
        }).collect(Collectors.joining("\n")));
        ...
    }
```

Exercise 4: Download jQuery and put it into `src/main/webapp/js`.
The updated `index.jsp` file reads as follows:

```jsp
<%@ page contentType="text/html;charset=UTF-8"
    language="java" %>
<%@ taglib prefix="c"
uri="http://java.sun.com/jsp/jstl/core" %>
<html>
<head>
    <meta charset="UTF-8">
    <script type="text/javascript"
        src="${mvc.basePath}/../js/jquery-3.5.1.min.js">
    </script>
    <title>Hello World</title>
</head>
```

```html
<body>
  <form method="post" action="${mvc.uriBuilder(
        'HelloWorldController#greeting').build()}">
    Enter your name: <input type="text" name="name"/>
    <input type="submit" value="Submit" />
  </form>
  <form>
   <script type="text/javascript">
     function submitAge() {
      var age = jQuery('#age').val();
      var url = "${mvc.uriBuilder(
        'HelloWorldController#ageAjax').build()}";
      jQuery.ajax({
        url : url, method: "POST",
        data : { age: age },
        dataType: 'json',
        success: function(data, textStatus,
                  jqXHR) {
      jQuery('#ajax-response').html( data.text);
    },
    error: function (jqXHR, textStatus,
              errorThrown) {
      console.log(errorThrown);
    }
  });
   return false;
 }
</script>
  Enter your age: <input type="text" id="age" />
  <button onclick="return submitAge()">
    Submit
  </button>
</form>
<div>
  <span>AJAX Response: </span>
```

```
    <div id="ajax-response">
    </div>
  </div>
</body>
</html>
```

Obviously, in the head's script tag, write the jQuery version you downloaded.

The `HelloWorldController` gets a new `@POST` method to receive the AJAX requests:

```
@POST
@Path("/ageAjax")
public Response ageAjax(
      @MvcBinding @FormParam("age")
      int age) {
  if(br.isFailed()) {
     br.getAllErrors().stream().
     forEach((ParamError pe) -> {
       errorMessages.addMessage(
         pe.getParamName()
        + ": " + pe.getMessage());
     });
  }
  userData.setAge(age);
    return Response.ok("ageAjaxFragm.jsp").
      type(MediaType.APPLICATION_JSON).
      build();
  }
```

The JSP fragment `src/main/webapp/WEB-INF/ageAjaxFragm.jsp` reads as follows:

```
<%@ page language="java"
    contentType="application/json;charset=UTF-8" %>
<%@ taglib prefix = "c"
    uri = "http://java.sun.com/jsp/jstl/core" %>
```

411

```
<%@ taglib prefix = "fmt"
  uri = "http://java.sun.com/jsp/jstl/fmt" %>

{ "text": "This is a JSP generated fragment.
            Your age is: ${userData.age}" }
```

Exercise 5: The observer class reads as follows (use any package and class name you like; the method names can also be chosen freely):

```
package book.javamvc.helloworld.event;

import java.io.Serializable;
import java.time.Instant;

import javax.enterprise.context.SessionScoped;
import javax.enterprise.event.Observes;
import javax.mvc.event.AfterControllerEvent;
import javax.mvc.event.BeforeControllerEvent;

@SessionScoped
public class HelloWorldObserver
    implements Serializable {
  private static final long serialVersionUID =
      -2547124317706157382L;

  private long controllerStarted;

  public void update(@Observes
    BeforeControllerEvent
    beforeController) {
   controllerStarted = Instant.now().
   toEpochMilli();
  }

  public void update(@Observes
    AfterControllerEvent
    afterController) {
   long controllerElapseMillis =
```

```
      Instant.now().toEpochMilli() -
      controllerStarted;
    System.err.println("Elapse = " +
      controllerElapseMillis + "ms");
  }
}
```

Chapter 8 Exercises

Exercise 1: Add these properties files to the src/main/resources/
book/javamvc/helloworld/messages folder:

```
## File Messages.properties:
title = Hello World
enter_name = Enter your name:
enter_age = Enter your age:
btn_submit = Submit
btn_back = Back
ajax_response = AJAX Response:
response_hello = Hello
response_age = your age is
```

```
## File Messages_de.properties:
title = Hallo Welt
enter_name = Dein Name:
enter_age = Dein Alter:
btn_submit = Absenden
btn_back = Zurück
ajax_response = AJAX-Antwort:
response_hello = Hallo
response_age = Dein Alter ist
```

(You can add other language files, if you like.) You can copy
Messages.properties to Messages_en.properties, but you
don't have to if you want to set English as the default. Add the two
classes—BundleForEL and SetBundleFilter—as described in the
text to your project.

As `index.jsp`, use the following:

```
<%@ page contentType="text/html;charset=UTF-8"
    language="java" %>
<%@ taglib prefix="c"
    uri="http://java.sun.com/jsp/jstl/core" %>

<%-- ${msg} is the localized bundle variable,
    registered by class SetBundleFilter        --%>

<html>
<head>
    <meta charset="UTF-8">
    <title>${msg.title}</title>
</head>
<body>
    <form method="post"
        action="${mvc.uriBuilder(
        'HelloWorldController#greeting').build()}">
    ${msg.enter_name}
            <input type="text" name="name" />
    <%-- Only if you added the 'age'    --%>
    <%-- field (from exercises):    --%>
    ${msg.enter_age} <input type="text" name="age" />
    <input type="submit" value="${msg.btn_submit}" />
    </form>
</body>
</html>
```

As `greeting.jsp`, use the following:

```
<%@ page contentType="text/html;charset=UTF-8"
    language="java" %>
<%@ taglib prefix="c"
    uri="http://java.sun.com/jsp/jstl/core" %>

<%-- ${msg} is the localized bundle variable,
    registered by class SetBundleFilter        --%>
```

```
<html>
<head>
   <meta charset="UTF-8">
   <title>Hello World</title>
</head>
<body>
   <%-- Only if you caught the error messages --%>
   <%-- (from one of the exercies)    --%>
   <div style="color:red">
   <c:forEach var="e" items="${errorMessages.msgs}">
       ${e}
   </c:forEach>
   </div>

<%-- If UserData has an 'age' field --%>
${msg.response_hello} ${userData.name}, ${msg.
 response_age} ${userData.age}
<%-- otherwise --%>
${msg.response_hello} ${userData.name}

</body>
</html>
```

Exercise 2: As a new App class, use the following:

```
package book.javamvc.helloworld;

import java.util.Collections;
import java.util.HashMap;
import java.util.Map;

import javax.ws.rs.ApplicationPath;
import javax.ws.rs.core.Application;

@ApplicationPath("/mvc")
public class App extends Application {
  @Override
```

```
    public Map<String, Object> getProperties() {
      Map<String, Object> res = new HashMap<>();
      res.put("I18N_TEXT_ATTRIBUTE_NAME",
          "msg");
      res.put("I18N_TEXT_BASE_NAME",
          "book.javamvc.helloworld.messages.Messages"
);
      return res;
    }

  }
```

In the SetBundleFilter class, you can then inject the
Application CDI bean to fetch the properties:

```
package book.javamvc.i18n;

import java.io.IOException;
import java.util.Map;

import javax.inject.Inject;
import javax.servlet.Filter;
import javax.servlet.FilterChain;
import javax.servlet.FilterConfig;
import javax.servlet.ServletException;
import javax.servlet.ServletRequest;
import javax.servlet.ServletResponse;
import javax.servlet.annotation.WebFilter;
import javax.servlet.http.HttpServletRequest;
import javax.ws.rs.core.Application;

@WebFilter("/*")
public class SetBundleFilter implements Filter {
  @Inject private Application appl;
  private String i18nAttributeName;
  private String i18nBaseName;
```

```java
    @Override
    public void init(FilterConfig filterConfig)
            throws ServletException {
        Map<String,Object> applProps = appl.
            getProperties();
        i18nAttributeName = (String) applProps.
            get("I18N_TEXT_ATTRIBUTE_NAME");
        i18nBaseName = (String) applProps.
            get("I18N_TEXT_BASE_NAME");
    }

    @Override
    public void doFilter(ServletRequest request,
            ServletResponse response, FilterChain chain)
            throws IOException, ServletException {
        BundleForEL.setFor((HttpServletRequest) request,
            i18nAttributeName,
          i18nBaseName);
         chain.doFilter(request, response);
    }

    @Override
    public void destroy() {
    }
}
```

Because the class no longer refers to project specific classes, it was also moved to a more general book.javamvc.i18n package location. The BundleForEL class rewrites to the following:

```java
package book.javamvc.i18n;

import java.util.Enumeration;
import java.util.Locale;
import java.util.ResourceBundle;
import javax.servlet.http.HttpServletRequest;

public class BundleForEL extends ResourceBundle {
    private BundleForEL(Locale locale,
```

```
            String baseName) {
        setLocale(locale, baseName);
    }
    public static void setFor(
            HttpServletRequest request,
            String i18nAttributeName,
            String i18nBaseName)   {
        if (request.getSession().
          getAttribute(i18nAttributeName) == null) {
          request.getSession().setAttribute(
          i18nAttributeName,
          new BundleForEL(request.getLocale(),
                          i18nBaseName));
        }
    }

    public void setLocale(Locale locale,
            String baseName) {
        if (parent == null ||
            !parent.getLocale().equals(locale)) {
            setParent(getBundle(baseName, locale));
        }
     }

    @Override
    public Enumeration<String> getKeys() {
      return parent.getKeys();
    }

    @Override
    protected Object handleGetObject(String key) {
      return parent.getObject(key);
    }

}
```

Exercise 3: Add the following to UserData:

```
private double rank;
// Plus getter, setter
```

The corresponding part in index.jsp reads as follows:

```
<form method="post"
  action="${mvc.uriBuilder(
  'HelloWorldController#greeting').build()}">
    ...
   ${msg.enter_rank}
   <input type="text" name="rank" />
   <input type="submit" value="${msg.btn_submit}" />
</form>
```

And, in greeting.jsp, write the following:

```
 ...
 <fmt:formatNumber value="${userData.rank}"
    type="number" var="rank" />
 ${msg.response_rank} ${rank}
 ...
```

Add values for the enter_rank and response_rank keys in Messages.properties:

```
enter_rank = Enter your rank:
response_rank = your rank is
```

(Add values for other languages if you want.)

The update for the controller class reads as follows:

```
@POST
@Path("/greet")
public Response greeting(
    @MvcBinding @FormParam("name") String name,
    @MvcBinding @FormParam("age")
```

```java
    @Min(1)
    int age,
    @MvcBinding @FormParam("rank")
    @FloatRange(min=0.0, max=1.0)
    double rank,
    @Context HttpHeaders httpHeaders
  ) {
    ...
    userData.setRank(rank);
    ...
}
```

@FloatRange is a validation we developed in another exercise:

```java
// ---- File FloatRange.java
@Constraint(validatedBy = FloatRangeValidator.class)
@Target({ PARAMETER, FIELD })
@Retention(RUNTIME)
public @interface FloatRange {
    String message() default
      "Value out of range [{min},{max}]";
    Class<?>[] groups() default {};
    Class<? extends Payload>[] payload() default {};
    String[] value() default { };
    double min() default -Double.MAX_VALUE;
    double max() default Double.MAX_VALUE;
    double precision() default 0.0;
}

// ---- File FloatRangeValidator.java
public class FloatRangeValidator implements
    ConstraintValidator<FloatRange, Number> {
  private double min;
  private double max;
  private double precision;
```

```
@Override
public void initialize(FloatRange constraint) {
  min = constraint.min();
  max = constraint.max();
  precision = constraint.precision();
}

@Override
public boolean isValid(Number value,
    ConstraintValidatorContext context) {
  return value.doubleValue() >=
        (min == -Double.MAX_VALUE ? min :
              min - precision)
      && value.doubleValue() <=
        (max == Double.MAX_VALUE ? max :
              max + precision);
  }
}
```

Exercise 4: Inside index.jsp, add this to the <form> tag:

```
...
${msg.enter_dateOfBirth}
<input type="text" name="dateOfBirth" />
...
```

In the controller, you have to add a String parameter to the @POST method, because there is no date converter. You therefore need to parse the String manually:

```
@POST
@Path("/greet")
public Response greeting(
    ...
@MvcBinding @FormParam("dateOfBirth")
    String dateOfBirthStr
    ...)
```

```
    {
  ...
  DateTimeFormatter dtf =
      DateTimeFormatter.
      ofPattern("yyyy-MM-dd");
  LocalDate ld = LocalDate.parse(
      dateOfBirthStr, dtf);
  userData.setDateOfBirth(ld);
  ...
}
```

Inside UserData, add the new date of birth field, together with getters and setters. As an additional getter, add getDateOfBirthDate() and return the date as a java.util.Date, since JSPs can't handle LocalDate objects:

```
...
private LocalDate dateOfBirth;
...

public LocalDate getDateOfBirth() {
    return dateOfBirth;
}

public Date getDateOfBirthDate() {
    Calendar cal = Calendar.getInstance();
    cal.set(dateOfBirth.getYear(),
        dateOfBirth.getMonthValue()-1,
        dateOfBirth.getDayOfMonth(),
        0, 0, 0);
    return cal.getTime();
}

public void setDateOfBirth(
    LocalDate dateOfBirth) {
    this.dateOfBirth = dateOfBirth;
}
```

In greeting.jsp, you can use the <fmt:formatDate> tag to output the date:

```
...
<fmt:formatDate value="${userData.dateOfBirthDate}"
    pattern="yyyy-MM-dd" var="dob" />
${msg.response_dateOfBirth} ${dob}
    ...
```

As a last step, add values for the enter_dateOfBirth and response_dateOfBirth keys in the language resources files.

Obviously, the age field is obsolete now and you can remove it, if you like.

Chapter 9 Exercises

Exercise 1: (1) No, an EJB can have only a local interface, only a remote interface, or both. (2) No, a no-interface EJB means it can only be used for local access. (3) No, a remote EJB can be accessed from the same application, a different application on the same Jakarta EE server, or applications from other servers on the same machine or anywhere in the network. (4) No, a stateful EJB *can* maintain a state. (5) No, a singleton EJB never gets instantiated more often than just once. (6) No, for local EJBs you can also use injection via the @EJB annotation. (7) No, only the remote interfaces must be exported if EJBs are used remotely.

Exercise 2: The build.gradle file of the library (JSE, plain Java) project reads, for example:

```
plugins {
  id 'java-library'
}
```

```
java {
    sourceCompatibility = JavaVersion.VERSION_1_8
    targetCompatibility = JavaVersion.VERSION_1_8
}

repositories {
    jcenter()
}

dependencies {
    // Use JUnit test framework
    testImplementation 'junit:junit:4.12'
}
```

The class reads as follows:

```
package book.javamvc.simplenojee;
import java.time.ZonedDateTime;
import java.time.format.DateTimeFormatter;

public class MyDateTime {
  public String date(String format) {
    ZonedDateTime zdt = ZonedDateTime.now();
    String outStr = "";
    try {
      outStr = (format == null || "".equals(format) ?
          zdt.toString() :
          zdt.format(DateTimeFormatter.
              ofPattern(format)));
    } catch(Exception e) {
      e.printStackTrace(System.err);
    }
    return outStr;
  }
}
```

The build.gradle file of the EJB project reads as follows:

```
plugins {
  id 'java-library'
}

java {
  sourceCompatibility = JavaVersion.VERSION_1_8
  targetCompatibility = JavaVersion.VERSION_1_8
}

repositories {
    jcenter()
}

dependencies {
    implementation 'javax:javaee-api:8.0'
    implementation files(
      '../../SimpleNoJEE/build/libs/SimpleNoJEE.jar')
}

task extractStubs (type: Jar, dependsOn:classes) {
    archiveClassifier = 'ejb-stubs'
    from "$buildDir/classes/java/main"
    include "**/interfaces/*.class"
}
jar.finalizedBy(extractStubs)
```

The classes and interfaces read as follows:

```
import javax.ejb.Local;
import javax.ejb.Remote;
import javax.ejb.Stateless;

import [...].MyDateTimeLocal;
import [...].MyDateTimeRemote;
import [...].MyDateTime;
```

```
@Stateless
@Local(MyDateTimeLocal.class)
@Remote(MyDateTimeRemote.class)
public class MyDateTimeEjb {
 public String date(String format) {
    return new MyDateTime().date(format);
 }
}
```

For the ellipses, you have to write the package you chose for
MyDateTime and the interfaces (see the next two listings).

```
public interface MyDateTimeLocal {
    String date(String format);
}
```

```
public interface MyDateTimeRemote {
    String date(String format);
}
```

For the EAR project, create it as described in the text. Make the
EJB project a subproject of the EAR project. Because the EAR
project needs to refer to the non-Jakarta EE project, add the
following inside the dependencies { } section:

```
...
dependencies {
  ...
  earlib files(
     '../SimpleNoJEE/build/libs/SimpleNoJEE.jar')
  // <- Assumes that the non-Jakarta EE project
  // is called SimpleNoJEE. Also adapt the path
  // according to your needs.
}
```

You can now run the ear Gradle task, fetch the EAR from the build/libs folder, and deploy it on the server.

For the client, first run the EJB stub generation task called extractStubs from the EJB project. Assuming that the remote EJB interface reads book.javamvc.mydatetimeejb.interfaces. MyDateTimeRemote, for the client class, you can take the following:

```java
import java.util.Properties;

import javax.naming.InitialContext;
import javax.naming.NameClassPair;
import javax.naming.NamingEnumeration;

import book.javamvc.mydatetimeejb.
        interfaces.MyDateTimeRemote;

public class Client {
  public static void main(String[] args) {
    String remoteServerHost = "localhost";
    String remoteServerPort = "3700";
    Properties props = new Properties();
    props.setProperty("java.naming.factory.initial",
      "com.sun.enterprise.naming." +
      "SerialInitContextFactory");
    props.setProperty("java.naming.factory.url.pkgs",
      "com.sun.enterprise.naming");
    props.setProperty("java.naming.factory.state",
      "com.sun.corba.ee.impl.presentation.rmi." +
      "JNDIStateFactoryImpl");
    props.setProperty("org.omg.CORBA.ORBInitialHost",
      remoteServerHost);
    props.setProperty("org.omg.CORBA.ORBInitialPort",
      remoteServerPort);
    try {
      InitialContext ic = new InitialContext(props);
      MyDateTimeRemote testEJB = (MyDateTimeRemote)
```

```
        ic.lookup("book.javamvc.mydatetimeejb."+
                    "interfaces.MyDateTimeRemote");
    System.out.println(testEJB.date(
            "yyyy-MM-dd HH:mm:ss"));
  } catch (Exception e) {
    e.printStackTrace(System.err);
  }
 }
}
```

Make sure you've added the stubs from the EJB project and the `gf-client.jar` from GlassFish's `lib` folder as library dependencies.

Chapter 10 Exercises

Exercise 1: (1) True. You administer a data source on the Jakarta EE server. The way this needs to be done is server product dependent, but once the data source is available, the access mediated via JPA is standardized.

Exercise 2: The ORM—Object Relational Mapper.

Exercise 3: (1) No, although DAOs help improve code quality. (2) No, the entity manager will take care of that. (3) No, this is the entity classes' responsibility. (4) Yes. (5) No, EJBs help improve DAO handling, but you don't need to use them if they don't fit your needs.

Exercise 4: (1) True. (2) No, you can provide the table name inside the `@Table` annotation: `@Table( name = "TAB_NAME" )`. (3) No, you can provide the column name inside the `@Column` annotation: `@Column( name = "COL_NAME" )`. (4) True.

Exercise 5: Create a table and sequence as described in the text. Add the table column header label `tblhdr_status = Status` to the `src/main/resources/book/javamvc/jpa/messages/`

Messages.properties file. Inside the index.jsp view, add the following:

```
<table>
  <thead>
    <tr>
      ...
      <th>${msg.tblhdr_status}</th>
      ...
    </tr>
  <thead>
  <tbody>
    <c:forEach ... >
      <tr ...>
        ...
          <td>${itm.statusLst}</td>
        ...
      </tr>
    </c:forEach>
  </tbody>
</table>
```

Update the User class and add a field for the status (comma-separated status list):

```
package book.javamvc.jpa.data;

public class User {
  ...
  private String statusLst;
  // + Getter / Setter
  ...
}
```

On the database side (package db), you have to add a little more structure and introduce a new Status class. This class was described in the text.

For the MemberDAO class, you have to add a (`varargs`) parameter for the status of a new user, or use the following:

```
package book.javamvc.jpa.db;

import java.util.List;
import java.util.Set;
import java.util.stream.Collectors;
import java.util.stream.Stream;

import javax.ejb.Stateless;
import javax.persistence.EntityManager;
import javax.persistence.PersistenceContext;
import javax.persistence.TypedQuery;
@Stateless
public class MemberDAO {
    ...
    public int addMember(String name,
        String... status) {
    List<?> l = em.createQuery(
        "SELECT m FROM Member m WHERE m.name=:name").
setParameter("name",   name).
        getResultList();
    int id = 0;
    if(l.isEmpty()) {
        Member member = new Member();
        member.setName(name);
        Set<Status> s = Stream.of(status).map(
            s1 -> new Status(s1) ).
            collect(Collectors.toSet());
        member.setStatus(s);
        em.persist(member);
        em.flush(); // needed to get the ID
        id = member.getId();
    } else {
        id = ((Member)l.get(0)).getId();
    }
```

```
    return id;
    }
    ...
}
```

Inside the controller, update the addMember() method and add a
new parameter for the status list. Also, inside the addUserList()
method, you must mediate between the structured status
collection from the database and the flat comma-separated status
list for the view.

```
package book.javamvc.jpa;

import java.util.ArrayList;
import java.util.List;
import java.util.stream.Collectors;

import javax.ejb.EJB;
import javax.enterprise.context.RequestScoped;
import javax.inject.Inject;
import javax.inject.Named;
import javax.mvc.Controller;
import javax.mvc.binding.BindingResult;
import javax.mvc.binding.MvcBinding;
import javax.mvc.binding.ParamError;
import javax.validation.constraints.Pattern;
import javax.ws.rs.FormParam;
import javax.ws.rs.GET;
import javax.ws.rs.POST;
import javax.ws.rs.Path;
import javax.ws.rs.core.Response;

import book.javamvc.jpa.data.User;
import book.javamvc.jpa.db.MemberDAO;
import book.javamvc.jpa.db.Status;
import book.javamvc.jpa.model.UserEntering;
import book.javamvc.jpa.model.UserList;
```

```
@Path("/hello")
@Controller
public class HelloJpaController {
  ...
  @POST
  @Path("/add")
  public Response addMember(
    @MvcBinding @FormParam("name")
      String name,
    @MvcBinding @FormParam("statusLst")
    @Pattern(regexp = "(\\w*(,\\s*\\w*)*)?")
      String statusLst) {
  if(br.isFailed()) {
      br.getAllErrors().stream().forEach(
      (ParamError pe) -> {
      errorMessages.addMessage(
        pe.getParamName() + ": " +
        pe.getMessage());
    });
  } else {
      userEntering.setName(name);
      userEntering.setStatusLst(statusLst);
      memberDao.addMember(name, statusLst);
  }

  addUserList();
  return Response.ok("index.jsp").build();
  }
  ...

//////////////////////////////////////////////
//////////////////////////////////////////////

private void addUserList() {
  userList.addAll(
    memberDao.allMembers().stream().
        map(member -> {
```

```
        int id = member.getId();
        String name = member.getName();
        String statusLst = member.getStatus().
            stream().
         map( Status::getName ).
         collect(Collectors.joining(", "));
      return new User(id, name, statusLst);
    }).collect(Collectors.toList()) );
  }
}
```

Exercise 6: @OneToMany, @ManyToOne, @OneToOne, and @ ManyToMany.

Chapter 11 Exercises

Exercise 1: Let it read as follows:

```
package book.javamvc.helloworld;

import java.util.HashMap;
import java.util.Map;
import java.util.logging.Logger;

import javax.annotation.PostConstruct;
import javax.inject.Inject;
import javax.ws.rs.ApplicationPath;
import javax.ws.rs.core.Application;

@ApplicationPath("/mvc")
public class App extends Application {
  private final static Logger LOG =
    Logger.getLogger(App.class.toString());

 @PostConstruct
 public void init() {
   LOG.entering(this.getClass().toString(),
     "init");
 }
```

```
@Override
public Map<String, Object> getProperties() {
  LOG.entering(this.getClass().toString(),
    "getProperties");
  Map<String, Object> res = new HashMap<>();
  res.put("I18N_TEXT_ATTRIBUTE_NAME",
    "msg");
  res.put("I18N_TEXT_BASE_NAME",
    "book.javamvc.helloworld.messages.Messages");
  LOG.info("Set 'I18N_TEXT_ATTRIBUTE_NAME' to "+
    "'msg'");
  LOG.info("Set 'I18N_TEXT_BASE_NAME' to " +
    "'book.javamvc.helloworld.messages." +
    "Messages'");
  return res;
  }
}
```

Exercise 2: Adapt the `server.policy` file as described in the text. Add the the `log4j-core-2.11.2.jar`, `log4j-api-2.11.2.jar`, and `log4j-appserver-2.11.2` files (or whatever version you downloaded) from the Log4j2 distribution to the GLASSFISH_INST/glassfish/domains/domain1/modules/autostart folder. Add a `log4j2.json` file to GLASSFISH_INST/glassfish/domains/domain1/lib/classes. Example configuration files are presented in the text.

To your project, inside `build.gradle`, add the following as a dependency:

```
dependencies {
...
  implementation 'org.apache.logging.log4j:'+
    'log4j-api:2.11.2'
}
```

Add a static logger field to each class and use it:

```
public class SomeClass {
private final static Logger LOG =
    LogManager.getLogger(SomeClass.class);
  ...
public void someMethod() {
  ...
  LOG.trace("Trace: ...");
  LOG.debug("Debug: ...");
  LOG.info("Some info: ...");
  LOG.warn("Some warning: ...");
  LOG.error("Some error: ...");
  LOG.fatal("Some fatal error: ...");
   ...
  try {
    ...
  } catch(Exception e) {
    ...
    LOG.error("Some error", e);
  }
 }
}
```

Index

A

Administrative REST interface, 34, 42
Application scope, 139, 148, 188
Asynchronous EJB invocation, 252, 253
Authentication, 19, 22, 66
Automatic timers, 253, 254, 258, 259

B

Bean validation, 23, 122, 193
BundleForEL class, 226, 238, 417

C

Component-to-EJB communication, 249, 258
Conditional branching, 152, 153, 177, 189
Context and dependency injection (CDI) technology, 23, 134, 135, 187
context.getTimerService(), 256
Controller, 1, 2
ConvertDateTime tag, 236
ConvertNumber tag, 235
Cookies, 153, 154, 189
createSingleActionTimer() invocation, 256
Custom converters, 237, 239
Customized bundle class, 226

D

Dependencies, Gradle, 66–69, 89
Dependent scope, 139
doFilter() method, 226

E

Eclipse
  adding plugins, 49
  configuration, 48, 49
  everyday usage, 50
  functions, 50
  Gradle multi-project, 76, 77
  IDE, 46
  installation, 46, 47
  Java runtimes, 49
  plugins, install, 47
Eclipse Gradle plugin, 55, 57, 75, 81, 88, 92
Enterprise Archive (EAR), 250, 258
Enterprise edition J2EE, 20
Enterprise Java Beans (EJBs)
  accessing, 246–248
  asynchronous invocation, 252, 253
  container environment, 241
  defining, 242–245
  dependencies, 250–252
  local access to session, 243
  projects, 248, 249
  session, 241, 242
  timers, 253, 255, 256

© Peter Späth 2021
P. Späth, *Beginning Java MVC 1.0*, https://doi.org/10.1007/978-1-4842-6280-1

Printed in the United States
By Bookmasters